To Joe Antka
My sincere thanks for your loyalty to my show
Jim Roselle

Dedications

To my mother and father and our family.
And to everyone who gave me the pleasure of their company.

Jim Roselle

To Bill, Matthew, Cait and especially Patricia.
And to Nancy, without whose patience and support this project
would have been impossible.

Walt Pickut

Copyright © 2014 Walt Pickut
All rights reserved

ISBN: 978-0-692-23930-8

Printed in the United States of America
Falconer Printing and Design Inc, Falconer, New York

The Best Times of My Life
By: Jim Roselle with Walt Pickut

Table of Contents

Dedications		
Preface	The Right Place, the Right Time – Walt Pickut	3
Introduction	A Most Gracious Man – Mark Russell	5
Chapter 1	A Nickel's Worth	7
Chapter 2	New York State Hall of Fame Inducts Jim Roselle	10
Chapter 3	Why Jamestown, Why Then?	17
Chapter 4	**The Seats of Power:** Bill Clinton, Ruth Bader Ginsburg, Andrew Young, Leah Ward Sears	18
Chapter 5	**Sex, the Sniper and the Survivors:** Dr. Ruth, Ernst Michel	33
Chapter 6	**People and Events that Decorated My Life:** Family, Neighborhood, Community, University	40
Chapter 7	**The Literary World:** Norman Lear, Billy Collins, Rita Dove, Margaret Atwood, Wes Moore, Joyce Carol Oates, Roger Rosenblatt	57
Chapter 8	**The Real Woman Behind James Bond's "M":** Stella Rimington	75
Chapter 9	**WJTN Around the World and My Kind of Town:** Dr. Daniel Bratton, The Soviet Union, Disney World, London	80
Chapter 10	**Tarzan's Real Jane and Lucy's Dad:** Jane Goodall, Donald Johansson	86
Chapter 11	**Tales from the Golden Age of Radio:** Wake the Town, The Cup of Happiness, The Times of Your Life, On the Air, There's an Audience, The Cookout Shows	101
Chapter 12	**Sports:** Roger Goodell, Clark Kellogg, Jim McCusker, Sharon Robinson	117
Chapter 13	**Commenting on the World:** David Gergen, Shields & Gerson, David Ignatius, Jim Lehrer, Mark Russell, Tony Snow	134
Chapter 14	**The Plane Left Without Him:** Steve Scheibner	155
Chapter 15	**Actors – Cinema Stars - TV Personalities:** Gregg Oppenheimer, Margaret Hamilton, Michael York	159
Chapter 16	**Religious Leaders:** Tony Campolo, Bishop Spong, Huston Smith	170
Chapter 17	**The Music Makers:** Judy Collins, Ray Evans	179
Epilogue & Acknowledgements		186
Farewell & Sign-off		188
Appendix I	The Boys of the Boys Club	189
Appendix II	A Poem	191
Appendix III	Timeline	192

Preface

The Right Place, the Right Time

Time always passes *someplace*, and the place can be as important as the time. The place gives it structure and meaning…context. And context is everything.

This is a story about the nexus of time and place with a man and his microphone.

Jim Roselle is a man whose time and place, he says, made him what he became. Those of us who know Jim also know that he is the man who made his time and place in history what *they* became; he created a context where history could be experienced in the making.

Jamestown, New York, in the years between the Great Depression and the opening of the 21st Century, gave birth to people who changed the world. Jamestown's contributions include Lucille Désirée Ball, Desi's red headed wife, the Lucy everybody loves…whose televised comedic genius still graces the airwaves someplace on Earth every hour of every day of every year in the universal language of good will; wholesome laughter and delight.

The City of Jamestown also gave the world a man whose language, though different, was as universal as Lucy's. He used the language of law and justice to defend everyone's most basic, human freedoms – including the simple liberty to laugh, love and live in peace. Robert H. Jackson, United States Attorney General and Associate Justice of the United States Supreme Court, led the prosecution of Nazi war criminals in Nuremburg after World War II. Jurists from around the world now study his life's work and writings at the Robert H. Jackson Center in Jamestown, his hometown. Every summer at Chautauqua Institution, about 15 miles up a country road from Jamestown, the Jackson Center stages the International Humanitarian Law Dialogs where human rights activists, world leaders, academics and jurists gather to review and debate cases tried in international tribunals and the International Criminal Court in The Hague. Jackson's judgments and writings have become an indispensable lens for the closer study of worldwide law, justice and mercy.

Chautauqua Institution has drawn thousands of such world-changing men and women together from around the globe for the last 150 years. They birthed the great Chautauqua Movement, and stood at the forefront of the new nation's intellectual life.

During a broadcasting career that, so far, has spanned 60 years, Jim Roselle has brought these two remarkable places together.

Jim introduced his listeners to the people who accomplished extraordinary and historic deeds in the world. With respect and affection, Jim interviewed the stars and chatted as old friends with the world's "superheroes". He invited his listeners to a seat of their own at his broadcast table, and inspired generations of radio fans. The tools of his art have always been uncomplicated: an inquiring mind, a microphone and a single radio station that understood what broadcasting could accomplish.

Jim often revealed his famous guests to be people like the rest of us, people who came from neighborhoods "where everybody knows your name", neighborhoods of ordinary children like Jim's long ago Franklin Street Gang.

What happens around Jim's microphone is the same thing that happens when neighbors get together for a back yard barbecue and when churches hold picnics on a summer afternoon; old friendships grow and new ones are made. Pretense, ceremony and deference to status simply fade away. That is what makes Jim Roselle unique among modern broadcasters and journalists.

Since 1974, Jim has welcomed more than 1,800 guests to his sidewalk studio on Bestor Plaza, Chautauqua Institution's village green. His guests have included world and national leaders in politics, warfare and religion, bestselling authors and poets laureate, film and television celebrities, Nobel Prize winners and NASA astronauts. But, Jim says, that might not even be the best part.

Jim's studio at WJTN, back in Jamestown, has a simple sign on its door: It says: "The Dew Drop Inn." That's where he works for 10 months out of every year – in his own hometown, not at Chautauqua Institution; that's only his "summer job".

Whether it's a local town mayor dropping in for a chat – no campaigning please – or a Girl Scout hawking her favorite cookies; a fire chief warning neighbors to watch their woodstoves for the first winter fires, or a neighborhood gardener extolling the virtues of back yard composting and worm farming… Jim treats them all like the celebrities he sees at Chautauqua. In the summer, he treats his celebrities the same way he treats his townsfolk, and they love it too. That's Jim Roselle's genius.

In the end, Jim credits his family and his community, more than anything else, for his success.

"People are people wherever you meet them," Jim says. "Every one of them is a story and every story is worth telling. If in my years on the air, people learned something they didn't know before, something they took home and used in their lives, then it was worth it. I want my listeners to get to know the people I've met over the years, especially the friends and family I grew up with, and the wonderful, amazing community that made it all happen."

In working on this memoir with Jim, I have found the experience inspiring. Yet, that says too little about the work. Jim has invited me, as he does everyone, to step away from the keyboard, the job, the self we all put on like work clothes every day, and to join his Franklin Street Gang of long ago where we are all as much family as friend – where everybody knows your name – and bring that experience forward into our everyday lives. Success is not determined in Jim's neighborhood so much by what you do, as it is by the kind of person you become in the time and place you've been given.

The following accounts are offered as Jim's invitation…not simply to observe his world, but to join in his experience of the amazing planet he shares with us.

Walt Pickut
Editor
The Jamestown Gazette
Summer, 2014

Walt Pickut is a native of Bloomfield and Upper Montclair, New Jersey, a sometime denizen of New York City, and happily transplanted long ago to Western New York for peace, quiet and community living the way it should be. He and his late wife, Pat, raised their three children here, Bill, Matt and Cait. Four grandchildren, Abigail, Grace, and twins, Jake and Mary, have also joined the clan.

In addition to serving as Editor of *The Jamestown Gazette*, a Chautauqua County weekly newspaper, Walt enjoys writing science fiction under the assumption that the genre is really only news of a future not yet arrived. He also writes non-fiction of many sorts as a freelance writer and stargazes at the nearby Marshal Martz Astronomical Observatory, serving on the board to extend remote access to the facility in classrooms countywide and nationwide, enhancing STEM education for students everywhere.

Walt is married to Nancy Marie, of Binghamton, New York, without whose collaboration this book would have remained merely a dream and a good idea.

Introduction

A Most Gracious Man
By
Mark Russell

Let me begin by saying that Jim Roselle is by far the kindest, most gracious, and yes, saintly man whom I have ever insulted.

Insult Jim Roselle? Let me count the ways: *The Jim Roselle Show* on WJTN can be heard from Jamestown, NY all the way to Mayville, NY and occasionally to Westfield, New York. On a clear day. The WJTN transmitter is powered by a union hamster running on a circular treadmill relieved by a substitute hamster on weekends. My snide digs have included a reference to Guglielmo Marconi, the inventor of radio. Marconi not only knew Jim Roselle but he was Jim's first engineer in the late 19th century. Part of early radio lore was the crystal set which (I never understood this) contained a cat's whisker. Little Jimmy didn't have a cat so he snatched a whisker from a department store Santa Claus who wound up not giving a damn what this kid wanted for Christmas.

And on and on over the years, while being interviewed by Jim plugging my bi-annual performances at the Chautauqua Institution amphitheater beginning in 1979. I soon had the impression that here was a folksy intellectual—not enough just to be folksy but his radio "studio" was a folksy front porch right in the middle of the folksy intellectual Chautauqua Institution. Jim even referred to his morning coffee as a "Cup of Happiness." Where I come from, a cup of happiness has a head on it. (Cue the snare drum).

Enough of the folksy. Let's just say that Jim Roselle is the last AM radio talk show host on earth never to utter the words "scumbag", "thug", "sleazeball", or "bottom feeder" when describing a public figure. He is your Jamestown neighbor who knows what is going on in Tibet. He's the guy with the groceries at the checkout counter who can rattle off the names of all 9 Supreme Court justices and not only because he has interviewed some of them including Oliver Wendell Holmes (oops -- there I go again).

What are Jim's politics? I haven't the faintest idea. Conservative Democrat? Liberal Republican? Vice versa? Card-carrying Yellow Dog, Boll Weevil? Libertarian? Search me? (Please don't, it's just an expression). Actually, Jim may have once been a Whig. (Oops).

This book is overdue and we should be grateful to Walt Pickut for honoring a man so deserving of the warm affection that Jim has in his hometown and from the world leaders, intellectuals, show folk and celebrities major and minor, far beyond Mayville, Westfield and Jamestown who have graced Jim Roselle's porch.

Mark Russell
September, 2013
Chautauqua

Mark didn't actually say Jim's program is for the birds, but…

Chapter 1

A Nickel's Worth

"*Cinque centi, Mamma?*" The little boy could have asked his mom for a nickel. "*Per favore?*" And he would have known enough to say *please*.

That could have been an awfully brave request, or a foolish one. The Great Depression was a slouching presence that walked the streets of the Western New York town where the little boy lived. It skulked in his mother's kitchen and picked his father's pocket. A nickel was a big deal in the USA in the early 1930s.

Josephine Roselle

A nickel could buy a working man a beer and a sandwich in the right tavern in the 1930s. Five cents could buy a housewife a good can of pork and beans. A pound of fresh peas would leave a thrifty shopper a penny in change and a fat head of cabbage would give back two. Or, as Mrs. Roselle would have also known, if she could add a penny, a nickel would buy her a fresh scented, creamy bar of Camay Soap, though she'd rather make her own...she was that thrifty.

The boy's mother would have known, however, that such a little beggar was neither brave nor naïve; he could ask because he knew his mother. Josephine Roselle was kind and wise; if a nickel was needed, really needed, she might find one. She could neither read nor write, nor could she, or would she ever, learn the language of her adopted country, America. But little Jim knew his mother was smart.

Neither Josephine Roselle nor Jim's father, Joseph, ever knew that their little boy, growing up in a country where it was said that any little boy could become president, would one day sit and chat with an American president-to-be as if they were boyhood buddies. They might not have guessed that he would hobnob with Nobel laureates, make movie stars laugh out loud or a famous explorer screech like a chimpanzee to the delight of more people than she could have counted.

Josephine knew, though - and that was enough - that Jim would make good use of a nickel if he wanted a nickel.

"*Grazie mamma,*" Jim would have said, pocketing his precious nickel and punctuating his thank you by letting the old kitchen screen door clatter shut behind him as he ran back to his gang. Jim Roselle knew that a nickel would buy him a month at the new Boys Club downtown, and *venticinque centi* – a quarter – would open the doors for a whole year. "My mother knew what love was all about. That club was my salvation." He still said so 70 years later. The Boys Club had become the neighborhood boys' home away from home after school, after dinner and when the streets were rainy or snow drifted – a place just like home and their neighborhood for the freedom and kindly mentoring it offered.

Joseph Roselle

Jim, however, did not ask his mother for a nickel that day. He didn't have to. Jim already had a job. In 1939, any 13-year-old boy could caddy at a local golf course and earn $1 for lugging a gentleman's hefty bag of irons, woods and putters around 18 holes. If he was good and the gentleman was more kindly than some, he could earn $1.25. Jim was a paperboy, too, hawking his papers, the *Buffalo Evening News*, on the corner of Second and Main in downtown Jamestown for five cents a paper.

Jim Roselle paid for his own membership in the Boys Club, and his parents were proud he could.

Jim's Franklin Street neighborhood of proud immigrant families, however, was the birthplace of aspiring people and many remarkable careers. One of Jim's boyhood friends, Frank Modica, two years younger, wanted to join the Boys Club too. Frank's mother, however, could not wrestle a full *venticinque centi* out of her family's budget. She asked whether the Boys Club would accept a nickel a month until she could pay for the whole year. Of course, the Boys Club accepted.

Years later, Mrs. Modica's boy claimed his piece of the American Dream as did many other of the boys who grew up on Franklin Street. Frank became a high-rolling, high-powered entrepreneur. He was Frank Modica, the man with *"the big ideas for a little property"* way out west in Las Vegas, Nevada. He had parlayed his nickels wisely, eventually becoming president and CEO of the famous Showboat Resort and Casino and conducting operations at the old Maxim, the Landmark and the Desert Inn Resorts and more, all across the city where "What happens here, stays here."

Jim's neighborhood was a good place to grow up.

Jim had been born with a misshapen back and a malformed foot that would eventually require the attention of many skilled surgeons and dedicated hospital staff through two intricate operations and long convalescences. The last convalescence, after the final surgery in his teenage years, appears to have served him well – for seven more decades. Jim never considered himself disabled, unable, or in any way less able than the boys in his Franklin Street gang.

That band of neighborhood boys, the ones calling themselves a gang, was more like a company of youngsters playing stickball in the street in raggedy sneakers, well loved "children of the neighborhood". Kindly "Mrs. Roselles" up and down the street might greet them with a cold glass of water or a breathlessly begged potty break any time of day before the streetlights came on and they all went home.

Jim (on right) and his brother Joe in their baggy knickers at play on Franklin Street.

Those were the days. The Great Depression didn't throw these kids into the streets; it opened the doors of their homes to fresh air, sunshine and a kind of camaraderie that created a lifelong band of brothers. Well into the second decade of the 21st century, those boys still get together. They don't play much stickball anymore, but they talk about their families, their children, grandchildren and great-grandchildren, their successful careers, the profitable businesses they built and the dreams of their immigrant parents that they turned into realities…because they were well loved children of the neighborhood in the United States of America in the early 20th century.

A half-century later Jim Roselle still understood how to befriend a stranger like the one who strolled into his new Chautauqua Institution neighborhood one sunny summer morning. The sandy-haired young man with a friendly smile sat down at a sidewalk café table with him. Jim had already heard a few whispers about the fellow. He was from Arkansas.

"I have to ask you this," Jim said. "It may come as a surprise, but I'm told you love the saxophone and you play a lot of good jazz with it."

"Well, I played a lot when I was a child," the young man said. Then his smile grew a little wider and a twinkle showed up in his eye. "And now I play with my daughter during her piano recitals," he added with fatherly pride and a chuckle.

William Jefferson Clinton had instantly become a member of Jim Roselle's neighborhood gang. Family, friends and fun, Jim knew, have more to do with friendships than station and status and formality.

That's the way it has happened in just about every one of the more than 1,800 radio interviews that New York State Broadcasters Association Hall of Famer Jim Roselle conducted at Chautauqua Institution for WJTN-AM in Jamestown for 40 years.

For Jim Roselle the world itself has become his Franklin Street gang. His is a story about the elevation of the common man to the nobility of great accomplishment. At the same time, it is the story of the common humanity shared by world leaders, pedestaled celebrities, celebrated scientists, athletes and astronauts and even a few famous rascals.

The famous network and cable newscasters of the world, the masters of broadcasting who uncover for us the opinions, insights and secrets of the nation's newsmakers and globetrotting dignitaries, do bring us the news we need to know, but they rarely bring us the people themselves.

That is Jim's genius. He learned it at 34 Franklin Street in Jamestown, New York. Jim's band of neighborhood buddies never left him behind just because he couldn't run as fast as the fastest or stand up as straight as some of them. And his parents, Joseph and Josephine – still new and proud from Sicily – always encouraged Jim to know he was as good a boy as any of the rest of them.

"Andare nel sole," my mother always told me, Jim recalls today. "Go in the sunshine." Outside in the neighborhood, in other words, was no farther from home than his mother's fragrant kitchen and father's tool-strewn workshop. According to Josephine Roselle, with a little help from our friends, we are all children of the neighborhood.

"Have fun and play with the other kids," she had said. Today Jim says, "I give my mother a lot of credit, she didn't smother me, she made me feel normal." No wonder one day, way back then, he took up a challenge and picked up a basketball. In less time than it would take for a line of cheerleaders to dance a halftime pom-pom show, Jim sank 58 out of 60 free throws from the foul line and claimed the famed and coveted Western New York Boys Club championship for himself.

The story of Jim Roselle's life, then, is more than a story about a wonderful, early 20th century childhood grown into a globe girdling network of connections, shared wisdom and friends. Jim's life is a parable of what can be. He says he never set out to be a role model, only a friend. If possible, a good one.

Today, though, no one can stroll down the street, a little past downtown Jamestown, to find Jim's old neighborhood. The houses there are still homes, but the old neighborhood is gone. Most of the dozen or so families whose names all ended in vowels, in the place some called Little Italy, are not there anymore.

One of the old Franklin Street boys, Joe Trusso, now an accomplished veteran of 37 years in the Chautauqua County Legislature, prefers to call the old neighborhood the "Little United Nations", ticking off the names of the Swedish and German and Jewish children who grew up there, too. "We might have been poor, but none of us would have traded our childhoods for anything in the world," Joe will tell you with a nostalgic catch in his throat. "This is the United States of America, and that's why our parents 'got on the boat' to come here."

Perhaps that's why today, when Jim Roselle welcomes someone to sit down at his microphone, he never quite says – but his guest always hears – "I knew you when… and we could have been friends. Let's start now." Jim recognizes and values the inherent goodness in everyone; the world-changing statesman and the deserving but unsung neighborhood hero alike.

Jim's story, then, is an invitation, freely offered with a hand of friendship and a Cup of Happiness – that special signature cup of morning coffee he sets down beside his microphone every day – to join him once again as a child of the neighborhood. Whether his guest is a world-famous dignitary, or back in Jamestown between Chautauqua's summer seasons, the mayor, a neighborhood gardener or the fellow who drives the snowplow, you know Jim's neighborhood is now as big as the world, and you belong.

At the end of the day, as the streetlights come on and we all go home, Jim will sign off as he does every day on his radio show, "Thank you for your company. Take good care of this day. Live, love and enjoy.

Chapter 2

New York State Hall of Fame Inducts Jim Roselle

The NYSBA

At Jim Roselle's induction into the New York State Broadcasters Association (NYSBA) in 2010, Joseph A. Reilly, NYSBA president, said, "Jim is a master interviewer, whether his subject is a professional athlete or a regular guy walking down the street. He's also been the voice of Jamestown for more than half a century, and now it's time to welcome him into our Hall of Fame."

Jim was inducted into the NYSBA, along with a slate of other famous 2010 inductees, and one 2011 inductee, TV personality Regis Philbin, at the traditional Tony Malara Awards Dinner during the association's 48th Executive Conference. While Regis Philbin holds the Guinness World Record for the most time logged in front of television cameras, his induction for the year after Jim reveals a notable similarity in their accomplishments. As far as is known, Jim holds the record for the most time logged on the same radio station's microphone—60 uninterrupted years at WJTN-AM, in Jamestown, New York. Jim, however, quipped to Regis, "Good job! But you know I got into the Hall of Fame before you."

To commemorate Jim Roselle's induction, the NSBA published a brief biographical sketch, expanded here and in greater detail throughout the following chapters.

Jim Roselle was born on Tax Day, April 15, 1926. Jim and his three brothers and three sisters grew up in a modest home at 34 Franklin Street, a few blocks east of downtown Jamestown, New York. Jim's parents had emigrated from Turturici in Sicily separately and did not meet until they both lived in Jamestown. They came because America offered a promise of better work than they could find at home. The plan was to save enough money for a comfortable life or a good start in business back in Sicily. After they met, married and started a family, they decided this part of the world was the best place to live.

After graduating from Jamestown High School in 1944, Jim Roselle attended St. Lawrence University where he received a bachelor's degree in business administration, while minoring in radio programming and production. It was his experience as a play-by-play broadcaster for S.L.U. football, basketball and baseball games that would be a springboard to a life of success.

In 1953, Roselle began his radio career at WJTN-AM in Jamestown, New York. Little did he know that what started as a part-time sportscaster's job was truly the beginning of a life of excellence in broadcasting and an ever deepening involvement in his hometown.

One day Jim learned that the president of his high school senior class, Charlie Goodell, who had already become nationally well-known, would be a featured speaker at the nearby cultural mecca, Chautauqua Institution. Jim asked his station manager if he could go interview Charlie on the air. The interview was so well received by listeners that the manager suggested Jim do it again next summer. "Why just once, why not all summer?" Jim asked, seizing the opportunity. "They have famous people there every week. Our listeners would love to hear them." Jim has been doing those "famous people" interviews for the last 40 years.

Today Jim says that so much of his success has to do with being at the right place with the right attitude when the right people come along. Whether it was fate, God's hands stirring the universe or good old-fashioned ambition applied to every opportunity, Jim says, "It worked for me, so why not you?"

Jim's broadcast excellence has sent him around the world to London with Jamestown Community College students, to the Soviet Union with Chautauqua Institution, to Austria, Germany and Italy with the Jamestown High School A Capella Choir and to the Macy's and Rose Bowl Parades and a week of live broadcasting from Disney World with the Jamestown High School Band.

Roselle is known for his interviews, most of which were broadcast from his Bestor Plaza studio at the Institution. Since the summer of 1974, he has interviewed hundreds of powerful speakers including Arkansas Governor Bill Clinton, political humorist Mark Russell, respected newscaster Jim Lehrer, naturalist Jane Goodall, *NBC*'s Tim Russert, sex therapist Dr. Ruth, U.S. Supreme Court Associate Justice Ruth Bader Ginsburg, television writer and producer Norman Lear, U.S. Poets Laureate Billy Collins and Rita Dove, evangelical sociologist Rev. Tony Campolo, singer-songwriter Judy Collins, novelists Margaret Atwood, Joyce Carol Oates and Wes Moore, essayist Roger Rosenblatt and NASA administrator Dan Goldin.

His style of interviewing is unique. Like other talk radio personalities, Roselle does detailed research on the subjects and people he interviews, and his knowledge and insight often surprise and impress his guests. It has been his disarming approach to these "on air conversations" that reveals the humanity of his world-famous guests.

"Good morning hometown Jamestown and all of its neighbors! Join me in a Cup of Happiness!" The community wakes up to his voice every day. It is the common person in the local community Jim relates to most, and he would be the last to boast of his community affiliations, passions and awards. He has been a member of the board of directors for the Lucille Ball Little Theatre for more than 30 years, the Jamestown Boys and Girls Club for more than 25 years, and more recently on the board at the James Prendergast Library. He's received the National Brotherhood Award from the National Council of Christians and Jews, the Paul Harris Fellowship Award from the Jamestown Rotary Club and has received the old, First Night Award from the Chautauqua Institution. He also has been the chairman for countless community events.

On his induction into the New York State broadcasters Hall of Fame Jim offered some reflections on a career and a life in broadcasting.

Radio became part of my life when I was young boy. I just thought, "That's one fabulous career. If there is a possibility, I'd like to go into radio and do that..." There's an old saying that goes, 'If you love what you're doing, you won't work a day in your life'. And I don't think I have worked a day in my life. It's a challenge every day. No two days are alike. You become part of the community. You can't be grateful enough to people who give you that opportunity to become part of their lives. I'm living the impossible dream. What more could a man in this business ask for?

Some thoughts from Tom Morgan: Jim's Secret Formula and the Hall of Fame

With WJTN kindly running my *Moneytalk* show [nationally syndicated on radio and in newspapers], Jim and I have been on the air together in Jamestown for 36 years. Of course, he's been on the air a few more years than that. I think his first Chautauqua interview was with Teddy Roosevelt.

Jim Roselle with Tom Morgan

Jim's magic formula is to be genuinely interested in you. Maybe it's your travels or your stories or your favorite book or movie. Jim will ask you about your career, your achievements and your family. But always, it is you.

Jim spends little air time talking about Jim. He is that rarest of celebrities in that he is most interested in his guest. He is like a combination of teacher, parent, grandparent and counselor because they are the kind of people who show an interest in us, and naturally, we appreciate them for it. And that's what Jim does, endlessly. We love him for that.

Jim has chatted with me on WJTN wherever I've been lucky enough to travel. I've spoken with him from a castle in Ireland to New Zealand and the Caribbean; from Cricket matches in London to places high in the Swiss Alps and the Canadian Rockies. Then there was Salt Lake City, Sicily and Bermuda; Manhattan, Croatia and Scotland.

When I called from Paris, I told him I was at a sidewalk cafe being served by a lovely young waitress. "Put her on," Jim ordered. I told her she would be on the air with America's best interviewer, with millions of listeners, and then I put her on. Fifteen minutes later I had to pry her off the phone. She was so thrilled.

I'm still waiting for my order.

If Jim had been at the right place at the right time, he could have been on network radio or television. He certainly had the talent. And he had the following. He could have been as famous as Larry King. If that opportunity had come, though, I suspect he would have chosen to stay at WJTN. He would not have been able to break off his love affair with Jamestown. He is Jamestown and Chautauqua's greatest fan and most ardent cheerleader. He is the voice of Jamestown and for a good part of the city, its soul.

Local News, Sports, Talk and Timeless Music

Jim invited me and my wife, Erna [Erna Morgan McReynolds], to the ceremonies when he was inducted into the New York State Broadcaster's Hall of Fame. As a matter of fact, Jim and Kathy were guests at our home as they traveled from Jamestown to the Hall of Fame ceremonies.

More humble and heartwarming acceptance remarks, you have never heard. He told us he was the luckiest of people. He described how blessed his life has been with friends, family and supporters. As I watched and listened to him, I pictured him as a young kid in Jamestown. Like a million kids in those years, he dreamed of getting on the radio, to talk with people and entertain them.

Well, he's the kid who followed his dream. For 60 years he has. Along the way, he has become an absolute master of his profession. He is simply the best.

Thank You and a Few Words on Retirement

My induction into the New York State Broadcasters Hall of Fame came about because of Merrill Rosen WJTN's General Manager (retired) and WJTN's Program Director, Andrew Hill.

I remember the day Merrill came in for a job in sales. He would ask what one show or another was about and then go out and sell par ads (*par*-ticipation ad: a given show host or celebrity would voice the ad. It cost a little more but listeners tended to trust the ad more, too). Merrill was amazing. He could sell ice boxes to Eskimos. He worked his way up from knowing nothing to becoming sales manager and eventually all the way up to general manager, a position he held at WJTN for many years. He was a real pro. He knew how to run a radio station – our success over so many years surely proved it – and he'd been very good to me.

It was Merrill's idea to put the nomination in. I really didn't know about it. He and my colleagues at WJTN decided to put together the resume of my career. They thought it should get some attention from the Broadcasters Association because of what I've done over the years, particularly the interviews and so many of the other events.

When I stop and think of what this community has done for me, I really would like to thank you, all of my listeners, for inviting me into your homes, your cars, your transistor radios and iPhones, and to do that on a daily basis or for whatever time you could afford… thank you!

I've got to be very grateful for that. You have kept me employed because of what you have done. People have asked me, "When are you going to retire?" And I say to myself, "Retire from what? Or to what?" I never developed a hobby that I could turn to; my hobby is my work.

But in fact, I did think of retirement once. The thought did come to me after a while and I thought, "Maybe it is time…" Then one day a lady came to me at an on-location show and looked at me for a minute. She wanted to be really sure that I was Jim Roselle.

"Yes, I'm Jim Roselle."

"I want to tell you something," she said.

"What is it?"

"Every morning I roll over in bed and turn you on."

I decided to postpone my retirement.

Jim Remembers… My First Radio Show

I give my brothers, Phil and Ross, credit for starting my career. Phil was a barber. He owned Roselle's News Stand, where he also did hat blocking - the Royal Hat Shop - and dry cleaning. He had a 6-chair shoe shine stand there, too. It was a top-of-the-line business in downtown Jamestown in the day when gentleman appreciated a shop like that.

When I graduated from St. Lawrence University in 1949, I had been sure my life would be in broadcasting, sportscasting in particular. I sent carefully prepared audition tapes of my very best work to radio stations in Vermont, Norfolk, VA; Bangor, ME; Paducah, KY and Amsterdam, NY. Silence was my only reply except for Amsterdam. I was sure I'd get that Amsterdam job, until they hired somebody else.

Si Goldman, at the time in sales at WJTN, regularly stopped by Phil and Ross's shop to get his shoes shined. After I graduated from college Phil kept saying, "Come on Si, give my brother a job." And he said it over and over.

And Si would answer, "Phil, there's no opening."

Si Goldman

Then one day Si came back and said, "Okay Phil, there is a high school football game, Jamestown High, and the sportscaster does not want to do the play-by-play. See if your brother wants to do it."

And that's how I got my first play-by-play game on the radio. Sometimes it had seemed like it would never happen - but it did.

Jamestown High played their home games at Municipal Stadium, just down the street. I'll never forget it. I went down to the stadium early for that Saturday night game because I was all excited. I had my spotter with me, my friend, Joe Pollino. I looked for somebody to direct us to the game.

"Where's the broadcast booth?" I asked a fellow who looked like he should know.

"We don't have a broadcast booth."

"Where am I going to go?"

"You have to wait for the engineer," he said. "He'll know."

He showed up. It was in a truck!

I sat inside at the broadcast board with my microphone while my spotter, Joe, stood outside where he could see the field better and relay players and plays to me.

That would have been about 1950, I was 24. It was my first part-time job in radio.

Joe, by the way, went on to attend Syracuse University where he played first team, defensive tackle with his teammate, Jim Brown, often called the greatest player of all time for his college and for his record-setting nine-year professional career as a running back for the Cleveland Browns. Joe Pollino later went to Washington, DC, to become Boys Club director for the entire city.

Jim Brown

After that first Jamestown High football broadcast, which I guess I did well enough to impress Si, I started doing a bowling show called "Alley Dust". It was on Sunday, giving scores of the week's bowling competitions. Bowling was very popular here, with at least six bowling alleys in Jamestown, Falconer and Lakewood, and leagues were there every night.

Sam Munella was a friend of Phil's. Sam owned a couple of the bowling alleys in town, the Palladium and the Pine Street Alleys. Sam told Si Goldman, "I'll buy it [sponsor the show], but I want Jim Roselle to do it." So here I was, doing bowling on Sundays and reading bowling scores. It was crazy!

I had to make calls and get the scores. Saturday I would call every bowling alley. "Give me your highlights; who was the high guy last week? Who had the best three games? What teams won? What teams are in first place? Did anybody pick up a 7-10 split? Did anybody roll a 300 game?" If so, that's what I would highlight.

I had this big vinyl record, a transcription with bowling sound effects of the ball rolling down the alley and smashing into the pins in the background. It sounded like you were at the alley. The show was 15 minutes long. I got three dollars!

> There's no opportunity so small it can't be turned into a stepping-stone.   Jim Roselle

...And My First Chautauqua Assignment

Charlie Goodell was the class president the year I graduated from Jamestown High School in 1944. When Charlie came back many years later, he was invited to speak at Chautauqua Institution, that was my first inspiration to broadcast from Chautauqua. Before then, every summer, I would read the Chautauqua summer program guide. I would only comment on the radio about whatever was going on there, about who was going to be there and what my listeners could look forward to.

But when the program for that year came out I looked it over and saw Charlie Goodell's name. He was going to be the lecturer for a subject titled "The Abuse of Government Power."

Charlie Goodell was a Republican. He had been appointed by New York's Republican Governor, Nelson Rockefeller, to fill the vacancy created by Democratic Senator Robert F. Kennedy's assassination. Richard Nixon, however, did not want Charlie as a Senator from New York because he was one of the first and loudest voices against the Vietnam War. Nixon supported James Buckley for the Senate seat, so Charlie had to run as an independent and did not win.

By the way, Roger Goodell, Charlie's son, now Commissioner of the NFL, was a busboy at Chautauqua when I was doing my show from the grounds. Roger was 15 or 16 years old, sweeping floors and bussing tables at the restaurant. Back then I wouldn't have guessed that by now I'd have interviewed Roger Goodell on the air as the Commissioner of the NFL.

I've had many unique opportunities like that in my years on the radio. The Charlie Goodell interview taught me one of the most important lessons of my career, one I've often repeated: "Never underestimate the value of relationships."

So I said to myself when I saw Charlie's name on the program, "I've got to go to Chautauqua. Charlie will give me an interview." Why not? He was my class president. We even played ball against each other. I felt confident I would get an interview. So I jumped right in my car, drove up to Chautauqua and asked permission to do my show.

I said I would just look forward to the local audience hearing their former senator and congressman. I think it is our duty as a public service to do that. They asked where I would do my broadcast from. "Well, I'm only 127 pounds," I said. "I don't take up much room, so how about the patio at the Refectory? I'll sit in a corner." They said they didn't see any problem with that.

I went back to the studio and walked into Mr. Willems office.

"Carl, I'm going to Chautauqua when Charlie Goodell gives a talk."

"You are?"

"Yes. Isn't it our job to do public service? Isn't it our job to bring out memorable stories? Let's do it."

"Do you think anybody will buy it?" He asked me. He was definitely a salesman.

"Even if they don't buy it, we are really obligated to do it. Let's do it."

"Okay," he said. "Let's get the engineering taken care of."

It was as simple as that. That's how it happened.

Si Goldman, my boss, was a special guy to me because he always gave me opportunities. He always said, "If you have an idea, let's use it. Don't be reluctant. Try whatever you want to be part of your show. If it doesn't work, try something else." I always thought that was a nice piece of freedom. He was right. That's how the Chautauqua interview broadcasts came about. It was just an idea. If it worked, he would okay it and endorse it, as long as I kept it rolling along.

So I stayed that whole week at Chautauqua. I only saw Charlie twice during the week as a guest, but in between I had nobody else planned. All of the lecturers and some of the performers usually stayed at the Institution's Wensley Guest House whose hostess was Winnie Llewellyn. I knew her as a teacher at the nearby Maple Grove High School. She was a very revered teacher and a kind friend. I asked her, "Can you talk any of them into coming on the radio? Maybe for 10 or 15 minutes? Do you think you can persuade them?" She certainly did!

She gave me [American cultural anthropologist] Margaret Meade that week and a few others. The next year she gave me Dr. Christiaan Barnard who did the first heart transplant in the world and so many more over all these years. What more could I ask?

Winnie Llewellyn on the air with Jim

The following Monday morning, I went back to work at the radio station and was immediately called into the office. Carl said, "We've got what you call feedback from your show last week. A lot of feedback! Do you want to do it again?" What a silly question that was! So I said, "I'll tell you what, Carl, only if we are going to do it every week. Why should it be just one week? Every week there is a different theme, a different subject. You have a goldmine of possibilities."

They decided I could, but I would have to leave room for other shows. We would do the Chautauqua programs Monday, Tuesday and Wednesday and then we would leave Thursday and Friday open for special shows that they sold back in Jamestown.

Joe Caprino, for instance, was a Jamestown furniture dealer who bought air time. He had a promotion about every week, and I had to be on location at his store. Over 37 years, I probably did 1000 or more of them!

At that time I didn't expect Chautauqua, starting from those three small shows a week, would still be here 40 years later. Now I go five days a week. It is a "mindfield." How could you possibly think someone at a local radio station would have the opportunity to chat with Nobel Prize winners, Tony Award winners, poets laureate, authors, historians and every other possible profession?

Chapter 3

Why Jamestown, Why Then?

There are no self-made people because we are all part of society. Accomplished people benefit from advantages created by earlier generations (of parents whom we didn't choose and taxpayers whom we've never met) and by the simple fact that they live in a country that provides opportunities that are not available everywhere. The successful thus owe quite a lot to the government and social structure that made their success possible.

E. J. Dionne

That is right! I'm convinced somewhere along the way somebody inspired each of us, made a decision for us that was right. There are people we've all got to look back on who created a possibility for us. We did all we could but we needed that moment, that assistance, that advice, that support.

When I stop and think about what Mr. Clemments at the Boys Club gave our little group, that Franklin Street group...the neighborhood boys who stuck together from kindergarten through high school...then you know there are no self-made people.

The obvious thing for people to think about is that I've been in the game this long, have had so many adventures in this game, I guess it's worth it to help people understand that there's more to it than just my job on the radio. I want people to look back with me and be grateful for so many people who made it possible. It's a way of saying thank you. My gratitude is endless.

I've got to mention the radio programming opportunities that the community gave me. All of these were subjects I could play with on the air. In many ways, as a matter of fact, it was the people in the community who created the programs.

We've got the Lucy Desi Center for Comedy, all of their events and their annual Comedy Festival, and we have our great minor league baseball team, the Jamestown Jammers. We have the Roger Tory Peterson Institute, the Fenton History Center, the Robert H. Jackson Center, the Lucile M. Wright Air Museum and the Chautauqua County Sports Hall of Fame.

The area itself has so much history. There were the pioneers of the community who left a legacy for all of us to enjoy. To name a few, they include; Reginald and Elizabeth Lenna and the Reg Lenna Civic Center along with the Lucille Ball Little Theater, both keeping theater alive in our area, and the Lawson Center Boating Museum, telling the story of the David S. Lawson family and the history of fishing and boating on Chautauqua Lake. Then there's the Lincoln Memorial in Westfield commemorating Abraham Lincoln's personal visit to thank a school girl for her kind letter.

Of course, we also have the link itself, the link to the whole world at Chautauqua Institution. What guy wouldn't like to have those things in his own backyard as a source to get those interviews? Where else would I get those opportunities? Jamestown is a one-of-a-kind place in this world.

Then I think about the music I've played over all those years and I remember Frank Sinatra's *My Kind of Town.*

> *Now this could only happen to a guy like me*
> *And only happen in a town like this*
> *So may I say to each of you most gratef'lly*
> *As I throw each one of you a kiss*
>
> *This is my kind of town...*

Chapter 4

The Seats of Power

Societies and families are just people related in some way and living together. Well ordered specimens of both team up, shape up and try to wind up in a better place from where they started. Jim Roselle interviews politicians out of that simple, homespun perspective.

I brake for politicians…As a group, I like them.
   Politicians are human. If you prick them, they will bleed. If you pet them, they'll lick your hand. They're filled with anxieties, contradictions and duplicities, but I wonder what groups, including journalists, salespeople, hammer dulcimer makers or Franciscan priests, are not…
   Every word they utter can be quoted. Smart people know they can advance their careers by bringing them down.

Politicians Are People, Too
Scott Simon
National Public Radio
July 4, 2009, 12:00 am

I will never ask a politician a 'Gotcha' question.

Jim Roselle, WJTN Radio

Arkansas Governor Bill Clinton: Blowing One's Own Horn

In June, 1991, Jim Roselle interviewed Arkansas Governor Bill Clinton. One month later Governor Clinton was nominated by the Democratic National Convention to run for President of the United States.
   As always, Jim wants to know about the man, not only about the office and the power. Personal interests and family matters matter more, so Jim simply invites his hometown radio friends along for a chat. Why talk to a man about politics until you get to know the man you're talking to?

Jim Remembers… My Question Behind the Questions

My involvement in the community over the years makes me wonder how a citizen can make his or her voice heard today in politics. The growing cost of getting elected, rising to hundreds of millions of dollars, might even be an anti-democratic force.

I can't help thinking, "How is the common guy ever going to be part of the process again?" He can't afford those expensive TV ads and radio ads by the thousands. Will the kind of money the major candidates have taken kill any opponent's campaign? And what happens when they win?

Do they go to their work relating to the people?

Here's the suggestion I have in mind. If I were a representative, once a month, if I had the opportunity and if I were invited, I would pick a family and go and sit with them and have dinner. I'd be delighted to go into their home and just sit and talk to the kids and talk to the parents. I'd ask, "What's it like to be a seventh grader?" I would ask what they like and don't like. I would get face-to-face with the voters. I would see their body language at the same time I heard their words. And a woman might tell me honestly that she has to worry about what to do from paycheck to paycheck. She would have to try to decide whether her husband and she could go out to dinner. Or could they take a quick weekend jaunt to the casinos?

I know I would learn a lot.

We had cookouts with listeners in their own back yards every week for 20 years. If you can get to know your audience, you can get to know your citizens. And it wouldn't cost billions to do it.

So I think it's important for people to get to know these people for who they really are. Do they care about the same things I do? I wonder if they have the same experiences as the voters do.

I think it's my job to bring that out, to let people meet them as if they really did come to dinner one night.

So when I had the opportunity to talk to Governor Bill Clinton, a young man everybody already knew was on the rise politically, I decided just to get to know the man first, and introduce him to my audience.

A Conversation with Bill Clinton

Jim Roselle: I'm sure, Governor that you realize that I'm going to expand this talk beyond political issues. You don't get Governor Clinton and only talk about national and international matters. Governor Clinton, my sincere thanks for giving us some time.

Governor Clinton: Thanks Jim, I'm glad to be here and I look forward to being on this program. Everybody around here says you're legendary, and I'll be lucky to walk out of here in one piece.

JR: Boy, I hope we got that on tape. Governor Clinton, I have to ask you this. It may come as a surprise, but I'm told you love the saxophone and you play a lot of good jazz with it.

Gov C: Well, I played a lot when I was a child and I have started in the last two or three years playing again and… The Four Tops are friends of mine. If they are anywhere where I am, I go play with them. I have two or three people like that I play with, and I play with my daughter during her piano recitals and that's about it. But I love it. It was a big part of my life at one time.

JR: Well, I will tell you the source of that information. That was Jim Walker of *Free Flight* who found out you love to have a great time with that instrument.

Gov C: I do. Some day I'd like to come here and just play with the band or the orchestra or something.

JR: I bet he'd like to have you sit in with him (Jim motions toward a local musician friend in the audience), you know, his flute and your sax. I would imagine a lot of great sounds would come out of it.

Then Jim turns to the politics of the day.

[But first…*A few 1991 memory joggers for 21st century readers:*
- ✓ ***January:*** *Operation Desert Storm begins against Iraq*

- ✓ **March:** *Motorist Rodney King is severely beaten by LA Police, seen on amateur video*
- ✓ **April:** *Victory in Persian Gulf War*
- ✓ **April:** *Johnny Carson announces '92 retirement date*
- ✓ **June:** *Apartheid repealed in South Africa*]

JR: Governor Clinton… I look at the nation and I guess I'd like to just ask a very simple question. You take it from there. Give me a report card on America…What grade would you give America for what we are experiencing right now?

Gov C: I give us an "A" for our role in the world, in our world leadership, in the Gulf War, in bringing down the Berlin Wall [1989-90] and for upholding freedom and democracy throughout the world, but I give us "C" for our ability to follow up on it because we have no money to help those countries that are struggling to become democracies…and a "B" for the conditions here at home.

We've got a decade now where middle-class people have seen their earnings decline while cost of housing and healthcare and the cost of college education is going through the roof. We've got the highest rates of infant mortality, teen pregnancy, and school dropout in the world of all the advanced countries. We're the only advanced country in the world that can't figure how to get health care to all of our folks, or inspire kids to go on from high school to college and to great jobs, and we've got some profound deficiencies in education and economic performance, so I'm very concerned about the long-term future of this country.

If we don't turn around our situation here at home, then 10 or 20 years now we will no longer be able to lead the world. America's leadership in the world depends on, more than anything else, the ability to keep alive the American dream here at home. And we're not doing a very good job of it.

JR: America was so fixed in on the Persian Gulf War, we became addicts of it through TV coverage, but… after the war was over suddenly the thoughts of Americans turned to domestic issues. What do we do here to take care of our problems? Are you supporting Lamar Alexander's educational reform bill? Do you like his ideas? [Lamar Alexander had been the 45th Governor of Tennessee ('79-'87) and was the Secretary of Education under President George H. W. Bush at the time of Jim's interview.]

Gov C: Lamar was my neighbor in Tennessee, and we served back-to-back years as chairman of the Governor's Association. He's a good friend of mine. I do think that the program has a lot of very good points…but it lacks opportunities that I think we need from the national government. For example, the president committed to give every eligible child in this country the opportunity to go to Head Start. But they're backing off…After World War II the G.I. Bill was instituted. The national government assumed primary responsibility for making sure the middle class as well as poor people can afford to get financing for college education. They are backing off of that. And those are not Lamar's fault…If you don't have kids getting off to a good start in school, and then you don't make it possible for the middle class and poor people to go forward beyond high school, we're going to have terrible economic consequences.

JR: The more things change, the more they stay the same. Thank you, Governor Clinton.

Associate Supreme Court Justice Ruth Bader Ginsburg: Home Cooking and Wise Decisions

It has been said somewhat facetiously, though often confirmed, that unless they have a book to sell, justices

Associate Justice of the Supreme Court of the United States, Ruth Bader Ginsburg on the air with Jim

of the US Supreme Court rarely give interviews.

In the summer of 2013 Jim was delighted to have a wide-ranging, nearly 45 minute, interview with U.S. Supreme Court Associate Justice Ruth Bader Ginsburg. Jim was very interested in the many ways which Justice Ginsburg broke stereotypes and forged her own path in her life and career and family.

Justice Ruth Bader Ginsburg was only the second female justice of the U.S. Supreme Court, following Sandra Day O'Connor, and she was the first Jewish female justice. When she entered Harvard Law school in 1956, her class of about 500 had only nine women in it. After graduation Justice Felix Frankfurter denied her a clerkship position because she was female.

Unrelenting in her passion for the law, however, she eventually forged her way upward until she was appointed to the Supreme Court by President Clinton, taking the oath of office in August of 1993. Her decisions and arguments are generally seen as siding with the liberal wing of the Court.

Jim's interest in the high cost of political activism for the average citizen returned in speaking with Justice Ginsburg because of her role in the Citizens United campaign finance ruling.

On the morning of Justice Ginsburg's interview Jim had scheduled Jim Johnson, executive director of Jamestown's Robert H. Jackson Center for an interview before Justice Ginsburg was due to appear. Jim Roselle, however, was not sure Justice Ginsburg would be able to meet him for her interview, so he extended his interesting conversation with Johnson to fill time. Out of the corner of his eye, Jim noticed a woman who approached the audience seating area slowly and sat quietly watching the interview in progress. Jim suddenly realized that it was Justice Ginsburg, patiently and politely awaiting her turn.

Not only was his guest patient, she was far more generous with her time than he had hoped.

Justice Ginsburg also advised Jim that anyone entering the judicial branch of the United States government needed a sense of humor. There's little doubt that members of the executive and legislative branches in Washington DC could use it too.

Jim knows that Washington sense of humor from firsthand experience. He learned it for himself one day from Liz Carpenter.

Jim Remembers… Liz Carpenter and Babe Ruth Go Shopping

Few people in government are as close to the First Family and the President as their speechwriters and press secretaries. They not only need a sense of humor more than most people, but bring it with them whenever they pack a bag to travel.

Liz Carpenter, an accomplished, professional newswoman and public relations expert, was Lady Bird Johnson's press secretary and staff director. She also collaborated in writing President Lyndon Johnson's speeches. Liz, who had also established the White House Humor Group, had a legendary sense of humor. Another fellow Texan, Governor Ann Richards, once described Liz as "…the tilt-a-whirl at the State Fair of Texas with all the lights on and the music. The only difference between Liz and a tilt-a-whirl is that, with Liz, the ride never comes to an end."

When Liz was staying at Chautauqua Institution one summer, I made the most of her quick wit by turning Mark Russell loose on her with a microphone in the broadcast booth. A hilarious pair!

I wanted Liz Carpenter for an interview on the show Russ Diethrick and I do every Saturday morning, *The Times of Your Life*, in our Jamestown, WJTN studio. After she agreed, I told Russ I had set up an interview for the next Saturday morning. Liz Carpenter was well known for telling great stories. When we invited her to Jamestown, she even created a memorable one herself.

I was scheduled to go pick her up at Chautauqua Institution and bring her to the studio, but I wanted a nice car for the drive. Russ got our friend, Les Ostrander, to loan us his 1922 Pierce Arrow. The car had once been owned by Babe Ruth. Les drove us to the Institution together in that magnificent machine to pick Liz up.

When we arrived at her door, everybody ran out of their cottages with their cameras when they saw us. They all wanted to pose with the car. They didn't even want to see Liz. She thought that was amusing, but since we had such a head-turning car at our disposal, she immediately dreamed up a few more uses for it.

We took Liz to the studio for the interview, and it went just fine. But driving back to the Institution, she asked us to please stop. She had seen a store. "I need a quart of milk," she informed us. Naturally, we stopped, and she got her milk.

She climbed back aboard with her purchase, and we drove on. Then she spotted another store, not very far from the Institution. "Stop! That's a grocery store. There are a few more things I need."

So, there we were, one fine Saturday afternoon, on a shopping trip for groceries with Liz Carpenter and Babe Ruth. I never heard about what she said to her neighbors about those grocery store bags she climbed out of Babe Ruth's beautiful car with.

In my business, there's a new adventure waiting every day.

Nancy Gibbs and the Presidents Club

Nancy Reid Gibbs, managing editor of *Time* magazine, is a native of New York City, and a life-long Chautauquan. She is widely known as an essayist, a best-selling author and a political and cultural commentator. With co-author Michael Duffy, she authored two *New York Times* Bestsellers, the more recent of which, *The Presidents Club*, she discussed with Jim Roselle at Chautauqua in 2013.

Gibbs graduated *summa cum laude* from Yale University in 1982 with honors in history. She earned her M.A. degree in politics, philosophy and economics at New College, Oxford, as a Marshall Scholar.

The climb to the top of her profession took the time-honored, traditional route, beginning at the bottom rung of the career ladder. She joined *Time* as a part-time fact checker in the *International* section in 1985. Within three years, she rose to the rank of writer with credit for more than 100 *Time* cover stories and won a National Magazine Award in 2002 including for her cover story on the September 11 attacks. She also won many other awards for her magazine writing before attaining the position of managing editor.

Jim and Nancy Gibbs discuss the elite Presidents Club

Gibbs has frequently appeared as a guest on radio and television, including the *Today Show, Good Morning America*, Charlie Rose, Jim Lehrer and Jim Roselle at Chautauqua Institution where she has appeared as a guest lecturer.

A Conversation with Nancy Gibbs

Jim Roselle: Welcome back to The Cove for the final week of the 2013 season, the Presidents Club Week. I'm asking the Breakfast Club to give Nancy Gibbs a warm welcome. [Applause] Nancy, it's good to see you again.
Nancy Gibbs: It's good to see you again, too, Jim. You've been here for 39 years, now, haven't you? All right then, it's official: You are a legend.

JR: Well, Nancy, you are a legend, too, and you are back where you belong, right here at Chautauqua.

NG: It's good to be home. I have been here just about every summer of my life, although I don't get as much time here as I used to. Those growing up years, when we could come in June and leave in August, was just a wonderful thing.

JR: I told you before and I'll say it again, I was so pleased years ago to meet your dad, Howard Gibbs.
It was a pleasure to realize, too, that he was serving as president of the national Boys Club.

NG: That's right; he spent his entire career with the Boys Clubs of America. He trained as a social worker and that was really his mission.

JR: Well, the boys club has played a very important part in my life. Your father became my good friend. And now, welcome back to Chautauqua to talk about your book, *The Presidents Club* [*The Presidents Club: Inside the World's Most Exclusive Fraternity*, Simon & Schuster, 2012].

NG: The last time I lectured in the amphitheater [*The Preacher and The Presidents: Billy Graham in the White House,* Grand Central Pub, 2007] it was about the role of religion in politics and what it is the [United States] presidents need spiritually. In the course of researching that book, which I did with my co-author Michael Duffy, we kept coming across these really interesting, offstage, back-channel communications among presidents and former presidents. Those were things that we had not come across before.

We started wondering about how much they actually talked to each other, and why has no one really told that story? We launched into that research and, five years later, this one is out now.

JR: How often did you have a conversation with the ex-presidents to get the detailed information about what their thoughts were or how they communicated with each other?

NG: Both of us are editors at *Time*. Between us, we had interviewed all of the living presidents. We could go back to them and talk about this, though it's not something they talk about a lot. This is kind of a private fraternity and we were knocking on a door that doesn't open very much. The thing that really struck us was the depth of knowledge that they have about the past presidents. When George W. Bush was in the White House he read 17 biographies of Lincoln. The presidents are really interested in the presidents. They study each other. They read the memoirs and diaries, letters and biographies. If you look on their bookshelves, it's all presidential history.

JR: Did George Washington, John Adams and Thomas Jefferson communicate with each other after they left office?

NG: Jefferson and Adams had famously feuded, but they ended up with an extraordinary correspondence after they were out of office. Their friendship was rekindled. Those are wonderful letters.

George Washington made the most important decision any president ever made: his decision to become an ex-president rather than stay on as a President for Life. The fact that he chose to serve just the two terms and then step aside set an important precedent.

John Adams was the first president to realize that a former president could be useful. In Washington, he had someone who was a national icon and a great military leader. In the face of increasing external military threats, he brought Washington back to command the United States Army again. That first relationship of president and former president set the precedent for what we saw all through history.

JR: Did Lincoln communicate with an ex-president?

NG: Lincoln was an interesting case. When he took office, there were five living, former presidents, the most there ever were in American history until Bill Clinton's inauguration when, once again, there were five. In Lincoln's case, the reason there were five was because his predecessors had all been thrown out quickly. There was a certain amount of, "Should we all get together and try to prevent a civil war?" That ended up not being possible. Until the modern age, there wasn't as much that a former president could do compared to what we now see them routinely doing.

JR: Did it all start back in 1953 when Herbert Hoover suggested to Harry Truman, "Let's start a Presidents Club."?

NG: This is one of my favorite stories. How is it that someone like Harry Truman becomes an ally, friend and partner of the man who was as politically, personally and ideologically as opposite to him as Herbert Hoover?

That became possible because, when Truman took office in the spring of 1945 and Europe was in shambles, Truman knew that there was probably no one in the country who knew more about humanitarian relief and about solving an engineering puzzle than Hoover. Hoover was an engineer - and a footnote here, just for you, Jim, Hoover was the founder of the Boys Clubs of America.

Hoover knew how to solve complicated problems. And Truman did not care that Hoover had left Washington as the most hated man in America. He simply said, "This is the guy I need. I'm bringing him back in. I'm going to get him to help me." The two men, then, throughout Truman's presidency, worked together very closely.

In 1952, Eisenhower was elected and Truman and Hoover were buddies. That's how it is that when Harry Truman greets Dwight David Eisenhower on the inaugural platform that morning, he says, "We should form a Presidents Club."

JR: How did Eisenhower fit into the picture?

NG: Truman and Hoover were very skeptical of Eisenhower. Truman and Eisenhower had an epic fight throughout that election, though they had once been friends and worked very well together. That Inauguration Day morning was frosty between those two men. Eisenhower nearly refused to pick up Truman at the White House. Traditionally, the incoming president picks up the outgoing president and they ride to the capital together. Eisenhower would not even get out of his car.

Hoover and Eisenhower did not have as much personal animosity between them, but they were ideologically quite different. Hoover was still an isolationist while Eisenhower had been the NATO commander and believed that America should station permanent forces in Europe for collective security. Neither Truman nor Hoover was crazy about Eisenhower as president.

JR: In your book, you talk about a residence for past presidents who come to Washington.

NG: Originally, Presidents Club was just a figure of speech we were using, but the more we looked into it, the more we realized this was much more real than we thought.

We discovered that there is, in fact, a clubhouse, an unmarked brownstone across the street from the White House, that right now only former presidents are allowed to stay in, and they have to call the White House for reservations. It was acquired for their use by Richard Nixon because he had many reasons to want to keep Lyndon Johnson happy. Johnson would call and ask for briefings, airplanes and the use of a place to stay when he came to Washington. Nixon finally asked a young military aid to find a place for Johnson to stay and work when he was in town. Nixon wanted a "clubhouse", mainly for Johnson, though, because Truman was not coming back to Washington very often and Eisenhower had died just a few months after Nixon's inauguration.

JR: Let's bring it up to date between Barack Obama and Bill Clinton.

NG: The things that Obama hoped to do were very different from what he found out was actually possible in the presidency. This is something all of them learn.

Once Obama had been in the job for a couple of years and had learned the kind of compromises that are necessary and inevitable, and learned the difficulty of keeping any promise, however grand or minor, that you make as a candidate, his understanding of Clinton and Clinton-ism changed very drastically. I don't think, however, that they are ever very likely to be best friends.

The best friend award goes to Clinton and George Herbert Walker Bush. That buddy movie is one to watch. They each say that the other one is the one who really reached out. Barbara Bush refers to her husband as the father that Bill Clinton never had.

This is why I like what Mark Twain said: "History does not repeat itself, but it does rhyme." You have George Herbert Walker Bush as president, followed by a president who never knew his father, who ultimately looks to the first man as a surrogate father. He is followed by the man who is the actual son of the first president, who is followed by another president who never really knew his father. You could call the modern presidency the "My Three Sons" of George Herbert Walker Bush.

As soon as he was in the White House, Obama made active attempts to get to know Bush 41, to honor him and go down to his presidential library to honor the Points of Light program. Bush would come to town and stay in the Clubhouse. Then he would go to the White House, but not to give advice or tell Obama what to do about anything. He just went to chat and tell him jokes to reduce the tension and make it all feel okay.

This was a classic case of a former president knowing what a sitting president needs; someone who he can let down his guard with.

JR: Tell the audience here, live and on the radio, the story of Winston Churchill going to heaven and meeting St. Peter at the gate.

NG: It's a story Margaret Truman told in the waning days of Truman's presidency. Churchill had come to Washington and there was a dinner at the White House for him.

Churchill, as you can imagine, was never one to let the conversation lag. He asked Truman whether he had given any thought to what would happen when the two of them found themselves at the gates of heaven confronted by the fact that they had, between them, agreed to drop the atomic bombs on Japan. That made for an awkward moment.

"Mr. Prime Minister, what makes you think you're going to be going to the same place as President Truman?" the Secretary of Defense, Robert Lovett, asked.

"I have faith in our Creator that he would not sentence a man without a jury of his peers," Churchill answered.

"A jury of Winston Churchill's peers at the gates of heaven? Who, exactly, would be on that?" Everyone at the table wondered.

The game was on. The Secretary of State decides said he would be Alexander the Great. Someone else decided to be George Washington. Another person decided he would be Thomas Aquinas. They all decided who they would be on this jury to decide whether Winston Churchill goes to heaven or not.

Ultimately, of course, Churchill decided to waive his jury rights and just let Harry Truman be the judge because he can count on the mercy of a man who knows what the really hard decisions are like.

In a sense, the Presidents Club is a club of people who, in different roles, at different times, have faced the impossible jobs. All they can do, sometimes, is choose the least bad option. When that is the job every day, there is no way one can leave that job without scars and regrets. Even if someone makes every decision right, the choices are going to weigh on him. I think that is what ties all of them together.

JR: President George W. Bush said, "I am going to just dance off the stage and let Barack Obama do his job." He wasn't going to criticize in order to give his party something of substance to use in their campaign.

NG: He has been remarkably consistent about that. He said, "President Obama deserves my silence. I don't think it is good for our country to undermine our president, and I don't intend to do so. I think the job matters more than the occupant, and I am not going to do anything or say anything or criticize in any way that will make his job harder. "

JR: Who did Obama call after the Navy SEALs got Osama bin Laden?

NG: Some of the first calls he made after the raid was successful were to George W. Bush and to Bill Clinton. Foreign policy bridges across presidencies. Vietnam, for instance, really started with Eisenhower and then went through Kennedy, through Johnson and to Nixon. In the case of the ongoing battle with Al Qaeda and bin Laden, it started with Clinton and went through Bush to Obama. That's why he called them first. He wanted them to know this had succeeded.

JR: What about LBJ's meetings with Eisenhower?

NG: That happened all the time. Johnson would call Eisenhower down on his farm in Gettysburg and say, "I really need to talk to you. I don't want anyone to think it is an emergency, so can you make up some cover story for why you need to come to Washington? Just slip into town and come to the White House and talk to me. Spend the night, and you can have the Lincoln bedroom."

Eisenhower, too, believed it was the obligation of all Americans to support their president. That is a really significant pattern that we saw all through.

JR: Let's bring in Jimmy Carter. He is the president who is making more trips to other lands trying to negotiate the best opportunity out of a difficult situation.

NG: He has had an extraordinary ex-presidency. He has sort of become a role model for all of the others. In September, 2013, Jimmy Carter becomes the longest serving ex-president in American history. I think Carter is one who has really shown those who followed what they can do.

JR: I want to give you the Chautauqua Question. Let's go back to the presidents who are not here any longer. What four presidents would you like to have with you for dinner some night?

NG: I certainly think both Roosevelts would be great companions. Of all presidents, probably the greatest storyteller was Lyndon Johnson. I bet he would be a great dinner companion. Obviously, Abraham Lincoln would, too, because when you have one of the most interesting presidents and one of the most interesting and fateful periods in our country's history, that is kind of an irresistible combination.

RG: If you could be a fly on the wall and witness any historic moment, where would you like to be?

NG: We had one of those moments recently in the decision of when and how to launch the Osama bin Laden raid. The stakes really could not have been higher. There was the risk of it going wrong, the risk of war with Pakistan, the risk of terrible loss of life and of terrible humiliation. Look at what happened to Jimmy Carter with the Iranian hostage rescue attempt.

Any moment like that – whether it was the Cuban missile crisis or the immediate aftermath of 9/11 or the Hiroshima decision – was about weighing impossible choices. Watching anyone doing those things in any role of life, but certainly watching the presidents, would affect all of us in an extraordinary way.

JR: Nancy Gibbs, thank you so much.

NG: Thank you Jim. Nice seeing you again.

A Conversation with Associate Justice Ruth Bader Ginsburg

Jim Roselle: I'm sitting next to United States Supreme Court Justice Ruth Bader Ginsburg. My heartfelt thanks for giving me an opportunity to let a local audience hear your story…not only the story of your life, as a Supreme Court justice, but as a mother and as a wife to Marty. It's a wonderful love story. I'd like to spend a little time on that if I may.

Justice Ginsburg: Yes, and I hope you will include my best-selling book in the Supreme Court's Gift Shop, *Chef Supreme*. My late husband was the Chef Supreme. And Mrs. Alito, wife of Justice Alito, thought that would be the perfect tribute to Marty.

JR: I read the part where, after he passed away, your daughter had to come and make sure that all the meals were prepared for weeks in advance, because he had done all the cooking.

JG: My daughter, Jane [a professor at Columbia Law], comes once a month, spends the whole day cooking and freezes individual meals for me. For most occasions when Jane was growing up, I was the everyday cook, and Marty was the weekend and company cook. Around about her junior year in high school Jane noticed a distinct difference between daddy's cooking and mommy's cooking and decided that *he* should not only be the weekend and company cook but the everyday cook as well.

JR: Well then, as long as you eat so well, how about telling us about your exercise plan. You now do 20 push-ups, don't you? At the age of 80?

JG: Yes I do. That's right…I started with my trainer in 1999 shortly after I had undergone surgery, chemotherapy and radiation for colorectal cancer. Marty said, "You know you look like a survivor of Auschwitz, you must do something to build yourself up." And that's when I started working with my trainer who now trains two Supreme Court justices. He trains Justice Kagan and me. His name is Brian Johnson.

JR: How did you get into that world of law?

JG: I was going to Cornell in the early 1950s. It was not the best time for the United States. It was the heyday of Senator Joe McCarthy who saw a communist in every corner. I was working for a professor of constitutional law and he wanted me to appreciate how far we had strayed from our basic values, from the right to think, speak and write freely. So I monitored "Red Channels," the latest blacklists and many other things.

The professor called to my attention that there were lawyers speaking up for these people before the House Un-American Activities Committee [HUAC], the Senate Internal Security Committee. So I came to understand that law might be a way to make a living while doing things outside myself that would make things a little better for my community and my country. That's what turned me on to the law.

JR: You mentioned the Joe McCarthy era. I remember viewing that on television and specifically Joseph Welch who made a statement that has been quoted quite often. He asked "Do you have any decency?" I remember that well.

JG: That was the beginning of the end for Joe McCarthy.

JR: You've been in the Supreme Court for almost 20 years.

JG: August will be the 20th anniversary of my Senate confirmation.

JR: The average person in America… I think I speak for them in a way…would like to understand your personal life as well as in the Supreme Court. But off duty do you socialize with the other justices?

JG: The court is the most collegial place I've ever worked in…There are many, many things that we do together…The court has two musicales every year and all of the justices attend. On a justice's birthday we have a toast led by the Chief and we sing Happy Birthday, with Justice Scalia usually leading the chorus because, frankly, he's the only one of us who can carry a tune. There is a lot of togetherness.

JR: You two are noted for your love of opera, you and Justice Scalia.

JG: We have been "supers" together twice at the Washington National Opera. [A super is a supernumerary, a non-speaking, non-singing role in an opera, like an "extra" in a film.] Another time I was a super with Justice Kennedy and Justice Breyer.

JR: Does the average citizen misunderstand what the Supreme Court does?

JG: The press tends to feature the constitutional decisions where there is sharp disagreement. But most of the cases we hear do not concern the Constitution. They concern the ordinary legislation that Congress passes in great numbers and often with less than a clear statement; there is room for interpretation. Those are 60 to 70 percent of our business, and we don't divide along so-called party lines…But because we are the highest court for the interpretation of United States law, which is mostly statutory law…sharp divisions are the exception not the rule. Twenty-five percent of cases we divide 5 to 4, while in at least 50 percent we are unanimous at least in the bottom-line judgment, and… a single opinion speaks for the entire court.

JR: Today there's still a very emotional argument going on about the Citizens United versus the Federal Election Commission case about making corporations able to give all of the donations they want without even identifying themselves. What are your thoughts on them putting that kind of money into elections today?

JG: I think my colleagues who decided that the First Amendment protects the right to speak through the money you give would say, "Nothing in that opinion suggests that there shouldn't be a disclosure requirement. It would be perfectly constitutional for Congress to say there is no limit on spending or contributions but all the people who contribute must be identified. Congress hasn't done that.

But in my view—I was a dissenter in Citizens United—I consider it one of the major errors that the court has made in recent years. Not tomorrow, and maybe not next year, but eventually I do think Citizens United will be overruled. I don't see how our democracy is advanced by allowing some people to spend with the sky as the limit and drown out the voices of people who don't have the wherewithal to make huge campaign contributions.

I think it has a tremendous effect on Congress, the people who have to run for office every two years. As soon as they get elected they have to start building up their war chest for the next contest. And I don't think that's healthy. Citizens United was a 5 to 4 vote. It would have gone the other way if Justice O'Connor had remained with us, because she was part of the majority. In fact, she wrote part of the opinion that upheld the campaign finance law decision that was overruled in Citizens United.

JR: You turned 80 in March of 2013 and the thought occurs to everybody; is Justice Ginsburg going to retire?

JG: As long as I can do the job full steam, I will remain on the court. When I sense that I'm beginning to slip, that will be the time for me to go. At my age you just take it year by year. I think I'm okay for next year and a year after that. I hope so, but I don't know… I've hired law clerks for the next two years.

JR: When you look back, what do you want the legacy of Justice Ginsburg to be?

JG: I hope it will be that I worked as hard as I can with the limited talent that I have to help realize what our Constitution starts out with…Some of the first words are, "To form a more perfect union…" I think that we have, over the last two centuries and more, made the union more perfect. The genius of the Constitution is that it has become more inclusive.

In 1787 when the Constitution was drafted, they wrote, "We the people…" but they were all white, property-owning men. Today 'we the people' includes so many who were once left out. Half the population was women, and there are people who were once held in human bondage and the Native Americans. America is ever more inclusive of different races, religions, national origins… I think that is what makes the United States a model for the world. I hope we will keep it, and I hope I can make some small contribution to forming that more perfect union.

JR: What advice would you give anybody in law school today?

JG: To the young women I would say, "What a great time to be a lawyer. There are no closed doors to you as there were to my generation. When I got out of law school there was no Title VII, there were no prohibitions of discrimination in employment, and I don't know how many employers told me, "Well we had a woman once and she was dreadful." My response was, "And how many men have you had that didn't work out?" A sense of humor really helped in those ancient days.

But now all doors are open. I would say to the young people, "You can be a lawyer and make a living, but if that's all you do you're kind of like an artisan, like a plumber working a day for a day's pay. But you have a skill because of your legal education to help make things better for other people." My advice would be, "Do something outside yourself. Whatever you believe strongly in, whether it's the environment, the equality of all persons in the United States—whatever is your passion—pursue that. Then you will be a true professional."

JR: Justice Ginsburg, thank you very much for this discussion and the pleasure of your company. Let's give her a nice round of applause.

Andrew Young
An Easy Burden

Andrew Young played an important role in the civil rights movement in the 1960s with Dr. Martin Luther King Jr. Young was a congressman from Georgia from 1972 to 1976, US Ambassador to the United Nations from 1977 to 1979, and Mayor of Atlanta 1982 to 1990. Andrew joined Jim Roselle at Chautauqua Institution in the summer of 2000. Jim Roselle—and all of his Franklin Street Gang—grew up in families where parents sacrificed for their children's futures and children simply accepted it as a fact of everyday life, a joyous, raucous and happy fact of life in families where striving for success was a badge of honor, not a burden.

Andrew Young, (1977)

Andrew Young's family was much like Jim's in that way; Jim and Andrew could understand each other. Jim muses that their stories practically made them brothers. He knew his listeners would welcome Andrew Young into their neighborhood, too.

A Conversation with Andrew Young

Jim Roselle: Andrew Young, if I read all of your background I won't have time for the interview. But of course we've got to acknowledge what you have accomplished in your lifetime. Former congressman from Georgia, former mayor of Atlanta, former representative to the United Nations, serving on many boards and the Olympic Committee for Atlanta. What haven't you done?

Andrew Young: The most important thing I have done was the eight years that I spent with Martin Luther King in the 60s. And then there were the three or four years I spent pastoring little churches in the South, in Alabama and Georgia.

JR: Why did you call the book you wrote two years ago *An Easy Burden*? [*An Easy Burden: The Civil Rights Movement and the Transformation of America* (with a foreword by Quincy Jones) Baylor University Press, 2008]

AY: People get the title wrong. They quite often say "No Easy Burden" but the truth of it is that it *was* an easy burden. I happened to have been born into a good Christian family where—they were not rich—it was taken for granted before I was born that I would go to college.

JR: How big a family?

AY: Just two brothers. We were good Congregationalists in the Deep South, which was unusual, but the Congregational educational heritage across the South made the first thing you thought about when a child was born was, "Where is he going to college?" or "Where is she going to college?"

JR: No matter what the economic circumstances?

AY: That was what my parents worked for. We didn't have a car and they never took vacations, but they put away money for our college. I was blessed with that kind of family. I also came along at a time after the World War II when Americans believed that all things were possible, and when the majority of people really wanted to do the right thing.

JR: Then you agree with the title of Tom Brokaw's book, *The Greatest Generation*?

AY: I really do. It's a pleasure that Tom wrote that book and gave it that title. I think the Marshall Plan, more than the war itself, was a symbol of the greatness of this generation. It was an effort at world leadership which John Kennedy and Lyndon Johnson applied at home. Also, in the early days, civil rights was a bipartisan concern. The Rockefeller wing of the Republican Party was probably more liberal than the Democrats in those days on race issues. It was the churches that helped put together the coalition of conscience that passed civil rights bills in 1964 and 1965.

JR: A work still in progress?

AY: A work still very much in progress. We found, and probably knew all along, that deeper than the issues of race were the issues of class. And in the underclass in America that has been somewhat exacerbated by the rapid growth of globalization. It means that that's a problem in the turn-of-the-century that is every bit as serious as the race problem was. I think those of us who have come up through this from the black side of poverty are more sensitive to the problems of white poverty. It's one of my few criticisms of Bill Clinton and Jimmy Carter. They were poor whites from the South, and they have done a lot for black people, but neither one of them addressed the problems of poor whites in the South. Lyndon Johnson did.

Johnson's poverty program was conceived largely, I think, out of his Southern white experience. It just happened to help; it made a big difference. It was branded by the Northern press as a big city effort to help the blacks and to create a welfare state. I think that Johnson was always mindful of his own poor background and the liberating effect his education had on him.

JR: Your book includes a picture of you marching along with Martin Luther King. Why did you choose that particular picture with a gun in the background?

AY: It's the most dramatic picture. I very seldom was in the front line with Martin. Most of the time I was at the back of the line trying to be sure everything was all right. Even though we were together for eight years, I probably don't have a dozen pictures of us together. We were walking on the street in Mississippi and somebody just framed it with the Mississippi state trooper.

JR: Was there any time in the marches with Martin Luther King that he was talking to you personally about the fear of assassination?

AY: He talked about it all the time. But it was never fear. We were together when John Kennedy was assassinated. He said, "You know, if they can't protect the president, we don't stand a chance." And then he would always turn it into a joke and say, "They're going to be shooting at me, but they'll probably hit you, Andy." He added "But don't worry. I will preach you the best funeral…" And then he would start preaching my funeral.

He always talked about death and he always laughed about death. Death was not something that he feared. In fact, he was stabbed in Harlem—after he wrote his book—by a demented woman. In order to remove the knife from his chest they had to cut his rib cage open. It left him with a scar in the shape of a cross on his chest.

"You fellas say you are ready to die for your country and to die for this movement," he would say, "but you don't really know what it is. Every morning when I brush my teeth I have to stare the cross in the face. I don't know whether this day is going to be my last."

JR: Andrew Young, thank you for telling us something about real bravery and inviting us into your life… Let's give him a round of Chautauqua applause…

Leah Ward Sears: Marriage, Divorce and the Chief Justice

Jim Roselle's friends often call him "The man who knows everybody."

After all, he meets the world's most famous people, many of whose stories make unexpected connections. Take the city of Nuremberg, Germany, for instance.

Leah Ward Sears, the youngest person and the first African-American woman to become Chief Justice of the Supreme Court of Georgia, was born near Nuremberg.

Another guest, Ernst Michel (Chapter 3, "Sex, the Sniper and the Survivors"), was an Auschwitz survivor and a War Crimes Trial correspondent in Nuremberg.

US Supreme Court Justice Robert H. Jackson, from Jamestown, NY, was the US Chief Prosecutor at Nuremberg.

And Leah Ward Sears' first judicial post was assigned by Jim's last guest, Atlanta, Georgia's Mayor, Andrew Young.

Jim's microphone is often a crossroads for such improbable connections.

Many of Leah Sears' successes came early and quickly. She earned her bachelor's degree at Cornell University at the age of 21 and her *Juris Doctor* at Emory University School of Law at 25. Andrew Young appointed her to an Atlanta City Court position at the age of 30 and a Superior Court judge by 33. In 1992 Governor Zell Miller appointed her a Georgia Supreme Court justice at 37. In June of 2005, Sears was elected by a bipartisan, landslide margin and elevated to Chief Justice of Georgia. Leah's husband, Haskell Ward, was the Deputy Mayor of New York City under Mayor Ed Koch.

Naturally, Jim was interested in anything that could have propelled Sears to such successes. He was especially curious about her views on family life.

Jim kicked off this interview in an unusual way, even for Jim. He introduced himself as "The other Jim Roselle."

"I'm not Jimmy Roselli the crooner," he said. "I hope you're not disappointed." Jimmy Roselli had been a popular contemporary of Frank Sinatra and Dean Martin.

[Before Jim opened the microphone, he played Jimmy Roselli's 1967 hit release, *When Your Old Wedding Ring Was New*.]

> *When your old wedding ring was new*
> *And each dream that I dreamed came true*
> *I remember with pride how we stood side by side*
> *What a beautiful picture you made as my bride.*
>
> Bert Douglas
> Written for the film: *Once More with Feeling* (1960)

A Conversation with Chief Justice Leah Sears

Jim Roselle: I thought it was appropriate for the week. You are in a situation where you deal with family situations and relationships. Are you trying to solidify those relationships?
Leah Sears: Unfortunately, as a jurist, I see them when they've broken down. I've seen judges come in on divorce matters, child custody, juvenile delinquency...

JR: I wanted to get to that one area of child custody. When a couple decides to divorce, things have changed over the years, obviously, but are the jury and the judge quick to give custody of the children to the mother?
LS: Years ago, the presumption was that the father would get the children because the wife and the children were the father's property. That then changed over the last 30, 40, 50 years. The presumption became that the mother would get custody of the children unless she was just flat unfit. I'm seeing nowadays, though, many, many more fathers being able to get custody of their children, even from mothers who aren't necessarily unfit, if the father would be a better parent.
JR: Do you ever inquire about the children's concerns; do they get to participate in the process?
LS: The whole analysis in a custody battle is what's in the best interest of the children. That's what you're trying to figure out. Most judges don't like children to participate because they believe children don't know what's in their best interest. It should be an adult who makes adult decisions for children.
JR: I'd like to get to the overall picture of family life today in America. Are you concerned about children out of wedlock?

LS: I am 52 years old now. I was born in 1955. When I was born, 20 percent of African-American children were born out of wedlock and about 8 percent of white children were born out of wedlock. Last year [2006] that number was 34 percent of white children born out of wedlock and 70 percent of black children out of wedlock, and that means they're not growing up with a mother and a father [2014 statistics are roughly unchanged]. Studies show a mother and a father provide the best setting for children if there's no violence. I know divorce happens, and I don't suggest we go back to a time when you can't get divorced, but we ought not to set out to create a difficult situation.

We have to acknowledge it is problematic. Everything is not okay. Every family form does not equal every other family form. Divorce is extremely traumatic; it's a great loss and a failure for many people. It's not just a wonderful thing… I can't say there are many times I leave divorce cases happy. I can think of one where they walked out, and they decided not to divorce; they stuck with it. One in 23 years of being a judge. So, I'm sorry to seem down, but I'm here now because I want other people to start thinking about ways you can cut my caseload down.

JR: Leah Sears, Thank you for sharing your time and your insights with us.

Chapter 5

Sex, the Sniper and the Survivors

Families can be whole… or lost in their entirety. But their values, their sense of purpose, can carry on through future generations; a lengthening shadow that stretches beyond the place where they once stood. Family tragedies rooted in hatred may even send survivors on missions of love. Jim Roselle was frequently awed by survivors' tales and sometimes even scandalously amused by their exploits.

That I survived the Holocaust and went on to love beautiful girls, to talk, to write, to have toast and tea and live my life - that is what is abnormal.

Elie Wiesel
Auschwitz Survivor, Author Political Activist

And now, somebody of a certain age, Jim, cannot hang from a chandelier anymore.

Karola Ruth Siegel Westheimer

The Girl Sniper

Karola was so small she might have been mistaken for a child. That's what got her the job.

At 4 feet 7 inches, she was only a little taller than her rifle and small enough to shoot from the tiniest of hiding places anywhere in the British Mandate of Palestine in 1945. The Haganah in Jerusalem, which later transformed itself into the Israel Defense Forces, had trained her as a sniper and an unobtrusive guide, hardly noticed even if seen. They had trained her, too, not to be susceptible to emotions, anxiety or remorse of any kind in her difficult job.

Karola Ruth Siegel's parents, Irma and Julius, were orthodox Jews. They were murdered in a Nazi death camp in 1941 when she was 13 years old. They had sent their only child to a Swiss sanctuary for safety two years earlier, but she knew nothing of their deaths until 1945. So many parents of the other children living there had suffered the same fate that the safe haven had become an orphanage by the end of the war. With nothing left for Karola back home, she decided to emigrate to the British Mandate of Palestine. There, she joined Haganah and nearly died in combat in 1948, the year of Israel's birth as a nation.

The girl sniper had already trekked some 2000 miles, counting the distance from her childhood home in Germany's heartland, in the sleepy country village of Wiesenfeld, through Switzerland, on to Jerusalem and then to Palestine's battlefields. Only two years after recovering from her injuries, she traveled to France where she studied and taught psychology at the University of Paris. Before she was 30, she moved again, this time to the United States to earn a doctorate degree. There she studied sex… human sexuality.

By 1980, Dr. Ruth's career had earned her a radio show, *Sexually Speaking*, which aired on *NBC Radio* from Manhattan, and from there in syndication across America. Dr. Ruth soon became a household celebrity on radios everywhere in the country.

Then, one summer morning in August of 2007, that girl sniper/sex doctor came to Jim Roselle's Bestor Plaza sidewalk studio. He invited her to his microphone, undaunted by the notion that she might sound like a "cross between Henry Kissinger and Minnie Mouse," (as a writer for *The Wall Street*

Journal had once portrayed her). Jim was prepared to meet this heralded and most interesting guest and hear what she would say to his audience.

"You couldn't help but anticipate the opportunity to talk to a lady who has given advice to so many people over so many years," Jim recalls. "She gave me a warm greeting and a big hug. Then we sat down and did the interview."

Passersby stopped by Bestor Plaza sidewalk studio to listen in.

A Conversation with Dr. Ruth

Dr. Ruth: I hear you are a legend…That's what they told me.
Jim Roselle: In my own mind? Maybe. Dr. Ruth, it's a pleasure to welcome you to Chautauqua and to this broadcast. I thank you very much for giving us an opportunity to meet you. You don't know how much time I devoted to thinking about the subject matter that we're going to be talking about.

DrR: I should hope so. Your whole lifetime?
JR: You have a program called *Sexually Speaking*.
DrR: True. (Dr. Ruth picks up a book from the broadcast desk) My Gosh, you got the book a long time ago. Wonderful. You did your homework. All right!
JR: I did a lot of reading, Dr. Ruth. Oh boy! (All laugh) You don't know how often, in my hometown of Jamestown, New York, the people asked me what my first question would be.
DrR: Let's have the first question.
JR: How's your sex life? (Long silence. Then Dr. Ruth, Jim and the sidewalk audience all laugh.)
DrR: I'm going to tell everybody here how old-fashioned and square I am. There is no answer to that question except to tell you, Jim, my late husband passed away a few years ago and I never permitted him to come to any of my talks. Not to the radio which I did 10 years in a row. Not to any lecture, because if I now would say, "Okay who has some questions in addition to Jim's fabulous question?" He would stand there and raise his hand, and I couldn't ignore him. I would have to acknowledge him and then he would tell you and your listeners in Jamestown and all of the people here, "Don't listen to her, it is all talk."
JR: Let's get serious for a moment… My question is, in one of your books you made a statement that generations ago people didn't concern themselves with sexual morality.
DrR: That's not so. They concerned themselves, but they never talked about it. It was very clear, though, for believing Catholics, Orthodox Jews, Protestants and anybody else who believed in a certain value, that they would not be sexually active before the night after the wedding ceremony.

The Victorian Puritan mother told her daughter the night after the wedding ceremony to lie back and think of England. There is nothing in it for you. Don't expect the earth to shake, don't expect the stars to twinkle, don't expect orgasms. That was the message. It's not that they weren't concerned with morality, there was an attitude that this is one part of life, but not like other things that you talk about.

I never ask a personal question. Now if you wanted to ask me a personal question about yourself, you have to come to New York, to my office. I have this very interesting way of dealing openly with all of those things, from erection to orgasm. But I never make it personal. Anybody who is here (Dr. Ruth motions toward the passersby) who wants to ask a question has to say "A friend of mine has a question." (All laugh). Now I don't know if it is you we are talking about. I'm very European and very old-fashioned in that.

However, we in this country have the best scientifically validated data about human sexual functioning that has ever been available…Here's an article in the *New England Journal of Medicine*. The study finds many still active into their 80s.

JR: In the generations way back, was it almost taboo to talk about sex?

DrR: You did not talk…You said about a woman, "She is with child." You wouldn't say the word pregnant. You certainly, now I'm going to shock you, I hope, even though I am never about shocking people, nobody would ever, ever talk about masturbation. And what we are going to do here…

JR: (interrupting) I don't think I've used that word in my entire radio career yet…

DrR: I know that.

JR: I don't know if I'm going to use it today yet.

DrR: Then don't use it. Only I can use it.

JR: I don't believe this is going on, I really don't.

DrR: So here's what we have to do in a place as fascinating as this Chautauqua. We have to bury some of those myths, but in good taste, never asking a personal question…I could stay here for a week, on your radio program, and talk about nothing else, only about all of those myths that have filtered down. One more about…

JR: Don't finish that sentence. A few years ago my career would've ended with that.

DrR: Mine too, so we would've ended both just like that. We would look for work together.

But on a more serious note, there is a myth that says that if a woman or a man brings themselves to sexual satisfaction, that hair will grow in the palm of their hands. I said that at the Harvard Law School, and guess what? Plenty of those attorneys looked at their hands.

[Jim, trying to catch his breath, turns the conversation in a different direction. He asks about her autobiography, *Musically Speaking: A Life Through Song,* in which Dr. Ruth says much about her own family matters.]

DrR: In there I'm talking about my coming out of Nazi Germany on a Kinder Transport to Switzerland into a children's home that became an orphanage. I have to tell you, walking around here just now; I passed by one house that has a lot of American flags. And that gives me pause to be very thankful, because if I had not been placed in Switzerland by a mother and a grandmother—my father was already taken to a labor camp on a train in Frankfurt am Main—I wouldn't be sitting here; I would be dead. If the allies, the Americans, the Australians, the Canadians had not entered World War II, I would not be alive. Hitler would have taken Switzerland.

I have this tremendous sense that I have to make something out of my life in order to justify why six million were killed. I was an only child. I have no family left. I came to this country on a visit, after I had traveled from Switzerland to Palestine where I was a sniper in the Haganah. I can still put five bullets in that red circle; I can still throw hand grenades. I was badly wounded in Palestine in 1948 on my 20th birthday. Shrapnel went through both my legs. That's why I'm short. I would've been short anyway… (Jim and audience laugh).

I was fortunate; I studied at *Sorbonne* in Paris. I was very poor but I was very happy. We were all poor so it didn't matter. We sometimes ate only two meals and we always shared. Then I was on my way back to Israel to be a director of a kindergarten. I thought I should visit these United States. I had an uncle in San Francisco who emigrated from Germany to Shanghai to San Francisco. That's how he was saved. I needed to check if he was as short as me. And look what happened. You people made me Dr. Ruth, and I have no complaints. I talk about orgasms and erections. (Jim and all laugh again, long and loud)

JR: Dr. Ruth, is society today obsessed with sex?

DrR: Look, I would not say obsessed, because that's a term that would imply a psychological disorder. Somebody who's obsessed would come to my office. I still do therapy five hours a week. And if they are obsessed with washing hands, for example, or with anything else as an excessive compulsive… I give them three names of psychiatrists.

We, in this country, have Masters and Johnson and we have the best knowledge, so we are not obsessed. But there's something that is given, by God, by nature, whatever you believe in, that is free and for people with a partner in a good relationship.

JR: Do you have any advice to give those of us here who are a little older?

DrR: Well, somebody of a certain age, Jim, cannot hang from a chandelier anymore. Next question?

JR: Is there a question after that? What advice do you give young people? We are hearing more and more that the sex life of today's generation begins as low as 13 and 14 years of age. What advice do you have for them? How can parents advise their children the best way possible? How should parents sit down with the children and talk about it?

DrR: Hear me loud and clear, I'm very concerned. I'm concerned about our young people walking around half naked, girls and boys with tight jeans down to their pubic hair because it is sexually arousing. And I want parents to be able to say, "No! Not in my house." Now I'm not saying that there will not be some kids who walk around like that, and going to the mall against their wishes, but I'm talking in generalities.

I'm very concerned about some of those "studies" that say at 13 years old they they're doing it in order to have a date Saturday night and to be popular. I'm very concerned. Number one, I'm concerned that we are going to see a rise in AIDS. In New York City where I live there are sex clubs springing up where indiscriminate sexual activity, both homosexual and heterosexual, take place.

Parents have an obligation, in my way of thinking, to be "askable parents," but also to be parents who says "No!" Even if it's unpopular. I'm very concerned about young people engaging in any sex play. I'm not even saying intercourse. I'm saying in playing before they are mature enough to have a relationship and to have that knowledge that this is something that has to be cherished and has to be dealt with, with a tremendous amount of delicacy.

JR: Who sponsored your *Sexually Speaking* show?

DrR: I was so happy, a Chevrolet dealer…I was very fortunate. I had bosses at *NBC*; Frank Osborne was one of them, who understood that I would have never let anything be advertised on my program that would raise my eyebrows. For example, I believe that abortion must remain legal. But I would've never permitted an abortion clinic to advertise in my program. That's where that fine line is. If I have to stand up and be counted, I take the risk - that's how I came out of Nazi Germany - I have to say where I stand, but not to advertise a clinic or anything questionable.

JR: I have just told the studio to eliminate *ABC News*. I am eliminating it just to get a few more moments with you.

DrR: Oh my God! That has never happened to me in my entire career. I love it. I've never had that happen to me.

JR: I only have what you call a once-in-a-lifetime opportunity, although I hope in your case it's not once-in-a-lifetime, I'm sure Chautauqua would like you back.

DrR: And I'll come back on your program. I promise you, I'll be back on your program.

JR: I don't need that in writing, do I? But Dr. Ruth, in all seriousness, how do you remain active after 80?

DrR: Okay, I'm 79, so, one more year I will be 80. Keep your mind active and, even if it's a little difficult, your body. I still, until two years ago, skied. I gave up now because you have to honor your age. I'm not saying you have to pamper, I'm saying you have to honor, you have to know what you can do and what you cannot do. The message is not going to be just about sex. Yes, sex is important, yes for some people it is sad because they don't have a partner, but keep your mind active. You can't look like when you were 25, you have to look in the mirror and say look at the faculties and the abilities I have now.

JR: What are you most grateful for, Dr. Ruth?

DrR: The most grateful I am for my four grandchildren because I can prove to Hitler and his cronies: "You didn't want me to be alive; you didn't want me to have a family. Now look at me. I have the best four grandchildren in the entire world."

JR: No you don't. Everybody here has the greatest. Everybody!

DrR: I have four, I'm satisfied with four. But first of all, to answer your question, that I'm alive. I could never explain to you how come. Millions of children were killed, I never forget it, but I could never explain to you how I, by chance, was in a group that was saved by Kinder Transport.

JR: What do you want to accomplish from this point on?

DrR: First of all, I want to stay in good health. Second, I want you to invite me again next year to be on your program. And I'm doing that documentary. I interviewed the first woman Bedouin physician gynecologist in the world, and I have it ready for my course. I'm teaching my fourth year at Princeton and Yale, a seminar on family life, not only sex. And I will have the Bedouin film ready. Now who would've thought that this little refugee, kicked out of Germany, would be a professor at Princeton and Yale? I wouldn't have believed it if you would have told me.

JR: Dr. Ruth, may I give you a great big kiss?

DrR: Yes. Right here on the radio. (Jim kisses Dr. Ruth on the cheek) That was nice kiss. All of you women here, (Dr. Ruth points to a woman in the audience) especially you, all of you women here who don't have a partner, right after this program make a line, and let him kiss you.

JR: Thank you very much.

Ernst Michel: Holocaust Survivor, Nuremburg Journalist

Ernst Michel escaped from a German concentration camp in 1945. He had been sent there at the age of 16. After nearly six years in some of the most gruesome of Nazi concentration camps, he escaped from a Gestapo death march just before the end of World War II.

Michel briefly worked for the Office of the Military Government of the United States (OMGUS) in Germany. He became a special correspondent for the new, post-war German news agency, *Deutsche Allgemeine Nachrichten Agentur* (DANA), and was assigned by the U.S. Military command to report on the Nuremberg War Crimes Trial. There, Ernst Michel met the top Nazi leader, Hermann Goering. The roles of prisoner and inmate had been grimly reversed. His articles, carrying the byline "Auschwitz Survivor number 104995" appeared in all German newspapers.

On September 11, 2006, the fifth anniversary of the 9/11 attacks in New York City, Washington, D.C. and Pennsylvania, Ernst Michel addressed a colloquium at the Robert H. Jackson Center's Carl Cappa Auditorium in Jamestown, New York, and afterward accepted Jim's invitation to take part in a broadcast conversation.

A major theme in Jim's life has been the realization that a single event, if taken as an opportunity, can radically redirect a person's life in remarkable ways. He is fascinated by people's stories of such events because, in many ways, they parallel his own experience of unpredictable, life-changing incidents, no matter how different the details may be.

A Conversation with Ernst Michel

Jim Roselle: Ernst Michel, thank you for this opportunity to speak to you on WJTN radio.

Ernst Michel: It's a pleasure to be in Jamestown, particularly at the Robert H. Jackson Center, which means a lot to me personally.

JR: You said there were three events that impacted your life forever.

EM: That's correct. The first one was when I escaped from the final death march on April 18, 1945. I had been 5 ½ years in the camps, and the war was coming to an end in April. As you know, the war ended in May of 1945 and we had thought they were going to just machine gun us. They marched us someplace instead. We heard the thunder of the battle, the allies coming from the West into Germany.

We took an opportunity there, two friends and I, to run away. Even the SS guards had to take a rest, and we had to take a stop in the middle of a small wood. We used the opportunity, if you pardon me, to put our pants down as if we were going to relieve ourselves, and then ran into the woods. They shot after us, but none of us got scratched, so we made our way to freedom. That was the first of the three major events.

The second one is the reason why I came to Jamestown. I've been asked to speak on my memory of Robert Jackson and the Nuremberg War Crimes Trial which I covered for the German news agency as a reporter for six months. To sit there, in the courtroom in Nuremberg and witness the leaders of the German government - those who survived - beginning with Hermann Goering, [Field Marshal] Keitel, and others being brought to justice was, without a doubt, the single most important event in my life.

The third was a different one. It took place after the war in Jerusalem when the survivors of the death camps for the first time met with 6,000 of their fellow survivors and their families. That was in 1981 to celebrate our survival and our new life.

Those three events, probably more than anything else that happened to me, framed my career and my life in the United States, ever since I arrived here in 1946.

[Jim had previously introduced Michel to his co-host for this program, veteran WJTN newscaster, Dennis Webster]

Dennis Webster: What are your recollections of Robert H. Jackson at that trial?

EM: I came to Nuremberg – remember, I was 22 years old – having never finished school and surviving five-and-a-half years in the camps, including Auschwitz. Then seven months after the war ended I was picked to become a reporter for the German news agency, *DANA*, at Nuremberg because I spoke and wrote fluent German.

WJTN newscaster and colleague, Dennis Webster

The first day in court in Nuremberg, I heard the name of the Chief Prosecutor of the United States. He made the opening statement about the crimes that were committed during World War II, crimes against humanity and waging war. Robert Jackson, whose name I had never heard before, made an opening statement that to me was one of the most brilliant accusations in any court that I have ever heard since. To me, his role at the Nuremberg trial as the chief American prosecutor was a highlight of my stay in Nuremberg.

DW: As you reflect on those events in your life, escaping narrowly on that death march and arriving at Nuremberg, is there something we did not feel because we were not there or we have forgotten over the years, Mr. Michel?

EM: Well, this all happened exactly 61 years ago. The trial started on November 20, 1945. I've been asked very often when I speak, "What are the lessons of Nuremberg?"

The lesson of Nuremberg was that the Germans almost succeeded. For the first time in all of human history the leaders of a country, a Western, civilized country, Germany, had as their objective to wipe out one people from the face of the earth, namely the Jews. These German leaders were brought to trial for the first time, and this has left an impact on international law until today.

Since then a word has been coined in the English language called *genocide*. Genocide is the destruction, willful destruction, of innocent people, men, women and children, by the hundreds of millions who have been killed, not in a war.

The lesson of Nuremberg is to try to find ways to deal with individuals who wage war today against innocent human beings for whatever reasons there are, all over the world. America, because it is a freedom loving country, does not want to accept these kinds of events taking place. This is the lesson that has been brought down from Nuremberg.

JR: At the time that those crimes were being committed by Adolf Hitler and the German regime, where was your family? What were you doing at that particular time when you were sent to the concentration camp?

EM: I was expelled from school in seventh grade; I never went back to school again because I was Jewish. It was not permitted. In 1939, when I was 16, I was sent by the Gestapo to my first forced labor camp in Germany. I spent the next five-and-a-half years in all kinds of concentration camps. I have no idea how I survived. It was luck, it was God, whatever you want to call it, but I was among those few who were lucky enough to survive one of the greatest tragedies in all of human history...Never in history has an elected government decided publicly to wipe out one people from the face of the earth.

JR: How did you get to America?

EM: I covered the Nuremberg trial that began in November 1945 and until June 1946, when I decided I could not live in the country that was responsible for everything that happened to me and my people and my family. I decided to come to the United States. I came here under the Harry Truman Displaced Persons Quota which permitted 100,000 young survivors to be able to come to this country, not only Jews but there were many non-Jews that came over here. That was organized by what the Jewish community called the United Jewish Appeal, and they arranged for me to come here.

This is where I began my new life. I'm one of those who owes a great deal to the United States of America. First of all, for winning World War II, and second for the kind of freedom that exists here. I only wish that youngsters who grow up in this country would appreciate what we have here more.

JR: Did you have a family, Mr. Michel?

EM: Yes, I had a family. My parents were killed in Auschwitz. The only survivor of my family is my sister who lives today in Israel. Her life was saved by Catholic nuns. They kept her in a convent until they were able to get her out of Germany. She wound up in Palestine before Israel became a nation. She lives there today and has four children, 15 grandchildren and 16 great-grandchildren. So out of the horror, there has come a new life.

I visit with her every year and I have brought my oldest granddaughter, Nauga, over here. She is now a soldier in the Israeli army. Every girl has to serve two years and every man, three years.

JR: We hear about people denying that the Holocaust ever existed. How do you deal with that?

EM: I've been asked whether I would be willing to debate with someone. I have refused to do that and so has every survivor that I know. There is no point in arguing with somebody who says this hasn't happened. I was there, I smelled it, I saw it, I saw my friends taken to the gas chambers and gassed. It happened to my parents. I am lucky enough to be one of those who were able to survive.

DW: Mr. Michel, you're obviously a very astute student of the geopolitical world. What do you think about the world today?

EM: Well, I will give you my very straight answer. I think we are living in very dangerous times. The leader of Islam has declared the whole of America has to become part of Islam. If not, the consequences would be very severe. Now you can't go further than that in indicating what a crazy world we live in today, that a leader of the *Al Qaeda* can threaten America.

Robert Jackson gave a wake-up call to the world that what happened to us in the 20th century should never, never happen again.

JR: Mr. Michel, thank you very much. This is *News Talk* 1240 WJTN in Jamestown.

Chapter 6

People and Events that Decorated My Life

The stories have to be told about all "the right people" in "the right places" at "the right times" that so often moved Jim's life in the all the right directions. Serendipity and synchronicity may only be new words for what have been called The Fates or what Jim may call Providence. But whatever it is, he knows he could not have done it by himself. He feels blessed to have been an observer of his own life as well as a willing eager participant with all the people and events along the way.

And you decorated my life
Created a world where dreams are apart
And you decorated my life
By painting your love all over my heart.

Bob Morrison & Debbie Hupp
As sung by Kenny Rogers

If the fiber of my life is brotherhood, it starts in the neighborhood where I was born.

Jim Roselle
NCCJ Brotherhood Citation Recipient, 1983

Family is one of Nature's great masterpieces.

Georga Santayana

Keep true to the dreams of your youth.

Johann von Schiller

First: The Family, My Father's Pushcart and the Rest of the Story
1. In the Beginning

My mother and father did not come from Sicily together, though they were both from Turturici on the northern coast of the island. They were Italian, but that was secondary; first, they were Sicilian. They just happened to wind up in the same town in Chautauqua County, New York. My father, Joseph Roselle, came first and lived with his sister. My mother, Josephine Parsaliti came a little later and lived with her brother, Pete.

My father, as a young man, had a fruit wagon. He would ring the bell going through the neighborhoods. "*Mele, pesche, pere. Verdure fresche!*" he'd call out.

"Apples, peaches, pears. Fresh Vegetables!" He sold whatever was in season – tree ripened fruit and fresh garden produce.

If it hadn't been for that pushcart of his, my father might never have met my mother. One day, while he was peddling his fruit and vegetables, he noticed an attractive young lady in the yard beside a house he stopped at. My father didn't have a lot of education, but in the custom of every good Sicilian family, he had been well schooled in proper respect for family traditions. He would not simply walk up to a young lady and introduce himself. He politely inquired of the homeowner, her brother, whether he may have permission for an introduction. Permission was eventually granted. He learned her name was Josephine.

Honoring another Sicilian family tradition – making sure each of his daughters was safe and well married – Josephine's father, Joseph Parsaliti, had come all the way to America. He stayed until he could go back to Sicily and report to his wife that all was well. Sadly, many years after returning to Sicily, his wife (my grandmother) died when a goat kicked her down a hillside in their own back garden.

When the news came to my mother – news her father delayed in telling her so as not to spoil her Christmas holidays – my mother began wearing the traditional black mourning clothes. She then settled onto her couch in near isolation for a long, long time. Eventually, my brothers and I had to talk her off that couch and back to life.

That permission, however, that my father had received so long ago to court the attractive young lady he had spied along his pushcart route – that young lady who became my mother – led inevitably to… as the man on the radio used to say… *the rest of the story*.

I'm one of the seven children Joseph and Josephine Roselle brought into the world. I have three brothers and three sisters.

My brother Phil was a barber who probably gave haircuts to half the men in Jamestown over the years. Phil and his wife, Janet (Fickiessen), are now both deceased. He had three step-daughters: Carol, Diane and Judy.

My brother Ross (deceased) married Nancy (Atwood) and they had a son and a daughter: Joseph and Betty Jo (Soldano). Ross had beaten all the competition as a teenager to claim the title of the Yo-Yo champion of Jamestown. Right after high school he started out as a shoe clerk, soon rose to store manager and then opened his own store. He stayed in the shoe business for 50 years. During those years, Ross and Phil also teamed up to open the Royal Hat Shop and Shoeshine Stand where their sister Anna's husband worked. Matthew "Mack" worked as the dry cleaning presser. It's all about *famiglia*, after all, isn't it?

My brother Joe (deceased) married Lois (Olsen, deceased). He had four children, Mark and Kathleen and (step-children) Lee and Joy (deceased). Joe worked at Crescent Tool in Jamestown for many years, but later moved to a new home in North Carolina. [The Crescent Tool Company was founded in Jamestown, New York, in 1907. It was eventually bought by Cooper Industries and moved to North Carolina. Joe moved there with Crescent.]

Joe was also the Boys Club middleweight boxing champion in 1943-44 at about the age of 15. He went to the Golden Gloves Boxing Tournament in Buffalo.

My sister, Grace Morrison (husband, Lawrence), passed away at the age of 91 and had four sons (Larry, Kevin, Carl, Raymond) and one daughter (JoAnn). My sister Sara Messina (husband, Carl), had 2 sons (Vincent, Carl) and passed away at the age of 85. My sister, Anna Paterniti (husband, Matthew), had one daughter, (Sara Ann). At the age of 95, Anna recovered from a serious fall with fractured bones and was able to return to the independent lifestyle she was used to at home and about town. Anna and I still get together every Saturday for lunch at her home and we call Joe in North Carolina. With us, it's always about *famiglia,* the family.

My three sisters did not graduate from high school. They all got married. Only two of us boys got high school diplomas, my brother Ross and I. Everybody went to work when they were young. My brother Phil left for Cleveland without my mother even knowing about it. I guess he was afraid she would stop him. He went to study how to be a barber and came back with all the skills. That's what he did all of his life.

Father worked for the city [Jamestown] laying bricks on streets, plowing the streets in winter, doing general repairs and other kinds of physical labor for the Department of Public Works. He worked hard. When he got done at the DPW every day, he and I worked together chopping and sawing wood in our backyard. We piled it up in a shed for people who might need it. He sold the wood to make a little extra money on the side. Sometimes we would walk to his garden way up on Swede Hill. He had rented a spot up there a half-mile from our home on Franklin Street. I pulled the wagon all the way back home loaded with potatoes, tomatoes, string beans and such for supper. We talked in Italian while we walked and worked. I remember it well. Those were good times with my father.

I made our table wine with my father too. Of course, I was more interested in eating the grapes than squeezing them when I was younger, but I could not touch them unless I was helping him with the work. One of my father's only pleasures, other than work, was to sit down and play cards with a couple of neighbors. They'd play the old, traditional card games, Brisca and Scopa. And of course, the jug of wine was always there, but never once did I see him inebriated.

I never had the opportunity to talk with my father one-on-one about the big things in life. I talked to him every day about every day things, though. Those were the days when my father taught me about being a hard worker and a good provider. That was the old way. It is still a good way. In those days boys and girls led a more home-based life. In the old country traditions I was raised with, such matters as dating and courting waited a little longer than they do today. He died before those things became important in my life

In those days there was no luxury. We had no discretionary income. You had to find ways to entertain yourself. I don't think my father ever went to a movie in his life. My mother did later on, though, after my father passed away. We talked her into seeing *The 10 Commandments* and *The Song of Bernadette.*

My father passed away from cancer of the prostate when he was 70 years old. I hadn't even known he was sick. I was still in my teens and he always looked the same to me. Then one day Pa was in the hospital and they operated on him.

He came back home and there he was, healthy again. We went out and did the usual things we always did together. We chopped wood and worked in the garden. I thought everything was fine. But it came back. I realized it one day when he had his shirt off and I saw how thin he had become. That's when I realized something was more than wrong.

My father died in 1945 when I was 19. My mother lived another 26 years as a widow.

2. Interrupted by Surgery

I had to have surgery on my spine. When I was 12 years old, in 1938, a local doctor told my mother that if the spinal curvature (present since birth) was not corrected, it would grow progressively worse until it left almost no room for my heart to beat or for my lungs to breathe.

Folks from the old country had a lot of superstitions. The old-timers would often stay away from doctors with the fatalistic notion that some things would either get better by themselves or *Dio si prende cura di esso,* it's better to let God take care of it. My father opposed the operation, but not because of the old superstitions. He was just worried. It could be a dangerous thing – "*troppo vicino al cuore,*" he said. The doctor might have to cut "too close to the heart". But when it came to her children my mother simply wouldn't accept old superstitions or arguments. Her boy would be taken care of by the best doctors she could find.

I had the surgery I needed that year. My mother came with me and stayed with me the night before the operation. The hospital could not budge her from my bedside. She had her mind made up to take care of me that evening before I went into the operating room. She mustered enough of what little broken English she could and told the nurse, "You care other people. I care my son."

I spent the next six weeks in the hospital to recover. Unfortunately, I caught the chickenpox while I was there. I had to be moved to the contagious section because I could not be in the ward with the other kids. My sister, Ann, came to Jamestown General with my mother. They had to stand outside my room and talk to me through a window. But that did not stop my mother. She was always there for me.

After I got better and went back to the ward they told me to remain calm and not too active. I wouldn't have any of that. There were other kids my age there so we got together and raced our wheelchairs up and down the hall. It didn't seem to do any harm.

Back at home, I spent another two or three weeks getting better before I could return to school. One day while I was still home, Miss Schaeffer, my fourth grade teacher who still remembered me these three years later, took me out for a ride and bought me some ice cream. I really liked her. I would have done anything in fourth grade to be kept after school. I was crushed when she got married.

I had come home with a plaster cast that stretched from my shoulder to my waist. The boys on Franklin Street loved to brag about how tough I was. If somebody new came down the street from a different part of town they'd say, "Go ahead and punch him in the chest. You'll see!"

Classmates had donated money to buy me a book to read while I was in the hospital. It was Jack London's *Call of the Wild*. My teacher, Miss Wheelock, was very encouraging about getting back to the classroom. She told me my friends would like to hear a book report about that book they bought for me, so I better come back soon.

I had been out for all of November and December, and I was afraid I had already missed too many days. I was sure I'd be kept back from my classmates the next year. They would go on to junior high while I was stuck in sixth grade at another school. I wouldn't even get to see them. One day while I was standing in the recess line, Miss Wheelock pulled me aside and spoke so no one else could hear her. "You'll pass, no matter what, just do your best." She took a tremendous load off my back with those few kind words. I did pass.

My mother never even hinted that my surgery should slow me down once I had recovered. She always told me *andare nel sole*. "Go in the sunshine, get some fresh air. Have fun and play with the other kids." I give my mother a lot of credit. She didn't smother me, she made me feel normal. In school, unfortunately, they would not let me play in the gym.

That didn't stop me either. I loved ping-pong and became the "under 18" Jamestown champ. In the Boys Club, I was the foul shooting champ at basketball. I once dropped 45 foul shots in a row and made 58 of 60 shots.

My second surgery, when I was 16 years old, was in Buffalo Children's Hospital. It was called a triple arthrodesis. My surgeon, Doctor Cleary, fused the three main joints in the rear part of my deformed right foot to relieve the pain and to improve my stability in walking.

The operation was in the summer, and my mother made every effort to come and see me as often as she could. Even though it was in Buffalo, my mother, believe it or not, left work at the hotel and went to the bus station on the corner of Cherry Street and Fourth. I don't know how she did it, but she got on the bus to Buffalo. I don't know how she asked for a cab, either, but she got to the hospital and there she stood again, waiting like she did before, right at my bed waiting for the day they operated. That's just how she was.

One day, two of my teachers, Miss Johnson and Miss Eckberg, came all the way up to Buffalo from Jamestown to visit me in the hospital. They brought me a present. It was a shoe box stuffed with candy. We kids weren't allowed to have candy in that hospital, so I thanked them, and we hid it under my bed. Pretty soon, though, all the candy was eaten…by my nurses!

I was there for 10 weeks after my operation this time. I got to know the other kids and, of course, we found ways to make it more fun to be there. The wheelchair races up and down the hallway once again came to the rescue for killing time. It was harmless enough…when we could get away with it.

3. No Interest under the Mattress

My mother could not speak, read nor write English. She could not read or write Italian, either. But she knew what love was all about. That's what she taught us best and that's how she took care of our family.

I remember she used to hide her money in an old chest in her bedroom. She'd gather a few dollar bills and put them away like most people did in those days. One day she asked me to count the money she had between the pillowcases and the bed sheets. It amounted to $600.00.
"Ma, you shouldn't have this here. You've got to put it in the bank."
"Okay. Take me to the bank."
My mother worked in the kitchen at the Hotel Jamestown. She was working in the early morning so I met her after work one day. I took her to the bank, and we deposited the money. I told the teller my mother does not know how to write. So the teller said when your mother comes to make a deposit all she has to do is make an "X". We will witness that transaction. And that's what my mother always did after that. On a payday, she would stop and maybe deposit a few dollars. I didn't keep track of it.

After a couple of months she asked me to check her bank book. I gave her the total and said, "Ma, they added two dollars and some cents in interest." She said "What's that?" I told her that's the money she earned because she put the money in the bank. She wanted me to read that book every week after that. She thought maybe they would do it steady like. That was my mother.

My story is all about people who were there for me, especially my family. My mother came over in 1909 right in the middle of the big immigration. Her brother, my Uncle Pete, was already here. They came here hoping to make some money, thinking they may one day return to Sicily. Although from the time my mother was born in 1888, she never went to school, she knew what her responsibilities were and what she had to do. She knew what she should teach her children; that was love and that was family.

At the age of 41, my mother gave birth to her last two children, twins, a boy and a girl. There would have been eight of us but the girl died at three months of age. My brother Joe who lived in North Carolina was the other twin. She always worried about me, just a little, because I was different. But she never let me think I was unable to play like the other kids.

Naturally, I spoke English because I was born here. My brothers and sisters did, too, but at home with our mother, we only spoke Italian. If my mother received a letter in the mail and it was in English she would take it to a neighbor friend and have it read to her. My mother had such other great qualities that those things made no difference at all in our home or in town. She knew that mother was the ultimate role in life, and she fulfilled it wonderfully. My mother was just a total mother.

4. A Little Help from My Family

Our parents taught us the dignity of hard, honest work. A laborer's toil deserved as much respect in their book as a doctor's job or a lawyer's profession. But I wasn't as strong as most boys my age so physical labor would not have been my best choice. So, among all our brothers and sisters, nobody chose college except for me. I chose St. Lawrence University.

My family didn't have a lot of money in 1944 when I graduated from high school, so I spent a year working to save up money for college. Though I might have made more somewhere else, Boys Club Director, Arthur Verry, gave me the opportunity to manage the game room. I wanted to start giving something back while earning something for myself. I started my freshman year at St. Lawrence University with the $700 I had saved in that year of work.

During that year I was interviewed by a gentleman named Hartwick from a New York State agency that would give a scholarship of $500 to someone with a handicap or disability of some kind if they could pass an aptitude test for the career they wanted. I chose radio and they sent me for that aptitude test. The strange thing was that it said I was best suited for mechanical drawing. I didn't even know how to draw! So they debated whether or not I should get the scholarship. They finally gave it to me in my very last semester. By then I had taken all the radio courses there were and I'd gotten my best grades in them. I had finally proven to their satisfaction that when I said radio, I meant it.

I could not have been more blessed than with the fellas I wound up with in my hall at St. Lawrence. They were the perfect mixture, from the onion farmer from Canastota to Bill, the wealthy student from Greenwich, Connecticut. My roommate was Bill McKeever. He was St. Lawrence's best pitcher, the perfect roommate for a baseball fan like me. I couldn't quite match him as a varsity athlete, but I did get to be the St. Lawrence University ping-pong champ. The fellows in my dorm were all the best friends I could have asked for.

Although my father had died in 1945, my mother and my brothers wanted to keep my college dreams alive. They all chipped in, one way or another, to help me finish. I got a part-time job on campus too. I was a soda jerk making ice cream sodas and sundaes in the campus center for a few hours a day between classes.

[College tuition at the end of World War II was typically $400-$600 per semester; generally no more than $5000 for a full four-year education. For Jim and his family that was a steep hill to climb.]

5. A Working Woman

My mother grew up in a time period when girls rarely went to school. But she was smart, very smart.

In those days common sense was the important thing and more important than anything else was The Family. *La Famiglia* was everything. A woman married and took over the responsibility to raise and care for her family. Most of my mother's life was spent in the kitchen, either at home or at the Hotel Jamestown. Some days she would come home and feed us then go back and work a banquet for extra money.

Things are different today for a lot of people, but I never met anybody who took more pride and found more satisfaction in what they accomplished than my mother.

The Hotel Jamestown kitchen where my mother worked was two floors below the radio station. Sometimes she'd have an extra piece of pie at the end of a shift. She'd dash up the stairs to the radio station, hand me the pie, and then hurry right back down.

One day I got a call from the hotel manager, Hillman Lyons, to tell me something had happened to her, and I better come down and help her right away. She had fallen and hurt her arm, but it seemed OK. A mild stroke followed and hospitalized her for a while. She didn't get worse, but she never got completely better again, either.

My mother's greatest concern was to return to work. She kept saying to me "Go tell Mr. Lyons I want my job back." She would not be consoled. My mother's determination was fierce. She believed in work and we didn't want to tell her she couldn't go back. I went to see Mr. Lyons and asked him to please come see my mom and try to reassure her. He was a wonderful man.

"Josephine," he said, "your job is waiting for you when you are better." She stayed at home for seven more years, and recovered enough to be up and around proudly tending to her home and family as well as she could. She never lost her spirit. She was bedridden only the last year. My mother expressed her last concern as a simple question, though we really knew it was more than that. "Are you going to take care of each other?" *La famiglia* had always been her greatest goal. She passed away at the age of 83.

Second: The Neighborhood
1. From Stickball to Microphone

Joe "Bronco" Trusso is another original Franklin Streeter, Jim's friend and another neighborhood success story.

A Korean War Air Force veteran, Joe's service sparked his interest in hometown service after he mustered out. In 1970 Joe won an elected seat in his Jamestown district on the Chautauqua County Board of Supervisors and the County Legislature. He took important leadership roles during his time in office and earned reelection for 37 years. On retirement in 2007, Joe received a Congressional Record commendation from New York Congressman, the Honorable Brian Higgins. (Congressional Record Vol. 153, Nr. 89 (6/5/2007) Extended Remarks-Page E1187. Online source: www.gpo.gov).

During the Great Depression boys like Joe, Jim and their friends had little to do around the neighborhood after school except for fair weather street sports and the Boys Club. Stickball and a game called "Nips" were staples of the day. Stickball was baseball with a stick instead of a bat and anything round with a little bounce to it for a ball. In those days, even the string around grocery packages was a small treasure. Boys collected it. They wrapped strips of Dad's tacky black electrical tape around tightly wound balls of the rough store twine and called it a baseball or a softball or even a football.

In stickball, down-the-middle line drives were preferred over hits toward what would have been right and left field, except a street doesn't have those. First and third bases might be fire plugs or lampposts with a manhole cover or a chalk drawn smudge in the middle of the road for home plate and second base. Stickball had hits and runs, innings and outs. Very few streets in any neighborhood had their own play-by-play announcers because nobody else had young Jim Roselle.

Nips is probably long forgotten by now in American neighborhoods, and its origin is obscure. Joe is even willing to credit its beginnings on Franklin Street to a borrowed *dreidel* from one of the Jewish boys nearby street in his "Little UN" neighborhood. Like a tape covered ball of twine, a nip—which is nearly *dreidel* shaped—is also a handcrafted thing.

"You take a square hunk of wood, maybe it's a leftover chunk of lumber," Joe recalls watching the distant scene in his mind's eye while his hands shape it in the air. "It's gotta be about five or six inches long. You whittle a point on each end. Then you write on each side in Roman numerals I, I I, I I I and IV—you know, one, two, three, four. You set it down on the ground and nick one of the points real quick with the flat end of a stick, maybe an old broom handle or a sort of straight hunk of a branch. The nip flips up into the air and you swing your stick at it. You whack it as hard as you can, as far as you can."

As he speaks, Joe is reliving the whole thing and almost knocks over his coffee mug in a wild pantomime. "If the fielder catches it, bang! You're out. But if it lands 'cause nobody catches it, the closest player takes one, two, three or four big steps or jumps or leaps—whatever number faced up when the nip landed—toward the hitter. He tries to hit the stick with the nip. That's how you scored it."

Nips, according to historians who study such arcane sports, is actually quite like a Lancashire game from the English Northlands. There it was called Nipsy or Peggy, or the even more obscure Knur, or Spell 'n Billets. The game traces all the way back to 12th century England. Flipping the nip was called "rising" it and the score, the distance from the nip's rising to its landing, was once measured in the old-fashioned units called chains. The ethnic origin of Nips on Franklin Street is probably as obscure as the neighborhood families' homelands are global. But nips and stickball brought fun and good play to the streets of Jamestown in the Depression Years.

Joe remembers that Jim played stickball, too, in spite of his limp. "Nothing ever stopped Jim. It might have been a nuisance, but never a handicap." But if Jim wasn't playing he was doing the sidewalk play-by-play. He was never merely a "pretend" announcer though; the street was a training ground for Jim and everyone who grew up there.

2. Jim Remembers… A Real Microphone

Bill Stern was my radio idol and my role model. [Bill Stern (1907–1971) was the pioneering sportscaster at the microphone for America's first remote radio broadcast of a baseball game in May of 1939. He also announced the nation's first televised football game later that year in September. Stern had also overcome a physical handicap. His left leg had been amputated above the knee in 1935 following an auto accident.]

I listened to Bill Stern doing college football on Saturday afternoons. I just thought what an exciting job he's got. There he is doing a game and describing it and giving us a chance to use our imaginations. TV wasn't here yet. Radio is full of imagination. And I thought, wouldn't it be fun to do a job you love just describing those games to people. You could paint a picture of the action like Bill Stern did. And I thought, I can't play professionally and I can't be a good writer about it, so why don't I try to be an announcer? In a way, I mimicked him. I practiced a lot.

If the guys were playing football in the neighborhood, I would pick up a stick, or whatever it was, pretend it was a microphone and while they were playing, I would do play-by-play and try to create the game, practicing to sound like Bill Stern doing my Franklin Street play-by-play commentary.

Remember football pools? You could play and bet money on how the games would come out? This was a New Year's Day. In those days there were only four bowl games; the Rose Bowl, the Cotton Bowl, the Sugar Bowl and the Orange Bowl. So I picked four teams to win those games and I bet $2. The odds were 17 to 1 and I picked the right teams.

I won $34 and hurried over to Peerless Photo on Cherry Street. I asked Mr. Swanson there, if I could put a down payment on a tape recorder. I said I would give him my $34 for a down payment and then I would pay a couple of dollars a week for the balance. "Sure Jim," he said, "we can do that."

So I got my Revere Tape Recorder and a spool of tape and I took it home. I couldn't wait to turn it on.

I grabbed a newspaper, picked two baseball teams and played a fantasy game right away. I just looked at the lineup and started the game.

Here's the starting lineup for the New York Giants...
Batting first is so-and-so, batting second… and so on.
Now here's the first pitch. It's a fast ball.
He hits a ground ball! It's a bobbler headed toward short.
Throw to first.
Out!

And whatever I dreamed up was the action of the game. I just got into that world. And that's the way I tried to get myself involved in the action, how I created the excitement. I always asked myself, "How can I be as exciting as Bill Stern?" I did everything in my power to accomplish that. Then I could play it back on my recorder and hear how I did.

By the way, my Giants didn't always win in my games. After all, I wanted it to be real.

Today, Bronco still recalls that recorder. "We could sing on that thing too, and replay it whenever we wanted. The thing was amazing. It was just fun for us, but for Jim it sort of started his career. There has never been anything Jim couldn't do if he set his mind to it. And he did."

Third: The Community
1. It Started with the Rotary

On June 7, 2013, the Jamestown, New York, Rotary Club honored Jim Roselle with a tribute.

Local attorney and long time Rotary Club member, Phil Cala, addressed a communitywide gathering he had organized with the Jamestown Rotary Club one evening in the summer of 2013.

Jim is a hero to one and all in this town," Phil said. "He's been part of the last 60 years of history in Jamestown. He has brought our whole community to a higher level."

Inasmuch as Jim's whole life has been one long conversation, perhaps it was no coincidence that a conversation between Jim and me one winter morning at Jones's Bakery kicked off this project. Later, I thought, 'Somebody ought to interview Jim.' It was a simple notion to interview the man who had interviewed so many thousands of people over the years. I realized that putting Jim on the other side of the microphone was long overdue.

It wasn't a new idea, but this time, Phil was determined, it was going to happen. He spent the better part of a springtime fielding the idea to his friends, at Rotary meetings, and around town. Finally, he pulled together all the people and resources he needed to create the special event.

On the evening of the tribute, Greg Peterson, also a Jamestown attorney and co-founder of, the city's Robert H. Jackson Center, the venue where the event had been staged, started to ask the first question of his long anticipated interview. Jim, however, interrupted him.

"Can I take a moment here, Greg?"

"I should have known," Greg said, laughing. "Go ahead. It's your night." Jim addressed the overflow audience before him.

"This community should be grateful that Greg had the original idea of what this Robert H. Jackson Center could become. Stop and think of what he has accomplished in bringing the best legal minds available in the world to

Greg Peterson, on another occasion, on the air with Jim

come here to honor Robert Jackson and to learn about his life and his work. There is no community that has the prize this man has given us. What community in this country, for example, can boast of having had three Chief Justices of the Supreme Court of the United States come to visit them?"

"You know," Greg said, "I've done interviews like this before, like when Dorothy Cotton [a leader in the African-American Civil Rights Movement] just threw me aside, ignored my first question and…" he yielded the floor back to Jim with a smile.

"I want to say this before this night ends," Jim said, "or I will be regretting the fact that I didn't do it. I would like to tell the audience here, the Rotary Club that is staging this event and everybody else, that I wouldn't be here if it wasn't for the Rotary Club. And I'll tell you the story."

Greg just settled himself back into his chair and relaxed. Everybody else did too.

2. Jim Remembers… The Right Place, The Right Time

The Rotary Club opened a Boys Club in 1939. They took an abandoned YMCA building, the Nordic Temple, which the Y had left behind in order to build their new home on Fourth Street. They opened a Boys Club in a building that had a pool, a gym and a game room. Their idea was that it appealed to what we call "the other side of the tracks," the kids who couldn't afford the Y. It would give them a facility where they could enjoy a lot of safe and constructive activities. They put themselves in a difficult position to find a director and the funds to guide that club along. And they did it. They opened that club. [For more about the founding of the Jamestown Boys Club and recollections by a number of early members, See Appendix I: The Boys of the Boys Club.]

As teenagers we spent all the time we could possibly spend at the Boys Club, from 2 o'clock to 5:30 every afternoon and 6:45 to 9 o'clock every evening. We even asked the director, Mr. Clemments, if we could play there on Sunday. He gave us that opportunity, of course, along with the responsibility to take care of the place while we were there. So I spent a lot of time at the Club, and that was our salvation.

The Club was our second home. We lived there. Mr. Robert Clemments ran the club for six years. He was also our teacher. He taught us teamwork, sportsmanship and values. After he left the Club in 1945 to operate a Boys Club in Brooklyn, he moved to Harrisburg, Pennsylvania. We missed him.

In 1951 Frank Morotto made a suggestion to me and our friend Blucky – Joe Panebianco, whose mom I had named "The Mayor of Franklin Street" – that we should go surprise Mr. Clemments and visit. So I called him and said, "Bob, we'd love to come and say hello to you. "Oh, we'd be delighted," he answered. "Roe and I would be happy to see you." And then, in a way kiddingly, I said, "Can you get me an audition at a radio station?" I asked because, frankly, I didn't have a full-time job. I was part-time at WJTN, 10 minutes a night. My first show was 10 minutes on Sunday. For three dollars. I did put that thought to him.

By the time we got there, I had completely forgotten about the question. I didn't even wonder if anything would happen. We sat down to dinner that night and suddenly he said to me, "Jim, I've got an audition for you tomorrow morning with a gentleman named Jack Hooper at WHGB. He told me go to the audition and then to take bus number so-and-so to get back. So I did.

Much to my surprise, they offered me the job on the spot. I was literally shocked. I just thought, I've got a lot of things to do, my first thought was that I've got to tell Si Goldman that I am not going to do part-time any longer, like it's a big deal, you know, so I gave him two week's notice. Secondly, I had to look for a place to live and make the arrangements. And, ladies and gentlemen, let me tell you, Mr. Clements said, "You don't have to find a place. You're living with us." [Long pause while Jim reflects.] So I lived with Bob and Roe for a year and a half.

That job in Harrisburg, Pennsylvania was extremely important to my career. I learned about music and how to spin records. I learned how to announce songs, chat between records and interview people. I got to talk ad lib on the radio and even learned how to do ads. I'd also been given one hour every Sunday afternoon for the *Italian Music Hour*.

I discovered that was a good time for radio. Television could not match it. On radio, people could call in, hear themselves and their friends could hear them. They could swap ideas and trade opinions with somebody who cared and might've been from his own neighborhood. TV couldn't do that.

At that station they would bring me someone to talk to. The first two guests I had were big sports stars. One was Chuck Bednarik of the Eagles, a colleague of Jim McClusker. They were on the Eagles team together and they won the national championship in the NFL. The other one was Robin Roberts, a Big 20 game winner for the Phillies. You see, we were near Philadelphia in Harrisburg. And then I had the king of polka music, Frank Yankovich. I went and introduced him at a concert. I had a polka hour on Sundays when all we played was polkas. So we introduced Frankie Yankovic the king of polkas.

Eventually, I wanted to come back. I missed my family, and I missed my friends. I thought I'd love to be back home. Fortunately I found a three-month job in Warren, Pennsylvania, and then a job opened up at WJTN in September of 1953. All of that is another example of everybody in the right place at the right time and giving you the right support. It also proves that a spur of the moment decision can redirect your whole life.

So here I am 60 years later.

Greg, and the audience, please understand… I wouldn't be here if it wasn't for the Rotary Club. Thank you very much.

3. Another Franklin Street Success Story

As significant as the Rotary and the Boys Club were, my old neighborhood was also the starting place for a lot of successful people. I think it had a very special quality that, though hard to describe, becomes obvious when you see what it produced. For instance, there's Joe Caprino.

Joe Caprino had emigrated from Italy after mustering out of the defeated WWII *Regio Esercito* – the Italian Royal Army – with his brothers, Pete and Al, both of whom were barbers. Joe continued to get his Army pension and it helped him start his own business as our neighborhood Radio Repair Shop. It was right there on his front sun porch. He was just around the corner from my house. You go up the street about three houses and there was Joe's. All he did was repair radios.

When his business started getting busy, he said, "Okay, I'll open a store." He opened it down on Second Street and sold Sylvania televisions. They had a lighted frame around the picture. He did so well that he opened an even bigger store to sell even more TVs.

Then he saturated the area with that sort of thing. He figured if his television sales were declining he'd better expend into furniture. So he built a wonderful furniture store, the best furniture store in town. He had promotions that would drive you out of your mind. "Look for the lighted searchlight in the sky," he said. It would be parked on the street right in front of the store. A car dealer tried to copy that, but when people saw the searchlight, they went to Caprino's!

Joe had married the sister of Tony Lucca, one of my old Franklin Street friends, and they had a son, Anthony, with cerebral palsy. Joe devoted his life to his son. When we had the sports dinners downtown he would invite the sports stars to his home so they could meet his son. Imagine in one night you're there with Joe Paterno from Penn State, Johnny Unitas of the Baltimore Colts, Henny Youngman the comedian and the Army Football coach, Tom Cahill. If only I had a camera or a ball to have it autographed or…

Joe Caprino bought a lot of my Chautauqua Institution shows. He also had a promotion about every week where I had to be on location at his store. Over 37 years there I probably did 1000 or more remotes. If I said it once, I said it 1000 times, "Go, Go, Go! See Joe!" Joe even tried to teach his parrot to say that. I told people not to say "Hello" when they answered their telephone; say instead: "Caprino's where the best costs less" and win a prize. The jackpot built up by two dollars a day.

Once a local fellow told me, "Jim, I called my mother in Florida while she was visiting her daughter there."

"Hello, Mom?"

"Caprinos, where the best costs less," she answered.

"Mom, you're in Florida!"

"Why not? They could've called me."

I wonder if there are some people who still do that.

Another one of the fellows from the old neighborhood was a guy named Tom Trusso. He became a police officer in Jamestown for 20 years. When he retired he bought the South Hills Golf Course and Country Club in Jamestown. He ran it for years afterward and it's still one of the finest in the area.

Franklin Street bred a lot of success stories.

4. Were They All Foreigners?

Bronco adds another remembrance of the world the way it looked from Franklin Street.

The word gang didn't mean what it means today in a 21st-century, inner-city way. We were just a band of kids who were friends. We were loyal to each other, our families and our neighborhood, no matter what. I think we all spoke Italian, because those were the families we came from, but we all spoke English, too. That was what we spoke in school and downtown.

Our neighborhood was safe. We never locked our doors. We didn't need to. Any home was everybody's home if he needed it. I would not trade my boyhood for anything.

Jim had a little gimp in his step, but who would've picked on him? He belonged to our gang. Franklin Street was no place for bullies in those days, but there weren't many neighborhoods a bully could have come from, anyway.

Jim was in the 'big gang' and I was in the 'little gang'. Jim was a couple of years older than I was. But sometimes we would do things together. We thought there should be at least one membership requirement for our gang. You didn't belong on Franklin Street if you didn't go for the Yankees and for Notre Dame. That's all there was to it. Except for Jim. He was for Notre Dame, alright, but he was for the New York Giants. But that was OK. He was Jim.

But I think the other reason our gang stuck together so well was because that's what we learned at home, too, from our parents.

The years 1935 and 1936 had some of the most extreme weather on record across America. Those were the terrible Dust Bowl years and hard winter years, too. On St. Patrick's Day of '35 we had a huge blizzard. The snow was higher than my head. Everybody still heated their houses with coal in those days, but the coal trucks just could not get through the snow to our homes.

All the men from every house on Franklin Street, and a couple of the other nearby blocks got out and started shoveling all the way to Center Street [nearly the length of 20 football fields]. They saved everybody because the coal trucks got through so nobody froze. That's how they all worked together. And it's not because we were all the same nationality, either. On Franklin Street and nearby there were Mr. Greendahl and George Sundholm who were Swedish, Bob Landrigan who was Irish, Afro-American families, Jewish families and all the rest.

We were all just neighbors and Americans. Nobody was a foreigner to us.

Before I started school, though, I only spoke our household Italian. After my first day at school, I came home and my father, my mother, my grandfather and everybody else were all waiting for me. They wanted to find out how things went.

I told them I didn't understand a thing. "I think they are all foreigners."

5. Jim Remembers… Something on Franklin Street Bred Success

It's interesting to realize that so many people who grew up on Franklin Street and the nearby neighborhoods went on to succeed in wonderful jobs, careers and professions.

A lot of us only learned English after we started school. But we learned it well. It became our native tongue. We did a good job with it, too. A lot of my friends from the old neighborhood became professionals and had great careers.

I can list dentists, for instance. There were Joe S. Panebianco, a root specialist, and Tom Raffa who went into general dentistry. Then there was Sebastian Ciancio. He was from Derby Street, which doesn't exist anymore. It wasn't far away, but it was part of what came to be known in Jamestown as "The Lost Neighborhood." An urban renewal project turned it into shopping malls. That was close enough, though, that we called it part of our neighborhood. He was really one, anyway, because his wife was a Franklin Street girl named Marilyn.

Sebastian became Professor and Chairman in the Department of Periodontology and Director of the Center for Dental Studies at the State University of New York (SUNY) at Buffalo. He wrote or co-wrote more than 100 publications in his field. He once told me he also did dental work for Saudi Arabian royalty. Every summer he chairs a dental conference at Chautauqua Institution for more than 150 dentists.

Jamestown educators were well represented from our neighborhood, too. William Gullotti was the principal at Persell Middle School in Jamestown, Sam Caruso was the principal at the Clinton V. Bush School and Sam Restivo became the Superintendent for the nearby Panama, NY, School System. Sam Restivo was also one of the founders of the popular Italian-American Golf Tournament, now bigger than ever in its fifth decade.

Not all of our neighborhood friends stayed home. Vincent SanFillipo, for example, went all the way out west, to California, but he was a successful school superintendent there for many years and still stays in touch with us back here. Tony Lucca spent his working life as a much loved and highly awarded high school English teacher in Brick Town, New Jersey.

Some of our neighborhood kids also became school teachers, lawyers, a judge, an FBI agent and two county legislators, Joe Trusso and Tony Raffa. Carl Cappa was a successful local businessman, owner of the Crawford Furniture Company, who quietly contributed to many charities and civic organizations, preferring to do his good work without publicity. His name, however, is on the theater at the Robert H. Jackson Center. Without fanfare, he also helped found Jamestown's St. Susan Center soup kitchen that now provides more than 100,000 hot, nutritious meals to the region's homeless and unemployed every year. Carl, however was not alone in his love for the community.

Every family in our neighborhood had a success story of some kind, and probably more than one. They were almost all first generation Americans.

I don't think it is hard to explain, though, because it's a combination of the good feeling you had in the neighborhood, the good traditions and the good discipline that your parents gave you. And my mother, like all the other mothers on our street, would be ready to make a pan of chicken broth or something hot and rich and say, "Here, take this next door to our neighbor, Mr. DeMarco, he is sick, or over to Aunt Mary who doesn't feel good today." When I had the operation on my foot, my mother came to visit me in the hospital in Buffalo and brought me a whole basket of goodies from the neighbors. They had all donated something to it.

Here's a picture of the old neighborhood you won't see very often now. My neighbor, Mrs. Marotto, was out in front of her house every day sweeping her sidewalk, and some days twice.

The girls in the neighborhood didn't all follow the old traditional ways, though. It was still pretty much a man's world when I grew up but a few of the girls were becoming more American and did well in careers of their own. Nancy Lucca, for instance, became a teacher. As a matter of fact, she's the teacher who gave me a crash course so I could pass my geometry test after I had missed so much school recuperating from one of my operations. I sat with her all evening, and she got me ready for that final exam.

That was a good place to grow up.

...And the Names Ended in Vowels

You have to remember that Franklin Street in those days was an ethnic neighborhood, like many others. The ethnic character was obvious when you heard some the family names on Franklin Street: Panebianco, Nicastro, Lucca, Trusso, Piazza, Riolo, Muscarella, Marotto, Pollino, Zerbo, Lisciandro, DeMarco and Schiera. Then there were the Morettis, the Purpuras, the Calalesinas, the Constantinos and the Paternitis.

I agree with my old friend Bronco that within a couple of blocks around us there were a lot of other nationalities, but right on Franklin Street, I remember only two families who were not Italian. They were Swedish. We wondered what they were doing there. That was our kind of neighborhood, though, and that was okay.

As often as we like to recall that ethnic stereotypes and prejudices were rare, they did exist.

One day my mother was walking down Foote Avenue with my brother, Phil. Someone yelled "Hi" to Phil from across the road but he added one of those old racial epithets that people sometimes pinned on people of Italian heritage.

That was a mistake.

Though my mother didn't speak English, for some reason, she understood that word. She had an umbrella with her that day and she took it walking with her across that street. She smacked the boy soundly with it and pronounced loud and clear, "His name is Phil."

That was my mother.

Fourth: The University Years
1. I Missed My Chance to be a Bookkeeper

I didn't take any college preparatory classes in high school. As a matter of fact, my guidance counselor, Mr. George Winslow, suggested a career in accounting or bookkeeping. It was work I could easily get in those days without a college degree. I took bookkeeping and typing and business and accounting. I hadn't prepared financially for college by the time I decided to go.

As a result, I stayed home for a year after graduation to work and help pay for my first year of college. I'm the only one of the seven children who went to college in my family. I realize I got a little extra treatment because of my condition. My mother treated everybody the same but there was a little more protection with me, maybe a little more guidance. She and my father decided that if I wanted to go to college, they would support that goal, partly because it did not involve a physical capability for heavy work.

I got a job that year at the Boys Club as the Game Room Director. I could've had a job at the local plant, though. They would have hired me as a bookkeeper at a good rate of pay. I chose the Boys Club job, though, at about half of what the plant would have paid me, because I believed I owed something to the Boys Club. At the end of the year, I had saved $700. That helped pay for part of my first term at St. Lawrence University. My mother and my two brothers all pitched in, too. They put some money in the bank that I had access to.

When I got to college, I realized there were still a lot of things I didn't have. We had to wear a jacket every night to dinner and I only had one sport jacket and one tie. I created some variety by borrowing a different tie every night. Then they changed the rules and nobody had to wear a jacket to dinner anymore. I was really delighted. That took the burden off of me.

During my first year, I was interviewed by an official from the State of New York. A teacher had told me that there is a fund in the state for handicapped people, and they might consider me for a scholarship.

A Mr. Hartwick from New York State interviewed me and included an aptitude test for the career I wanted. I said I wanted radio so they sent me for that test. I was amazed when I saw what came out of that aptitude test. They said I had the right aptitude for mechanical drawing. "I don't even know how to draw," I told Mr. Hartwick. In the end, they didn't give me the scholarship.

They interviewed me each year though. They didn't give me anything the first year or the second year or the third year. The scholarship would have been $500 each year. They kept asking me, "Why did you choose that career?" I guess I had to prove it to them.

It wasn't until the very last term when they finally decided I was going to be in radio. They had to admit it. I had taken all the radio courses, and I got my best grades in them. After all that, when the payment came due for that last term, New York State sent my check late. After the semester started the Finance Office let me know I'd have to go home if there wasn't a payment soon. I had to go track it down myself.

St. Lawrence University had also given me a job. I made $.75 an hour. On mornings when I didn't have classes I went to the soda fountain where I got to make kids a milkshake or whatever they wanted. It was for three or four hours, five days a week. I did that for a whole term. I guess I made about $15 a week.

We had a wealthy young man in our class named Bill "Shorty" Lehren. He came from Greenwich, Connecticut, and his father owned a big toy company called Wolverine Toys. He had whatever he needed, yet sometimes he had to borrow money from me. We became friends. He liked baseball and was famous among the students for his ability to recite from memory all of "Casey at the Bat". He knew I was a real serious New York Giants baseball fan, and he thought I would enjoy seeing the Polo Grounds and Madison Square Garden. He took me to New York City once.

There was a track meet at the Garden and Glenn Davis of Army was there, half of the famous running back duo of Davis and Blanchard. He ran the 60 yard dash in a track meet that night, so I got to see the great all-American. Then we drove past the Polo Grounds and found that the Giants weren't home but the Dodgers were, over at Ebbets Field.

That's why I said I couldn't be more blessed than to be with the fellows that I grew up with in my hallway. It was the perfect mixture with the toy empire heir, the onion farmer from Canastota and the math whiz. The whiz was so good that he never even had to take the final exam; his professor thought it would be a waste of time. He was my roommate.

I was the radio guy. I was not the bookkeeper guy.

2. No B.M.O.C.

When I was at St. Lawrence, most of the guys I was friends with didn't try very hard to play Big-Man-On-Campus (the proverbial BMOC of the era), especially when it came to dating.

I really didn't think I had any hope of a girl paying attention to me. My friends and I would look at those big, athletic guys. They were so handsome the rest of us didn't even want to ask for a date. We didn't want to know how many rejections we'd get. I guess you could say I was – a lot of us were – a little timid in the dating area.

After I had been at St. Lawrence for a while, I met a girl who said, "I'm going to teach you to dance." We went down to the radio studio and I played some records…she was really trying to teach me. It was great, not like a date, just having fun with somebody who wanted to be a friend, just a natural kind of thing.

But you know, because the guys I palled around with didn't go out on many dates, we were together just about all the time. Nobody separated us. There was only one, a fellow named Mike Tornatore, who dated a lot. I called him the Italian Stallion. He was a handsome guy and he was – get this – an onion farmer from Canastota.

3. Adventure: A Family Heritage

When Jim Roselle talks about his childhood, two ideas often come together in a charming and most telling way: Jim's admiration for his parents, and the importance of a mind always open for adventure… not necessarily the grand and daring sort, but adventures in the human spirit, people at their best and most inspiring.

Jim's childhood buddy, Joe Trusso – eventually a Chautauqua County Legislator and still a close friend – says, "It's all about *The Boat*. All of our parents came over on *The Boat*. Our neighborhood was made up of people who took their lives in their hands, left home as young men and women, often still in their teens, knowing they may never see their parents and friends again, sailed across the ocean to an unknown land and worked hard so their children could grow up in a country where they could do great things. Most people don't think of it this way today, but our parents were adventurers. They passed that spirit on to us."

4. St. Lawrence University Play-by-Play

At St. Lawrence they let me do the play-by-play sports broadcasting on the college radio station. That's basically what I wanted to do, but that's certainly not all I learned.

I learned about play production for radio, too. I had a part in a play that a student wrote for VE Day, Victory in Europe Day. It was a beautiful radio play. The college sent his script to WGY in Schenectady and they liked it so well they wanted us to come down and put it on their 50,000-watter [the highest transmission power allowed in radio broadcasting]. And I had a little part in that play. Wow! What a thrill it was to get on a 50,000-watter.

We did the play at St. Lawrence with sound effects. When we got to the WGY studio the production manager said we didn't need those. The organ would give us all the sound effects we needed. We wondered how the heck he was going to do that. But he did. And so there we were thinking, my God what a thrill. A 50,000-watter, WGY Schenectady! We learned a lot about real world broadcasting that day.

When I first started my radio classes at the university I did whatever my professor wanted me to do. Her name was Professor Gertrude Pasel. She later told me, "James, you were five minutes away from me telling you to follow a different career." She changed her mind, though, after hearing me do the play-by-play for a basketball game.

At home I had prepared by quickly tuning in Madison Square Garden, right there (Jim motions toward the old console radio that his parents had owned, now in the corner of his own living room). I listened to Marty Glickman do play-by-play from the Garden. I watched how he handled the play-by-play describing a game and made up my own for practice:

The ball's inbounds!
He dribbles up court into the offensive zone
He's by the keyhole, passes over into the corner, a bounce pass, the shot's up.
No good! It hits the rim. Rebound goes to the defender...

I tried to make it all visual; I tried to make the listener see what I was seeing.

She found the excitement in my voice and the style that I was using. She liked the fact that I created a sense of excitement in the game. In my mind, I thought I sort of went overboard a little bit. I was trying to copy all the sportscasters I had admired for so long. I just had to fine tune it. But she heard something there, and that made all the difference.

When I graduated from St. Lawrence University in 1949, I was sure my life would be in broadcasting, sportscasting in particular. I sent carefully prepared audition tapes of my very best work to radio stations in Vermont, Norfolk, Bangor, Paducah and Amsterdam. Silence was my only reply except for Amsterdam. I was sure I'd get that Amsterdam job, until they hired somebody else.

Chautauqua County, right here at home, as it turned out, became my turning point, the place where I finally broke into radio. It was that day in Phil and Ross's Royal Hat Shop, where gentleman got their hats blocked, their shoes shined and their hair cut, that Si Goldman gave me my first break at WJTN.

Sometimes it seemed like it would never happen – but it did.

5. Fraternity Life

I joined Sigma Pi in 1945 and helped revive it after the war years. The building that became the Sigma Pi House had been used as a USO Center during the war. We took the house over and began rebuilding the membership. The GIs were coming back to the States and to colleges everywhere on the G.I. Bill.

The fraternity voted me treasurer and we had a big job of fundraising to do. Before we graduated we had laid the groundwork for a $25,000 addition to the house.

Fraternity life was good then, and the parties were fun, but not really as raucous as some of the stories people tell. It was a place to make friends and enjoy a side of college life that was a little more relaxed than the study side.

My step-sons, Tom and Phil Nalbone, enjoyed the stories I told them about my college days at St. Lawrence. I told them about the sports, the professors and many other things, including the fraternity parties. It all sounded so good that Phil asked for a catalogue when he was planning for his life after high school. Bill Daly, the dean of admissions looked over his grades and said, "Phil is just the kind of student we want."

Phil, and later, Tom, applied to St. Lawrence University, earned scholarships and graduated from my *alma mater*.

Chapter 7

The Literary World

It's all about communication. Jim Roselle doesn't draw cartoons and he doesn't write plays. He simply talks. Authors, playwrights and poets commit their words to paper for others to read for years to come. Jim commits his words only to the air; they occur and then they are gone. He understands the art of communication, though, the same way the literary world does; words in any form are valuable only when they make a lasting impression where they land, and then they have worth. Jim invites his guest artists of the written word to a conversation with his listeners.

Everything tells me that the world would be an exquisite place to live, were everyone able to respond to life as Jesus did. I call that 'mamaloshen.' That is a Yiddish word meaning straight talk mixed with common sense. Actually it goes deeper than that. 'Mamaloshen' is the understanding that comes when one's common sense derives as much from the soul as the mind. The Sermon on the Mount is simple mamaloshen. And anything that ain't mamaloshen doesn't square with my religious sensibilities.

Norman Lear

I don't sit down in the morning and try to commit an act of literature before lunch.

Billy Collins

I was pirouette and flourish,
I was filigree and flame.
How could I count my blessings
when I didn't know their names?

Rita Dove
Poem "Testimonial" from On the Bus With Rosa Parks

A typical biography relying upon individuals' notorious memories and the anecdotes they've invented contains a high degree of fiction, yet is considered 'nonfiction'.

Joyce Carol Oates

When it is time for you to leave this school, leave your job, or even leave this earth, you make sure you have worked hard to make sure it mattered you were even here.

Wes Moore

Jim and Norman Lear in the broadcast booth

All in the Family with Norman Lear

Norman Milton Lear was born in 1922, before the Golden Age of Radio and long before the era of television, the medium by which Jim says Norman Lear changed the thinking and imagination of America as a creative writer and producer. Lear pioneered a new era of innovative and mold-breaking television comedy with productions such as the

1970s sitcoms *All in the Family* and its spinoff, *The Jeffersons, One Day at a Time, Good Times, Sanford and Son,* and *Maude.*

Lear was also a passionate political activist, founding the advocacy organization *People For the American Way* in 1981. He also championed spirited defenses of First Amendment rights and supported many progressive social and political causes. Backing up his passion for good government by and for the people, Lear also engaged in and supported many well known philanthropic projects with his time, personal influence and wealth.

As a producer and writer, Lear is often credited with a deep and instinctive understanding of the American media audience. It was an concept Jim Roselle also understood well, though he had come to it in a different way.

Lear was a keen observer of his public. He studied his audiences to see how they responded to the comedy that he and the other writers wrote. Jim, on the other hand, had placed himself within his audiences, broadcasting from their homes and back yards, from their businesses and shopping centers, as he fondly recalls *Tales from the Golden Age of Radio*, Chapter 11.

Jim asked Norman about Archie Bunker because he had come to know Archie's family and his neighborhood from the inside. And that's exactly what Norman Lear was counting on happening in every one of the more than 65 million American living rooms with a television set in the 1970s.

A Conversation with Norman Lear

Jim Roselle: Good morning everybody and welcome to the center of the universe, welcome to the front porch of the Hultquist Building here at Chautauqua Institution. I'm going to frankly and honestly say at this moment, I am awed by the opportunity to sit next to a gentleman who has changed the thinking of the world and people's lives.
Norman Lear: My God, did I do that?

JR: I'm sitting next to Norman Lear. I am so pleased that you have given me this opportunity.
NL: I couldn't be more pleased myself. Look what I'm looking at here. (Norman looks out across Bestor Plaza.)
JR: Does it bring a TV show to mind?
NL: Actually, it does. I wrote it a year ago. But I can't get arrested with it.
JR: First of all, let me say thank you to Roger Rosenblatt who is going to be the narrator on the stage for the entire week. It's a week called, "Roger Rosenblatt and Friends." Roger, it's a pleasure to see you again. This is the third time you've had an opportunity to bring your friends to Chautauqua.
Roger Rosenblatt: Yes it is. Every other year, and in the interim years, I put myself in a mental institution. I'm fine after that.
JR: I heard you say you are running out of friends.
Roger Rosenblatt: I ran out of friends before any of this, except for Norman Lear. He and I have been friends for 30 or 35 years. We were friends from the moment we saw each other, and it just grows and grows.
JR: How has the literary world changed in recent times?
RR: Considerably, especially with the advent of e-books and publishing online. It's very, very difficult for somebody to get a book actually published. The publishers themselves don't know what to do with the profession anymore. They don't know whether they should publish in e-books only, or a combination of e-books and print. It's the same problem as in newspapers. We are in a very odd, transitional time in publishing. It affects what writers choose to write.

But, you know what I'm going to do now? I'm going to leave this stage to you and Norman.

JR: We'll see you again, Roger. (Jim addresses audience.) Give him a nice round of applause.

NL: What was his name again?

JR: Norman Lear, when you look back at the early 70s when you wrote *All in the Family,* were you aware of what the impact of that show would be?

NL: I can't say that I was. I loved the show. You know, when you are working that hard - one show is going on and you've got three shows in the pipeline that you're writing and trying to get ready - there isn't a lot of time to think about the impact of the show. But when the press got hold of it, and the mail started to come, I began to realize its impact.

JR: The reaction was immediate. The critics were right there saying they thought it was groundbreaking. You said, "America, go look at yourself in the mirror." Was it an attack on racism and prejudices?

NL: Well, a lot of people didn't think so. A good deal of the press... Laura Hobson, if you remember, wrote *Gentleman's Agreement.* She was the reigning authority on racial issues at the time. She wrote a big *New York Times* piece which just damned the show. She thought it was altogether wrongheaded.

JR: Wasn't Richard Nixon one who commented on that?

NL: Richard Nixon was the guy who said, among other things, "How could they make such a fool of such a good man?" (Norman laughs)

JR: Can you give us an insight into how you put the show together? How did you choose Carroll O'Connor for the role of Archie Bunker?

NL: Interestingly enough, I came to California... I was casting in New York... And the actor that I thought had a name that could play the role was Mickey Rooney. I knew his manager and I called him. He said, "Wait a second, Mickey's right here and you can tell him." I said I'd rather not tell him, but I'm coming out to California, and I'd rather meet and talk to him about it.

Anyway, he put Mickey on the phone. Mickey referred to himself in the third person.

"It's the Mick, what you want? You are Norman Lear?"—We did not know one another— "tell me about it. What's the show?"

"Well, it's difficult to describe this character. I'd rather do it in person. It's a sensitive kind of thing and..."

"No, no, no. You want to tell the Mick something, just tell him." And he forced me to tell him.

"Well, he's bigoted. He speaks about people with racial slurs; he's that kind of guy. Antediluvian."

"Norman," Rooney said, "they're going to kill you in the streets. They are going to shoot you dead. You want to do a show with the Mick? Try this: Vietnam vet, short, blind, large dog." That was a show he wanted to do.

JR: How did Carroll O'Connor come into the picture?

NL: I had seen him in a picture that Blake Edwards made. He was one of 30 actors that walked into the addition. They had all seen a script. Carroll walked into a room I had taken to meet these actors. He opened his mouth and in two sentences I knew. He knew a cab driver who had a sound that he thought was right. He was doing that cab driver and it was dead right for me.

JR: How do you get Jean Stapleton to be Edith Bunker?

NL: I had seen her on Broadway in a show. She was an actress I had called in.

JR: And the children?

NL: I made it twice for *ABC* with exactly the same script, Archie and Edith were the same characters, but with two different young people each time. It was a gift from the gods I found Sally. I had known Rob since he was a little boy and he was just right. The heavens were smiling.

JR: You were so successful with that show, you changed the thinking and the language of America.

NL: I seriously doubt that. It's just the foolishness of the human condition. Don't you think we are foolish? I think we are funny as hell.

JR: But you are also a serious person, Norman Lear.

NL: Yes. That's how I know we are funny.

JR: Are you concerned about the Citizens United decision by the Supreme Court?

NL: I can't imagine anything to be more concerned about.

JR: What should we do about it?

NL: Should we have an America where people can buy the country and can buy the government? It doesn't seem like the America I understood this to be.

JR: One of my favorite questions here at Chautauqua is: "If you had an opportunity to have dinner some night, what four people, living or dead, would you invite?

NL: Jesus, (George) Bernard Shaw, Lady Gaga... I am quite serious about that. This young woman knows something we don't know. I am really curious about it. And you. You do this very well.

JR: I've got this on tape, Norm. Thank you very much. Are you seeing Chautauqua for the first time?

NL: Yes

JR: What was your impression?

NL: I think it may be the biggest enclave of people who get along in the world. They more than get along. Everybody seems to have the same appetite and interests here. It's a community that comes together in order to be together. It's quite wonderful.

JR: Norman, you are trying to get the young people in this country to vote. What successes are you are having with that?

NL: Well, you know, we were touring a copy of the Declaration of Independence around the country for a couple of years. We know we registered over 6 million in the course of those years. Those were hard figures, but how many others, I don't know.

JR: I'm going to repeat what I said when I started this interview, Norm, that I am awed that you gave me this time to have a conversation with you.

NL: You know, I've noticed it took every bit as much of your time as mine. So we break even there. And I have had as good a time as you. And that proves we break even.

JR: Should I end it by saying what Carroll O'Connor would say?

NL: What would he say?

JR: I think I'm outta here!

NL: Or... Case closed!

JR: Case closed, then, Norman Lear. Let's give him a nice round of applause.

NL: A real pleasure, Jim.

Billy Collins
(With Roger Rosenblatt)

William James "Billy" Collins was selected as Poet Laureate of the United States to serve between 2001 and 2003 and has received many additional awards and accolades as a poet.

He has published many collections and anthologies of poetry and has been a Distinguished Professor of English

Billy Collins and Jim enjoy a "Chautauqua moment" before air time

at Lehman College in the Bronx for more than thirty years. In advanced studies, Collins earned an M.A. and a PhD in Romantic Poetry from the University of California, Riverside.

Billy Collins' good friend, Roger Rosenblatt, is a popular and respected writer and journalist for *Time* magazine, an author and playwright and a professor at Stony Brook Southampton. He both earned his PhD from and taught at Harvard University.

As serious and dignified as Collins and Rosenblatt's resumes appear, they happily belie such gravitas when they get together at Chautauqua Institution and especially on the air with Jim Roselle.

A Conversation with Billy Collins and Roger Rosenblatt

Jim Roselle: What a pleasure it is to welcome a friend. I think I can say that, though right now he's pretty busy with the audience. Roger Rosenblatt, good morning.
Roger Rosenblatt: Good morning. How are you?

JR: Fine, thank you, and thank you for arranging this week of writers for Chautauqua.
RR: It's such a pleasure. All of these folks are such wonderful writers and great friends. I hope the conversation is worthy of Chautauqua.
JR: You're going to be on stage with them?
RR: I hope so; otherwise they wouldn't know what to do with themselves. They're kind of a dumb bunch, actually.
JR: How far back did you get acquainted with Billy Collins?
RR: Billy and I have known each other about 10 or 12 years. We go to the Southhampton Writing Conference together. It is probably the best in the country. We all, lots of writers, teach there for 12 days…just to see if the writers get a little better at the end than I am. At the start, we do a lot of drinking and a lot of singing too…and the singing increases in direct proportion to the drinking.
JR: Can we teach others to be smart? Scientists took a poll of thousands of people. The biggest percentage of them had not read a book in one year, had not even touched a book in one year.
RR: I guess other forms of learning have taken over. Maybe they read the papers on the Internet and maybe that's the future. I never think that one form of art will ever drive out another, or that technology will, for that matter. I remember when people thought the advent of television would drive out radio.
JR: My brother, Phil, said I better find a new career when TV came in.
RR: (Roger points into the audience and interrupts) You know, there's a guy walking by here looks just like Billy Collins.
JR: And there he is. It is Billy Collins, Poet Laureate of the United States for the years 2001 to 2003. Billy Collins, let me welcome you to Chautauqua Institution and to our broadcast. We thank you for accepting our invitation.
Billy Collins: Thank you.
JR: How does a poet see Chautauqua? Is there a quick idea for a poem here?
BC: Well, usually I use things I see. I might take away an image…like the image of Roger in shorts or something…some kind of little picture. I would write "My Day at Chautauqua" on the top of the piece of paper and try to respond to that as a kind of essayist or memoirist.

But clearly I've never seen a place like this. It's quite a… You know I have a poem I called "*The Chairs that Nobody Sits In.*" You know those chairs on lawns and by lakes and no one ever sits in them? But here at Chautauqua everyone sits in them, so it's a great place to sit. The chairs seem to be fully occupied.
JR: What gives birth to an idea for a poem?

BC: Less than what could be called an idea. I'm not sure I've ever had an idea. Things go through my mind, but I don't think that any of them really, really qualify as an idea.

JR: What about some emotion?

BC: Well, that is a problem, too. What really gets a poem going is a bit of language, a phrase…you know we are all writing about the same things. There may be five things to write about, maybe six. We just try to find new metaphors for writing about these things.

My sense of reality is always looking around opportunistically for new metaphors. When I was a teenager I started writing poetry because I'd had my heart broken by this insensitive 19-year-old, 10th grade girl, which began the whole thing.

Originally poetry was a system - a way of storing information with the mnemonic devices. Then, after literacy was invented, it was a way to get the woman. When that failed, it was a way to lament the fact that you couldn't get the woman.

As a teenager I was experiencing feelings of confusion and alienation. These were never before experienced in the history of mankind. These must be recorded. Otherwise, I'll be forgotten. And shortly thereafter I realized that everybody had the same emotion engines.

That didn't stop me from writing, though. Just because I had nothing to say, it didn't mean I didn't want to keep writing. There are other motives than getting women, like becoming well known, so…

JR: You keep coming back to women during this…

BC: Yeah, we have to because they are there.

JR: What was the first poem you wrote?

BC: I was in the back of my parents' car. I was an only child then. I spent many pleasant hours in the back of my parents' car. Even today, I can recognize an only child on the highway. They have a very distinct look, boys particularly. The parents are driving, and in their back seat, there is a child with a distant look, the whole backseat to themselves, and a certain smug look about them, as opposed to three kids back there with ice cream all over themselves,

Once, when I was about 10, we were driving up the East Side in New York City and I saw a sailboat sailing against the current of the East River. I had a literary reaction to this, and I asked my mother for something to write with. I asked my mother for my father's hand to write on. We didn't have paper in our family. We were poor. I don't know what I wrote, but I remember wanting to get this written down. That's basically called observational poetry.

And that's basically what lyric poetry has been like for 300 years. You see something - there are some daffodils, for example - and you write something down that you felt in reaction to the daffodils. That was listening literature that I committed at the age of 10.

JR: Billy, you have picked out the best poems of 2006. How do you do that?

BC: Good poetry is very accessible. But the real disturbing part about accessibility in poetry is that everyone has access to writing it without any practice or knowledge.

It's as if people think they can just grab a cello, get up on the stage and start screeching on it. No one would just start painting without even knowing how to use linseed oil. But all you need is a Bic pen and a piece of paper and you are a bard in self-expression. It's too easy. You would practice the cello or you could practice tone and color and other skills in painting, so you need to practice writing, too.

The practice of poetry requires deep reading of poetry. I have students - bless their hearts - who say, "I don't really read poetry because it's going to compromise my objectivity and originality." That is the least of their worries.

JR: When did you first get what you would call recognition for your poetry?

BC: You get little dribs and drabs and then you get on this kind of morphine drip of attention that you seem unable to do without. But I guess when this nice man from Congress called me up and said, "You are the poet laureate," that removed most of the lingering doubts about whether I was a poet or not. That was confirming my deepest suspicions about myself.

JR: What did you think your responsibility was?

BC: I had no idea. And I think if you took this microphone around and asked people what they think the poet laureate really is they would be a little nebulous about it.

Howard Nemerov, the past poet laureate, said what the poet laureate basically does is for one year he goes around and tries to explain what the poet laureate does; he tries to explain it to himself and to others.

So there's this tiny checklist of things you do. There's an office in Washington in the Jefferson Library, a beautiful office near the Capitol which you can see right over your shoulder. You also give a reading and a lecture at the Library of Congress. Other than that, you're free to stare out your window at the Capitol.

JR: You're a professor of English at Lehman College. For how many years now?

BC: I began teaching there when the earth was cooling, the ground was still a little warm…

JR: Did you mention that because you are concerned about global warming?

BC: Yeah, I mean, first of all… Hey! That was a good segue there, you *are* the boss!

As someone who's interested in the language, I don't think it should be called global warming. Warming is to comforting a word. I think it should be called something like global roasting or global baking, or something with global death. You know global warming makes it sounds sort of cozy.

The reasons people are very slow to react to the crisis of global warming, are twofold.

First, the enemy is invisible. You can't really see the pollution. You have footage of polar bears on diminishing icebergs, but you don't really see it in your daily lives, so the enemy is invisible.

The second reason we're slow to respond is that the people we're trying to save have not yet been born. So we're doing it for a generation that doesn't exist, and we can't see the enemy.

JR: What are your thoughts Roger?

RR: Well, that's a very smart way of looking at it.

JR: Ladies and gentlemen, let's have a big round of applause for Roger Rosenblatt and Billy Collins. Thank you very, very much.

Rita Dove
Consultant to the Library of Congress

Rita Dove was born in Akron, Ohio, into a family of high intellectual and profession achievements. Her father, Ray, was a research chemist with Goodyear, the first African-American chemist in the American tire industry. Rita's mother, Elvira, with a passion for reading, had achieved honors in school and shared her enthusiasm for the written word with her daughter, which Rita carried into undergraduate, graduate and post-graduate studies in the U.S. and abroad in Germany.

Rita Dove received the Pulitzer Prize for poetry in 1987, served as Poet Laureate Consultant in Poetry to the Library of Congress from 1993 to 1995 and a year later was awarded the 1996 National Humanities Medal by President Clinton. President Obama presented her the 2011 National Medal of Arts. Dove was the first African-American appointed as poet laureate. She also served as "special consultant in poetry" to the Library of Congress for its bicentennial year from 1999 to 2000. Her poetry also earned her many other awards along with 24 honorary Doctorate degrees.

With her husband, Fred Viebahn, an award-winning German-born novelist, poet and journalist, Rita is also an avid ballroom dancer and performer. They have one daughter, Aviva Dove-Viebahn.

Though Rita Dove's family and Jim's were so very different in many ways, they each grew up in a home that encouraged reading. Later in life, Jim served for many years on the board of directors of Jamestown's Prendergast Library and has frequently entertained primary school children throughout the community with classroom readings, conversations and encouragement to travel the world through books. Early reading experiences were also essential to Rita's early development.

A Conversation with Rita Dove

Jim Roselle: I read about when you were given word that you were going to be the poet laureate. You said, "It's crazy, but I've got to take it anyway." What did you mean by that?

Rita Dove: I knew that being a poet is like being the most introverted, quiet, private thing in the world. And then to become the poet laureate seems to be the most extroverted, outward thing in the world. That's what I meant by being crazy. I wanted to stand up for poetry, but at the same time I really wanted to be in my room, writing. But I knew that I had to accept the position. I was called at that moment and that was my time to stand up and say, "Okay. Here I am."

    JR: Where did that little poetry affair start, Rita?

    RD: With learning to read…and learning that just putting these little squiggles on the page could make a story that could lead me anywhere in the world or in time…and being encouraged to see that it was really fun.

    At the same time music was part of the school curriculum. We had to go and play the tonettes and that was another passion. I loved the idea that you could join together with other people and make this glorious sound. So I grew up doing both music – I played the cello – and reading. It all just seemed part of learning and just becoming a person in this wide world.

    JR: You know that commercial that says, "What's in your wallet?" You know what I say every time I hear that? I say, "My library card."

    RD: Mine too! It is so important. My parents let us go to the library at any time. And there were books in our house and my parents didn't restrict me from reading any of them. I think they figured if I was old enough to understand it I was old enough to read it. I felt this incredible freedom of just being able to roam those shelves and just read anything.

    JR: What's the first poem that got your attention?

    RD: It was actually a book in my parents' library that was called Lewis Untermeyer's *Treasury of Great Poems* [first published January 1, 1901]. I still remember the cover. It was purple and gold. One of the first poems that caught my eye was a long poem called *Barbara Fritsche* [John Greenleaf Whittier, 1864]. It told the story of a woman who stood up for the flag of the United States. I still remember two lines:

> … Shoot if you must this old gray head
> but spare your country's flag, she said…

    I was just thrilled. I don't know why, but it did. That was the very first poem that I remember. [It has been reported that when Winston Churchill passed through Frederick, Maryland—Barbara Fritchey's hometown immortalized by her exploits—with President Roosevelt en route to the retreat now called Camp David in 1943, Churchill recited the entire poem for his traveling companion.]

    JR: Billy Collins has put a very lighthearted touch to poetry. A lady came to me after hearing him and said, "After listening to Billy Collins I'm going to read a poem before I go to sleep every night." She said it as if she was saying, "I'm going to have a nice glass of wine before I go to sleep every night."

    RD: So many people are afraid of poetry. People would say, "I don't know much about poetry but…" Or "I really don't understand poetry." And then they would tell me an incredibly moving story about the first poem they ever read.

I think many people are afraid they will *get the wrong answer*. What Billy has done and what Robert Pinsky has done with his *Favorite Poem Project*, and what many other poets laureate have done, is to awaken people to the fact that poetry is about everyday life, it's about every one of us.

JR: Rita Dove is the author of the book, *Sonata Melodica*. It's a story of a violinist.

RD: It's different than a lot of poetry books because it is, in a certain way, a novel inverted. It is told through a poem about George Bridgetower who was a mixed race, prodigy violinist in the 18th and 19th centuries.

The miracle about the whole story is that he existed and that we know very little about him. But his claim to fame is that he met Beethoven and Beethoven composed a sonata for him, a violin sonata, which we know as the Kreuzer Sonata. It was originally called the Bridgetower. They got into an argument, though, and Beethoven, being Beethoven, did what he does so well: he destroyed his dedication.

JR: I asked John Tesch [American pianist and composer] what poem he would recommend that I read. He said, "You have got to read *Forerunners*. I've read it a thousand times, and every time I read it my socks were knocked off."

> The harbingers are come. See, see their mark:
> White is their color, and behold my head.
> But must they have my brain? Must they dispark
> Those sparkling notions, which therein were bred?
> Must dullness turn me to a clod?
> Yet have they left me, *Thou art still my God*…

> George Herbert, Wales. 1593–1633
> From: *The Temple* (1633)
> Stanza 1 of 6

RD: That's what a great poem does, every single time.

JR: What was the first poem you ever wrote?

RD: I can give you the line from the first poem that I wrote that I was really excited about because I didn't know the ending until I wrote the ending. And that was when I was 10 years old. It was an Easter poem, and it was about a rabbit with a droopy ear. It started out:

> Mr. rabbit was big and brown
> but he always wore a frown.
> He was sad because Easter was here
> because he had one droopy ear.
> They were the handsomest ears in town,
> except one went up and one went down…

I had this dilemma with the droopy eared rabbit and I didn't know exactly what I was going to do with it, but the poem rhymed and I kept going and finally he solved his problem.

JR: We are glad you ended up on that seat, right here and for this opportunity you gave me today, Rita Dove. Welcome to Chautauqua.

RD: Thank you.

Margaret Atwood
It's All About Your Experience

Margaret Atwood is the author of nearly seventy volumes of poetry, novels, children's literature, non-fiction, edited works and dramatic scripts. She has earned many national and international awards for her writing. Born in 1939 in Ottawa, Margaret Atwood grew up in Canada and completed her undergraduate studies at Victoria College, University of Toronto and her master's degree at Radcliffe College in Cambridge, Massachusetts.

Broadcasting from The Cove at Chautauqua Institution Jim was delighted to welcome Chautauqua's author of the week, Margaret Atwood, to his broadcast microphone. Her work, featured that summer by the Chautauqua Literary and Scientific Circle, CLSC, was *The Handmaid's Tale* [McClelland and Stewart, 1985].

A Conversation with Margaret Atwood

Jim Roselle: Margaret, welcome to Chautauqua. You are so prolific, over 60 books and still counting…
Margaret Atwood: Yes, but some of them are short.

JR: Where does all of this energy and creativity come from?
MA: First of all, I've been doing it for a while. So, it sort of accumulates. If I had done those 50 books in five years, then you might have reason to be surprised, but it's over a much longer period of time. So where does the energy come from? I'm a writer and what I do is write. We don't get the retirement slip when people say that's enough of you, you can stop now. Or, they might say that but you don't have to listen.
JR: I agree. It is lifelong.
MA: You do sometimes get worse. But it started out worse, got better for most of your career, and then you might get worse again. Think of it as a bell curve.
JR: Is there a moment when you suddenly don't feel you can create?
MA: That has happened several times. And at those times, luckily, I was writing in several different forms. So I stopped writing the thing that wasn't working, and I wrote a travel piece or something else like that.
JR: But there is always something in place…
MA: It's something like being a piano player. You can practice every day.
JR: Your book was selected as the book of the week here at Chautauqua. When you received that information what was your first thought?
MA: I'm the ice cream of the week! The flavor of the week. Being any 'thing of the week' is a bit problematical. A week is kind of short, don't you think? On the other hand, it's very thrilling so many people, all at the same time, will be reading the same book, discussing it among themselves and then will be able to discuss it with me later today.
JR: Did you need a lot of imagination to create that story in Handmaid's Tale?
MA: It was not such a stretch. I didn't put anything into that book that has not actually happened at some time, some place in history. I didn't want people telling me that I had a weird, twisted imagination. I wanted to be able to say, "Well, that has been done." It hasn't all been done in Cambridge Massachusetts, which is where the book is set, but it's all been done somewhere.
JR: What prompted you to tackle that subject?

MA: A couple of things. I was an early science fiction reader. Among my formative influences were George Orwell and HG Wells, Ray Bradbury and Aldous Huxley. When you have admired something, you always want to give it a try yourself. So that's number one.

Number two, I have never believed people who say, "it can't happen here." I've never believed that. I was born in 1939, so I did grow up during the World War II. One of the things that were true about that war was that England was extremely unprepared for it when it began. They had thought it wasn't going to happen again.

And there could never be a totalitarian government in the United States. I don't believe that either. A question would be - if there were to be one - what form would it take? That's among the questions that I was asking myself.

I was lucky to be able to study with the great American literary historian, Perry Miller, when he was at Harvard, which is one of the reasons the book is in part dedicated to him. America began as a 17th century Puritan theocracy, not as the democracy that we are taught about that dates from the 18th century. It began in Cambridge, Massachusetts, as a theocracy. I just went back a bit in time, as well as forward in time.

JR: When you stop and think of that moment when someone recognized your ability, your writing talent, what was it?

MA: You're going to think this is funny, probably. I have a couple of people who did. One was my aunt who wrote Sunday school stories. She was my literary relative.

The second one was my Brown Owl in Brownies. My Brown Owl was a very spectacular individual. To get these badges that you got in Brownies you would write little booklets. So I wrote these little booklets to get Brownie badges. My Brown Owl saved them. I thought she was long gone, but it turned out that she was the aunt of somebody I met who said your Brown Owl is my aunt. "What you mean 'is'? I asked, "She can't possibly still be alive." But she was.

So we went off to see Brown Owl. She was in a retirement home. We had tea with her, and we had a lovely time. At the end of the tea she said, "I have something that I would like to give you." She brought out the little booklets that I had written for her when I was nine. She had saved them all those years. So there they were again.

She was one of my 'first readers', and you can say she was an appreciative reader because she saved them all. Then a terrible thing happened. She was so excited by my visit that she died in her sleep three days later. My friend said, "You killed Brown Owl." Anyway, she died happy. She was about 95.

JR: Early in your career, there were a number of rejections. What was that first rejection like?

MA: Oh, let me count the ways. I think we are probably talking about poetry early on, but I had some more spectacular rejections a bit later. I did write a novel in 1963 when I was 23. I wrote part of it during my day job, because I could do my day job quite quickly, and then I could type my novel and look as if I was busily doing my job. I think my boss knew, but never minded. I wrote the novel and submitted it, and it did get rejected.

But it was ahead of its time. It ended with a female protagonist wondering whether or not to push the male protagonist off her roof. It was an open ending. Everyone in publishing was pretty much a man in those days. And this nice man took me out for a drink.

"We can't publish your novel," he said, "but could you change the ending?"

"No, I don't think so."

"Is there anything we can do?" Then he patted my hand. I think he thought it was my autobiography.

JR: I took a book out of the library that was posing the question, "Why do we write?" It had 20 authors who wrote about the reasons why they have to write. Why do you have to write?

MA: Because that's what I'm good at. It's too late now for me to be a ballet dancer, it makes me dizzy.

I am a writer. That's what I do. If two roads diverged in a yellow wood I might have turned out to be a botanist because I grew up in a scientific family, not a literary one. My brother turned into a biologist. If I had taken that road I would be cloning your genetically modified food right now. I went the other way, though.

JR: Was there a book when you were young that you read that inspired you in some way? In your childhood did you read something that fascinated you to say, "Wait a minute, I might want to do that?"

MA: In my early childhood my reading came through my mother reading aloud to me. About 1946, my parents ordered by mail order the complete book of Grimm's Fairytales, with all the eyeballs and blood and stuff in it. When it arrived, they thought they had made a mistake, that this would be too frightening for young children. But not so. I read that from beginning to end. Then I became an avid reader.

I didn't think about becoming a writer until I was 16. I had a very good high school teacher. I put her into a book. She is dead now. Her name was Betsy Billings, and she is in a book called *Moral Disorder* in a story called, *My Last Duchess*. That's her, it's her outfits, it's her method of teaching, everything. She was very inspirational to a lot of people. She did make one famous remark - she read an early poem of mine - "Well dear, I can't understand this at all, so it must be good."

JR: Do you love poetry as well as nonfiction and fiction?

MA: I do. Being from a family with some neurophysiologists in it, I suspect the different kinds of writing come from a different part of the brain. I think the poetry part is a lot closer to music than mathematics and certain kinds of oral patterning.

JR: Have you heard the saying, "There is a poet in every pocket?"

MA: I haven't heard that saying. It's probably true, though, because I think poetry is very connected with our early learning of language. There probably is a poet in every pocket, but it may not be a very good poet, but I'm sure there is one.

JR: As always, a huge thank you for giving us your time here to be on our broadcast.

MA: It's such a pleasure. And congratulations to you on your wonderfully long radio career.

JR: Thank you very much, Margaret Atwood.

Wes Moore and The Other Wes Moore

Wes Moore's first book, *The Other Wes Moore: One Name, Two Fates* [Spiegel & Grau, 2011] became an instant New York Times bestseller and a Wall Street Journal bestseller. Moore is also a youth advocate, a businessman and a US Army veteran combat paratrooper.

Wes's widowed mother raised him and his sister in difficult circumstances. Like the other Wes Moore, he struggled through behavioral and academic issues in school, but unlike him, graduated Phi Theta Kappa as a commissioned officer from Valley Forge Military College and Phi Beta Kappa from Johns Hopkins University where he earned a bachelor's degree in International Relations and went on to study International Relations as a Rhodes Scholar at Oxford University.

Jim understood growing up with limited resources and the powerful influence of family and neighborhood. Wes Moore's experience, however, was quite different from Jim's, a circumstance Jim found fascinating for both its similarities and its differences.

A Conversation with Wes Moore

Jim Roselle: Good morning again. I'm going to be talking to Wes Moore, the gentleman who wrote the book called *The Other Wes Moore* [Spiegel & Grau, 2010]. We are going to find out about him and that other Wes Moore. It's a pleasure to welcome you to Chautauqua.
Wes Moore: It is an honor to be here and an honor to sit next to you. Thank you.

Wes Moore and Jim share a common conviction that strong families breed success

JR: It's an interesting title. "The Other Wes Moore" means you knew somebody with the same name, in the same neighborhood, but you were not aware of it at the time.
WM: There were wanted posters in my neighborhood saying the police were looking for Wes Moore, and if you see him do not approach him because he is assumed to be armed and very dangerous.

That was the first time I learned about this other Wes Moore. The more I learned about him, the more I realized how much more we had in common than just names. That was the initial trigger that led me into a now almost decade-long conversation with him.

JR: But that young man made the wrong choices, and you made what I would call the right choices.
WM: Well, I was definitely blessed. Wes and I both grew up in single-parent households. We both had academic and discipline troubles growing up. What happened in many cases was this: I found myself surrounded by people, starting with my mom and my grandparents, and eventually a wonderful string of role models and mentors who showed the world was bigger than what was directly in front of me.

They showed me that second chances can mean something. A lot of the opportunities that I had – that Wes did not have – continued to compound until eventually, he made this tragic decision which led him to the murder of a police officer.

JR: He went into the world of drugs and crime.
WM: In 2001, he received life without parole for the murder of Sergeant Bruce Prothero.
JR: Where is he today?
WM: He is in the Jessup Correctional Institution, a maximum-security facility on the outskirts of Baltimore City. He has been there ever since sentencing and will be for the rest of his life.
JR: Is there no chance, that even on good behavior, they would reconsider?
WM: At this point, it would take nothing short of a presidential or gubernatorial pardon. But when you're in prison for the murder of a law enforcement officer, pardons don't come. At this point he finally understands what his punishment really means.

But that is why the book has such impact. It is being made part of curriculum in schools all over the country and college students are doing service projects around the tenets of the book. That's inspiring.

Wes's fate is sealed. The thing I want to do is to make sure these avoidable tragedies don't have to keep on happening.

JR: What are the odds in neighborhoods where people offer young people big money for drugs and crime? How do we rectify that situation?
WM: Kids will do what they see. There are a couple of things we fundamentally have to address. First, there needs to be a larger and a more sincere incorporation of not just second chances, but of leadership.

When I was younger I got sent to military school because I had a lot of issues. I had a mandatory year in military school which ended up turning into five years.

JR: You mean you were a bad boy?

WM: I needed a little bit of discipline. In military school - I'm not saying this is a panacea for everyone and everything - they taught leadership starting very early.

For instance, suppose I was in charge of a squad. If someone in my squad shows up late for class they will not be asked, "Why are you late for class?" The question they are going to ask is, "Who is your squad leader?" And they are going to come and find me because I am the squad leader, I am the one in charge. I need to have an answer.

And then with a graduated sense of responsibility, you become a platoon sergeant, or a first sergeant, or a platoon leader. They help you grow this sense of responsibility.

The drug game on the streets is really no different. Kids don't start off as kingpins. They start off as lookouts standing on the corner. When they see a cop roll by or someone who doesn't belong in the neighborhood, they just call and alert their people. Then they become a runner, or a house man, or a lieutenant.

That same graduated sense of responsibility that exists in the military structure, or the Fortune 500 structure. So the way we have to combat that is, A.) Understand it, but then also, B.) Make sure that we are taking the proper countermeasures in order to grab kids when we know we can grab them, and bring them back into the fold.

JR: It sounds like you have given many commencement speeches.

WM: I have. I ask them, "What is your influence, and what is your obligation to make sure that you are serving others? How do you make sure that you matter?" Education can't simply be about what you learn. Education also has to be about what you give. If the only thing you have to show after high school or college is a diploma, then you missed the point.

JR: Do you occasionally visit Wes Moore?

WM: I don't see him every time I am in Baltimore, but probably about once every month or two, and I write him more often than that.

Some people say, "I don't know why you're in touch with him still, don't you know he's a murderer?" I tell people, with all due respect, "I know why Wes is in prison, and I did not reach out to him to write a book, so why would I stop reaching out to him?

JR: What does he think about what he did? Does he have remorse for it?

WM: Wes read the book, and he had two main reactions to it. First, he said it's amazing how much research went into it. I did hundreds of hours of interviews with Wes, his friends and family, my friends and family, to make sure I was really getting the facts and the feel of the story right.

The other reaction he had was that it made him realize how little he has done with his life. When Wes was 23 years old he heard a judge tell him, "You are going to spend the rest of your life in prison." He's now spent the last 11 years, every day, in a 6' x 8' cell thinking about both what he did and what could have been. He deals with that every day.

JR: Has he ever considered suicide knowing he has got the rest of his life there?

WM: He has never expressed to me that he has considered it, but I know there are days he wakes up and he says, "What's the point?" He knows where his destiny is. He knows it because of the tragic death of Sergeant Bruce Prothero.

You know Wes also has four kids, and when Wes was 32 years old he became a grandfather. Even though he is not in close touch with them there is still a point to living because of this.

I also do know we receive thousands of letters from parents and teachers and students about the book and the impact that it is making. I cross out the names and photocopy letters and send some of them to Wes so he can see the impact that this story is having on the lives of others. And I know for him that has been very motivational, very touching.

JR: Is Dr. Martin Luther King's "I Have a Dream" speech one of your favorites?

WM: One of the things I find interesting about the "I Have a Dream" speech is that people sometimes actually miss the point.

It was not simply about what we can be. It was also a celebration of what we already are. Progress has been made, but there is also an underlying thread that says we still have work to do.

JR: For your next visit to Wes Moore do you have questions that you still want answered?

WM: I don't go there with an agenda anymore. But I know our worst decisions don't separate us from the circle of humanity. I have learned so much by my relationship with Wes. I have a greater appreciation for my life and a greater appreciation for the people who are involved in my life, for the people who sacrificed and are able to hold onto my dreams for me to grow up and be able to then hold onto them for myself.

JR: I sometimes refer to them as "the bridges we have to cross" to get where we are going. So, along the way, what bridges did you cross and who were the people that made it possible to get where you are today?

WM: I had countless bridges. And, to be honest, I still have bridges to this day. One thing about this idea of choices is that it doesn't stop when we are kids. I'm going to make 20 decisions before the end of my day today that will determine what my tomorrow looks like. I have people around me every single day that are helping to shape what my tomorrow will look like. I think our job at that point is to appreciate them, is to love them and is to thank them, because it's never easy to go through that process alone. It's impossible to go through that process alone. Having a greater appreciation of the people who will help to make that happen, helping make it possible is important.

JR: Wes Moore, thank you so much.

A Conversation with Joyce Carol Oates (And Roger Rosenblatt)

Jim Roselle: Roger Rosenblatt, do you realize what it means to have you on the air with me?

Roger Rosenblatt: I do. Sometimes I awaken in the morning and look in the mirror and say the same thing. "Do you know how lucky you are to be looking at me?" Then I get over it, and I can start my day.

Joyce Carol Oates on the air with Jim

JR: You know… it occurs to me that I have never asked you about your childhood.

RR: I didn't have a childhood.

Actually, that's almost true. A lot of people my age in Chautauqua will recognize this, particularly the men. My parents didn't recognize childhood as a condition of life. The idea was that you were born and as soon as possible you were an adult. I remember my father talking to me about it once.

"Roger, that's no way for a 12-year-old boy to behave."

"Dad, I'm six."

The idea of childhood as an isolatable stage of life came in the 1960s when it came with a vengeance. Everybody wanted to be a child, and grown-ups wore jeans.

The idea of childhood has changed. I think it had more profitable consequences than bad ones because people started to pay attention to the needs of children more than they had before – child abuse and childhood diseases for instance. There was a lot of silliness attached to it, too, including the rampant immaturity of adults. When I was a child there wasn't any childhood. There was only some vague pre-stage to adulthood.

You can remember the way they used to dress babies as grown-up as possible.

JR: The guest today, Joyce Carol Oates, has done, without question, a remarkable amount of work, whether it be novels, poetry, essays or drama. How many have you written?

RR: Twelve.

JR: Joyce Carol Oates has written, I believe, more than 100.

RR: There is no need to be unkind about it.

JR: But how does anybody have that time and that ability to do it?

RR: The interesting thing about Joyce is not that she has written so many books, but that she is such a stunningly good-looking woman that when she comes on the stage you're amazed – not that she has written 100 books – but that they are so good. She would be, and I told her this, a major writer of the 20th and 21st centuries if she had written one book or one novel or one play or one essay or one poem.

She has done so much for our benefit, but too many people like to emphasize the output. It is simply the output of an amazing writer. And she is extremely sexy, as you can see. She is really quite a lovely person. (Turning to Joyce) and you are, too, Joyce.

JR: One of your books, Roger, which I've read and appreciated…

RR: I knew there was at least one.

JR: *Where We Stand: 30 Reasons for Loving Our Country* [Harcourt, 2002].

RR: Oh, I hated that book! That was written in response to the conservative response to 9/11. But if you found something brilliant in it, by all means quote it.

JR: I was going to but as long as you introduced us, I'm going to talk to Joyce Carol Oates instead.

RR: It's about time.

Jim Roselle: Let me first sincerely thank you for the opportunity to talk with you, Joyce Carol Oates. I could read this bio, and it would take the rest of the program. I want to devote as much time in our conversation with you as I can. You have local roots here.

Joyce Carol Oates: Yes. I was born in Lockport, New York, and I lived all my life until the age of 18 on a small farm south of Lockport, just north of Buffalo.

JR: You pay a lot of attention to your childhood, to the memories you have from there, the imagination it created for you. You talk about games that I played, myself. I was trying to tell my kids and my grandkids about the funny games we played. I mentioned one day that we played a game called Palm, Palm Pull Away, Get Your Horse and Run Away. They thought I made that up.

JCO: That's probably a variant of the game children have played through the millennia. But we did play it in upstate New York.

JR: And you also played the familiar games of tag and hide 'n seek. Why did that leave such an impression on you?

JCO: I write a lot about my childhood memories, so that's part of it. I was a sort of tomboy and I loved to travel around outside. So this is just part of the fabric of memory.

JR: You have done such a remarkable piece of literary work. What is your day like? What will you be doing after today to get back into your writing career?

JCO: On a typical day I work through the morning. I can work until about 1:00 or 1:30, then I have a break. I don't think there's any particular mystery or mystique about being a creative artist. You basically have to do it. People have ideas and all sorts of dreams and notions but unless you actually do it and put some time in, nothing gets done. So it's a matter of discipline.

JR: In your book, *The Faith of a Writer: Life, Craft, Art* [Ecco-Harper Collins, 2003] you said that if anybody wants to write, "Write your heart out! No matter what."

JCO: Yes. Write about things that matter to you, and keep writing no matter what. Don't let anything stop you.

JR: Even though you may be disappointed in what you're doing, and you want to say I just can't keep doing this?

JCO: There may be some people who are not writers, but who are visual artists or something else. Just writing itself is not the absolute. There are other ways to be creative. I happen to think that one can be very creative in one's personal relationships, in creating a family, which my mother did. She didn't write the books.

JR: I remember reading that one of the great influences in your life was the book *Alice in Wonderland*.

JCO: Oh yes, that and *Through the Looking Glass*. I was eight years old and that was a book that came into the house. It wasn't that I was choosing among Dickens and DH Lawrence and Tolstoy and I chose *Alice in Wonderland*. Simply, that was the only book I had.

JR: The first book you wrote was?

JCO: *By the North Gate* in 1963 [Vanguard Press].

JR: What inspired you to write that?

JCO: Well, I had been writing for a long time. I was even writing when I was a little girl. What inspired me to write this book were many, many influences. It was a collection of short stories, not a novel. I had been writing when I was in my late teens and early 20s.

JR: You write a lot about violence in dysfunctional families. Why?

JCO: Well, not all the novels are the same. Some novels hold more with violence and others don't. It depends on what you mean. My most recent book is *Wild Nights*. It's about five American writers, and it is not really about dysfunctional families or violence, especially. I write about human beings who do different things, and some of the things they do once in a while are violent, but I would say that my subject matter is the human soul.

JR: And the conflicts that every individual faces in life are fascinating to you. I'm thinking of today, the issues that we deal with now. Has terrorism in the world given you any reason to write another novel?

JCO: Well, shortly after 9/11 I did write a novel called *The Tattooed Girl* which is not about 9/11 but it is about the issues of 9/11. It's about ethnic hatred. Someone in the novel is very anti-Semitic and just hates Jews but has never actually met a Jew. So a confrontation between an anti-Semite and a Jew is sort of the essence of that novel. My feeling is that when people get to know one another these ethnic hatreds fade away. They're only based on not knowing. They are based on ignorance.

JR: What about the situation today where race has become part of the political campaigns?

JCO: Race has always been with us. Race is the great issue in this country, going back to the early 1800s when there was beginning to be a movement for abolition. The country was violently divided between the abolitionists and the pro-slavers.

People who come to Chautauqua would have been quite abolitionist and against slavery. Issues of race are not new to this country. I think today, obviously, for an ethnic minority American it's the best time in our history. Not too many decades ago you would not see Barack Obama in any public position, whatsoever.

I think it is thrilling and very exciting and the entire world is looking at us. But prior to this, when Hillary Clinton was doing her campaign with some mixed results, that was a historic time, too. A woman, a frontrunner, a leader and a politician – no matter if you didn't like her – the fact is that she was there. And she is very, very resilient and certainly determined. A woman and a black man… It's just astonishing. So I think we can be proud of ourselves for having come so far.

JR: I want to ask you about a passage that you quoted from Henry James: "We work in the dark. We do what we can. We give what we have. Our doubt is our passion and our passion is our task. The rest is the madness of art." Why is it called the madness of art?

JCO: Because there is a certain frenzy, a certain craziness of art. Most art is very eccentric and wild and weird – like the dreams we have at night. Our dreams are often very surreal and mysterious. They are not like our daylight experience at all. When they fall asleep at night, they inhabit worlds that are very antithetical to their own, daytime worlds. Their dreams are extreme tapestries of great beauty and mystery, but they are not sane tapestries. Dreams are more like *Alice in Wonderland*.

JR: Why did you write under another name of Rosamond Smith?

JCO: I actually wrote under two pseudonyms. The other is Lauren Kelly. The Rosamond Smith and Lauren Kelly novels are psychological suspense novels. They are a little different from my usual novels which tend to be quite densely populated. I do a lot of research. Mysteries and psychological suspense novels tend to move much more quickly and to be more cinematic.

JR: Something that struck my curiosity was a book written by Billy Collins, the poet laureate. It was called *Taking the Clothes Off Emily Dickinson*. What do you think of a title like that?

JCO: His poem is very playful. It's about the feeling of great fascination poets and other people have for Emily Dickinson. It is like deconstructing Emily Dickinson and trying to figure her out. I think the title is meant to be funny and somewhat prurient but not exactly serious. He's really writing about apprehending and trying to appreciate this mysterious woman. I think she may be the greatest American poetess who ever lived. So it's an act of homage, I think.

JR: You have received so many awards, Joyce Carol Oates, and yet you said it's a minor part of your life.

JCO: Certainly awards are not a major part of one's life. Why did anybody think they are?

JR: The public puts you on a pedestal.

JCO: No, the public thinks what the media says. The media has very limited views of people. The most wonderful, important thing about a certain person is that he is a great father, but he is also a famous person; it's the same they emphasize. I know people in the entertainment world who are very famous. Some of them are remarkable people, but not because of the fame; it's because of their character and the good that they have done for others. The media is very distorting.

The media is also very cruel. The media puts somebody on a pedestal and then brings that person down. It is just part of a theatrical exploitation of human beings. I wrote a novel called *Blonde* which is about Marilyn Monroe. That is the quintessential story of a person exploited by the media.

JR: Should young people be more exposed to poetry in today's educational system?

JCO: Yes, certainly to poetry and prose. Young people should be more exposed to all the arts, including music. Many public schools have dropped their music programs and maybe their art programs. I think that writing is very central to the curriculum, and that will not be dropped. But music is also very important and that is being dropped all across the United States. That's very sad.

JR: With all your work, where do you find time to enjoy your casual life?

JCO: I do have a personal life, as most of us do. Anyone you interview here has a personal life that he or she may not make public. All you really know is the public life.

JR: When you think of people who want to be writers, what is the advice you would give them?

JCO: I don't know what you mean by wanting to be a writer. If you have a story to tell or a memoir to offer or something to tell, you should tell it. To be a writer is like saying you want to be an opera singer. It is very grandiose and somewhat pretentious. How about beginning with just one little project? One thing at a time? Should you say, "I want to be a great artist" or should you say, "I want to paint one painting?" Do one thing at a time.

JR: How would you describe it to somebody who has never been here before?

JCO: Chautauqua is an institution and a tradition that believes in educating and stimulating the mind in terms of family, not just adults who might go to adult education school but children as well – all generations. It's unique that way.

JR: Joyce Carol Oates, we thank you so much.

Chapter 8

The Real Woman behind James Bond's "M"

Coming of age in a neighborhood cemented together by trust and respect should be natural. It is not. A half century after Marshall McLuhan predicted the Global Village it is still not a cohesive, coherent place. The globe is not yet a neighborhood like Jim Roselle's Franklin Street. Good will and ill will cross borders in mixed measure; eternal vigilance remains the price of freedom. That's why there are spies. What they do is as necessary as it is alien to the average citizen, even among neighbor nations and allies.

One of the objects of terrorism: that we live in fear and under a police state.
Stella Rimington

The role of women has always been undervalued in the spy world, always undermined in terms of recognition. Unfairly so. It's a world that needs women.
Helen Mirren

Stella Rimington: Britain's Top Spy

MI5 - Defending the Realm

MI5 dates back to the First World War when the department was the fifth branch of the Directorate of Military Intelligence of the British War Office. MI1 though MI4 were eventually withdrawn or taken up into other government branches. MI5 joined with Scotland Yard's Special Section in 1931 and was renamed the Security Service which now employs about 3,800 staff operatives responsible for domestic intelligence. MI6 has continued as Britain's Secret Intelligence Service.

Dame Stella Rimington, DCB (Dame Commander - Most Honourable Order of the Bath), at one time Britain's top spy, worked in all three of the British Security Service branches: counter terrorism, counter espionage and counter subversion between 1969 and 1991. She rose to the rank of Director General of MI5, serving in that capacity from 1992 to 1996. Rimington was the first female Director General of MI5, and the first DG whose name was declassified on appointment. In retirement she became an acclaimed novelist writing spy thrillers drawing widely on her deep knowledge of domestic and international espionage.

Rimington's memoir *Open Secret* [Arrow Books, 2002] was followed in 2004 by her first novel, *At Risk* [Vintage Crime/Black Lizard]. She has since published six more highly popular "insider" spy novels.

During Jim's interview with Stella Rimington he was reminded that the best laid plans, no matter how well begun or how carefully staged, can run headlong into a brand new crisis at any time. Jim's urgent change of plans one day didn't threaten to derail national security like Dame Stella's did, but a choice between urgent alternatives is the kind of thing both Jim and his listeners could relate to.

Jim Remembers… A Trip Instead of a Journey

I tripped, fell down the cellar stairs and banged my head on the concrete floor, one afternoon. I just got up, though, and went about my business.

    I drove my car over to the AAA office to make reservations for a trip Kathy and I were planning. We were going to Denver to visit my daughter. It was just something I had on my mind to do. Although I had bled a little from my scalp, I thought it was only a little thing. It had already stopped, I thought. When I sat down to talk to the AAA manager, my friend Roger, he looked at me kind of strangely.
    "Do you know that you are bleeding?" He asked. "It's coming from your nose."
    "Well, I just fell."
    "Holy mackerel," he said, handing me a tissue. "Come on, I'll take you to the hospital." That surprised me. I felt fine. The little headache, I was sure, would go away soon too.
    "Well, thanks Roger. It's okay. Really," I said. "Maybe I'll have my wife take me." I realized Kathy was still at work so I just drove home and called her.
    "Hi Kathy, Roger just told me I have a nosebleed. He thinks I should go to the hospital, but I don't really know if I should."
    "I'm coming right home, and you're going!" Kathy had decided. I didn't have a choice.
    The doctors in the emergency department checked me over, and as I suspected, at first they didn't seem alarmed. Then Kathy spoke up.
    "I'm not a nurse or anything," Kathy told them, "but I watch the ER program on TV a lot, and I think you ought to look into his ears."
    They were probably about to do that anyway. An intern started to take a look. A moment later they bundled me right up and whisked me away to Buffalo General Hospital where they had the specialized facilities they decided I really needed.
    After five days of neurological tests, x-rays and constant observation I was finally allowed to go home, but not until my doctor told me that the worst bleeding had been inside my skull. Considering the area I had impacted, it had nearly cost me my power of speech, had they not intervened when they did.
    I took a little time off after that. I had broken my clavicle, too, and I had to wait for that to heal. My commitment to work, however, and the kind of plans other people are counting on, has always been such that even my friends and family just roll their eyes and say, "That's just Jim. He'll most likely not change his plans over any 'less important' things."

    It's the same sort of determination that, years later, Jim heard from Stella Rimington the day an emergency made her decide between being a spy and being a mother. Either decision could have left a long-lasting scar on either her nation or her personal history.
    Remembering back to his own incident, Jim now admits there had been at least a bit of lasting damage. "Oh, yeah," he confesses, "There was some damage: a little crack where I hit the cellar floor. But I spackled it. It's okay now."
    Jim's sense of humor sometimes surfaces in his interviews, too. He began this conversation with Stella Rimington by playing the 007 *James Bond* theme music.

A Conversation with Stella Rimington

Jim Roselle: Did you mind that I played that as the opening to our interview?
Stella Rimington: I'm quite used to it, I must say.

JR: The James Bond theme for Stella Rimington, Director General for four years, 1992 to 1996, of the British Security Service, also known as MI5. But you don't want to be referred to as the female James Bond, do you?

SR: No, I don't, I've fought all my life to make people know that British intelligence is not about James Bond. It's about people carefully assessing and analyzing information and taking appropriate action, not going around the world with guns killing people.

JR: Let me be the first to welcome you to Chautauqua and to America. By the way, have you been here before this visit?

SR: I never have been to Chautauqua before. I've been to America many times, but this is absolutely fantastic.

JR: You found something you didn't expect to find?

SR: I didn't know what I was going to find, apart from a good look at the website, but I don't think anybody could imagine a place as wonderful as this.

JR: What is the difference between MI5 and MI6, Britain's two intelligence services?

SR: MI5 is responsible for our domestic security, in other words, its job is to defend us against serious domestic threats to the home base. MI6 is a bit more like the CIA. Though there are some huge differences. It goes out around the world and gathers foreign intelligence. It is then fed into MI5, assessed and appropriate action is taken. We have a third intelligence service called GCHQ, which matches the American NSA, so it's our technical intelligence service as well. Those three form British Intelligence.

JR: When you were Director General back in the early 90s was there any great concern about terrorism yet?

SR: Yes, we had the IRA for many, many years. That had been our main terrorist target because they had been blowing up the streets of London and killing British soldiers. During my career I spent a lot of my time fighting against the IRA. By the time I became Director General, we were already beginning to see the first twitchings of what we're now calling Middle Eastern terrorism. It was already obvious, coming out particularly in places like Algeria, that there were extremists intent on attacking what we refer to as the West. We had a lot of experience with certain countries who used terrorism in those days as an arm of their foreign policy. They were killing their dissidents on the streets of London, and we were trying to stop them.

JR: But it's more severe today.

SR: I think it is very different today. When we were working against the IRA we knew a lot about that organization. It had a headquarters, we knew who the people were, we knew broadly where they were, and we knew exactly the kind of thing they would do, because they were not suicide bombers.

Now I think we are facing a much more diffuse and difficult terrorist threat because I don't think anybody is entirely clear on what they actually want. And we've got groups of young men in Britain who were born and educated here, are British citizens, but have been turned against the country and are prepared to carry out the most appalling atrocities with no thought about who their targets are. That is all very difficult to combat and to foresee.

JR: Tell us about the "Umbrella Incident".

SR: Georgi Markov, a Bulgarian dissident, was stabbed with a poisoned pellet out of an umbrella while walking across a bridge in London.

I remember it particularly well because I was the duty officer for MI5 that evening. In those days life was so relaxed in the duty office you could spend the weekend at home, provided you were near a phone. We'd just been having my daughter's fourth birthday party and were all relaxed with a glass of wine when the phone rang. It was the police to say they got a man in the hospital who claimed he'd been stabbed by an umbrella.

"No, no, that's ridiculous," I said. "These things don't happen." But it had. It was a Bulgarian intelligence service plot to kill this man because he'd been very critical of the Bulgarian president.

JR: Can we defeat terrorism by the military alone?

SR: No. The phrase "The war on terrorism" implies you can defeat them by military means, but you can't. You need a combination of tactics. One is prior intelligence to prevent their attacks. In Britain that's police action; we regard terrorism as a crime to be tried in the courts. International liaison is another thing, including military action where you need it. You also need political cooperation to ultimately defeat terrorism.

JR: How do you stop the recruitment of the jihadists?

SR: Only do that by attacking the reasons why a young man who lived in Birmingham in the UK, for example, will decide to go and kill people in the street.

I think in the UK we've failed to integrate our minority communities to the extent that you probably have here in the US. And people are allowed into the country whose sole aim is radicalizing young people. They exploit the situation in Israel, Palestine and Afghanistan, for example, and accuse our intelligence services of torture. All these things feed young people who are looking for a cross, looking to be martyred. All those things have got to be tackled.

JR: You invented a character named Liz Carlyle for your novels. When did you decide to write spy novels?

SR: First, I wrote my autobiography which caused a bit of a sensation. Then, having done that, I thought I'd have a go at my first spy novel which was published in 2004, several years after I left the service.

I invented Liz Carlyle to be the antithesis to James Bond because she's a thinking woman, sort of spiky and feisty. She thinks and analyzes the issues that she's facing. And this is, I think, very true to life. Liz Carlyle is a member of the team and that makes it very much the way MI5 works. It's not one man like James Bond going off to solve the problems of the world.

JR: Looking back on the British Intelligence Service, it was commonly known as a boy's club network, but you're the first woman to rise to that particular position of power.

SR: When I got there, it was a boys club all right. Women were only allowed to have what was effectively only a second class career. I was recruited as a clerk typist in India, even though I had a degree and a postgraduate diploma. When I got back to London, I discovered they were running two career structures, the men were the intelligence gatherers and the women were the helpers.

Our job was to sit at our desks and do the papers even if we were quite bright. They would let us do some intelligence analysis, but never out on the streets doing the intelligence work. That gradually changed. I joined just as the 60s turned into the 70s.

Along came the 70s with Women's Lib and sex discrimination legislation. Gradually they had to realize they had all these bright women around and they were keeping them under. Gradually we were allowed to try our hand at the intelligence work. Some of us turned out to be quite good at it. We've brought that absolutely essential thing, which was the diversity of approach. Then, you know, the world changed.

JR: How did you meet your husband?

SR: I met my husband on the school bus, actually. We were both at school at Nottingham. He was at the boys' school, Nottingham High School, and I was at the girls' school, Nottingham Girls' High School. Then we lost touch when he went to Cambridge and I went to Edinburgh University. Quite by chance we met up again and got married. I was working as a historical archivist, my first profession, and he was in the British civil service.

After we'd been married a couple of years, he got posted to the British High Commission in New Delhi as a First Secretary dealing with aid to India. He said to me, "Come on, let's go." So I said "Great!"

and gave up my job. In those days women were programmed only to work until they got married or until they had children. I thought I would never work again and went off to India to be a diplomat's wife.

But that's where I got tapped on the shoulder, which was the traditional way of recruiting people to British Intelligence because it was all so secret. You had to wait for somebody to sort of sidle up to you and say something.

JR: How have your children affected your work?

SR: I've got two daughters whom I had while I was working in MI5. With my first daughter I took three months off - all you were allowed in those days. With my second daughter, my husband was again on a foreign posting. We were in Belgium, so I had her there. One was expected to come back really quickly and to work 24 hours a day seven days a week if that's what the job required.

One of my daughters was a baby and I was meeting a man from one of the East European embassies who was thinking of defecting. I had arranged the meeting. We were going to meet at a safe house. It was all very covert.

The telephone on my desk rang, and it was the nanny calling to say that my younger daughter, Harriet, had gone into convulsions. She called an ambulance, and asked me to meet them in the hospital.

Who was I going to let down? Here's this man waiting for me, and here's my daughter who may be deathly ill. So I rushed off to the safe house, explained to this man what had happened, actually borrowed money from him for a taxi and got to the hospital in time.

Fortunately my daughter wasn't seriously ill; she simply had a high temperature, so that worked out all right. But, you know, those were episodes of the kind that occur when you're trying to be a mother and a full-time intelligence worker.

JR: Who are your heroes?

SR: The main one is Winston Churchill. I was actually born five years before World War II broke out. We spent quite a lot of our time in areas that were the subject of bombing raids. My brother, who is three years older than I am, spent a lot of our time in air raid shelters with me listening to the bombs dropping. So the guy who won the war for us, Winston Churchill, is a great hero of mine.

People who lived in the South of England could look up to the lovely blue sky and see our boys - some were only 18 - in these tiny little Spitfires, face to face with the Germans. They were fighting the Battle of Britain to stop Hitler's Nazi Germany invading our homeland. Winston Churchill epitomized the way this small island was fighting for all of us.

JR: Well, Stella Rimington, we thank you so much for giving us this wonderful opportunity and the pleasure of your company.

SR: Thank you. It's been great.

Chapter 9

WJTN around the World and My Kind of Town

Contrast creates clarity. T. S. Eliot once said, "We shall not cease from exploration, and the end of all our exploring will be to arrive where we started and know the place for the first time." Jim Roselle's community enthusiastically supported the broadcasts he originated across the nation and around the world for many years. Exposure to the wider world enriched his listeners' appreciation of their own hometown.

We hope…to have programming…where we have Christian, Jew and Muslim come together and have a better sense of understanding for each other's point of view, talking about issues of life and death and human relations…not theology and politics.

Dr. Daniel Bratton
Past President (1984-2000)
Chautauqua Institution

My Kind of Town

When I think about how our city responded to sponsorship opportunities, like the trips around the United States and around the world, I'm simply left with that song title again: *My Kind of Town*.

I think most businesses probably think of advertising as a way to get their name out in the public and boost their sales. That's the way it is supposed to work, and a radio station is a great way to do it. I think, though, based on years of experience and really getting to know the people who advertised on my show, there's at least one more reason: they really want to support the community they are a part of. I guess you could say, "Customers are neighbors too."

Our town's merchants sponsored – and listeners supported – broadcasts from Disney World, the Rose Bowl in Pasadena, London, the Soviet Union and many more remote locations over many years. As a matter of fact, many of those trips and broadcasts came about because listeners initiated them; a lot were planned and carried out by them, not at the station's suggestion. The town also supported wonderful local events like the popular Italian-American Charity Golf Tournaments.

We started the broadcast with just five minutes of golf scores per half hour. I did the first ones. Now they are complete shows, and I still do them. Sam Restivo, another one of our Franklin Street neighborhood kids founded the tournament along with Sam Paladino and Gino Micciche. The Italian-American has a wonderful Brotherhood theme that tells you just what kind of town this is. Every Italian player must invite a non-Italian partner to play with him or her. The IA, as most people just call it now, has benefited our local health care system, WCA Hospital, to the tune of nearly $1.2 million. It started small, but by now in its 44th year, the tournament typically raises $50,000 every year.

That's my kind of town!

Jim Remembers… The Soviet Union

I went to the Soviet Union with Chautauqua Institution for 13 days in October of 1988.

Chautauquans went there to discuss various issues from our standpoint with counterparts in the Soviet Union. We brought women from Chautauqua to meet with Soviet women about women's issues in their country. We also brought men from the State Department to meet with men from their State Department. They discussed nuclear weapons and other matters of importance between the United States and the Soviet Union.

The conference was held in Tbilisi, Georgia. We also spent a couple of days in Leningrad and in Moscow. I had a roommate from the State Department, Tom Robertson. Each day, he went to a conference and came back in the evening. I made a phone call to access the international phone lines and put him on the radio so he could describe to Sheila McCarthy at WJTN and her listeners what the conference had been about for that day. I also remember one day that he borrowed a tie from me. He wanted to wear a different tie because, apparently, he hadn't brought enough. I sent him a new tie for Christmas to thank him for his company.

At another time, the Soviets sent a delegation here to Chautauqua Institution for the same purpose. They came during the Institution's summer season when Dr. Daniel Bratton was president.

A Conversation with Dr. Daniel Bratton

Dr. Daniel Bratton in the USSR

Jim Roselle: Welcome back to Bestor Plaza for this special moment on our broadcast. I am privileged to have Dr. Daniel Bratton, the President of Chautauqua Institution, on with us. Welcome, Dr. Bratton. Please let me put the other half of the family into the picture here, too. How has Wanita [Dr. Bratton's wife] enjoyed the experience here?

Dr. Daniel Bratton: Oh, she has enjoyed it enormously. She's really a miracle worker. She really is because not everybody knows that she has her own career. She goes off to work every morning as a psychotherapist in Jamestown. We entertain a lot. I bet over 1000 people every season come through that house... Many times she rolls in the driveway from work and the occasion has already started. People are bustling all over the place, and she manages all that. She enjoys it enormously, but she's ready for retirement too.

JR: That brings up a question: of all the personalities here, of well-known figures that you have entertained, any funny or fascinating anecdotal material there anywhere?

DB: Not really...
JR: Any accidents that occurred? Spilling a drink on their lap or anything like that?
DB: No, I really can't think of anything (laughing), I'd have to go back and really cull my memory, Jim, to find something like that. It really has been great. We had dinner at our house on Monday with Steve and Cokie Roberts. They're just a delightful couple. Most of the really top notch people that have come here are like that. There have been very few occasions where somebody who is a big name comes in and turns out to be a dud as far as their personality is concerned (laughing). We have been so lucky in that regard.
JR: Then there was the Russian conference... And I have to, of course, thank you because I came along for the Russian trip to Leningrad and Tbilisi, Georgia which is one of the great experiences of my life. Did that put Chautauqua on a world level, may I ask?
DB: I think so. And it proved to this institution what it was capable of doing programmatically because that was an opportunity that just fell into our lap. We had to take advantage of it. We had no

operational staff with which to pull off the first two experiences. By the time we had the 1987 program here, I had hired somebody to help with it. It just proved what we are capable of doing. Yes, I think it got us international acclaim we had not had before.

JR: You talked to me previously about your hopes for the religious world to get together. You were working on programs in the future. Where is that at this point?

DB: That is called our Abrahamic Initiative. We are seeking the funds right now to make a long-range commitment to that. Ross Mackenzie, who retired as director of the Department of Religion, is directing that initiative. We hope over several years

Wanita Bratton conferring with Soviet counterpart concerning women's issues in the USSR

to have programming both here and off the grounds in the off-season where we have Christian, Jew and Muslim come together and have a better sense of understanding for each other's point of view talking not about theological issues but issues of life and death and human relations and civil liberties and women's rights and all those kinds of things. We hope, down the road, and I can't even say when it might happen, there would be a Soviet type experience held in Cairo or in Jerusalem or at some point where Christians, Jews and Muslims lived together on a regular basis.

[According to the Chautauqua Institution's website, www.ciweb.org, Tom Becker became the 17th president of Chautauqua Institution in November of 2003 following Dr. Bratton's retirement. Becker carried out programmatic initiatives instituted during Tom's tenure...including the five-year people-to-people exchange with the Soviet Union and the decade-long Abrahamic Initiative that promoting dialog among Christian, Muslims and Jews on critical topics.]

JR: We look forward to that if it does occur.

DB: You'll go if that does happen.

JR: Another question that brings up, Dr. Bratton, is whether those who come here are aware of what is in place here?

DB: Most of them are aware of Chautauqua as an idea; they are aware of the Chautauqua Movement that occurred, the Chautauqua Circuit, they know there is an Institution in Western New York State, but they have no idea what it's like.

JR: What do they say to you after their appearance?

DB: Most of what I hear – I'm talking here mostly about the morning lecturers – tell how invigorated they were by the audience, that they really feel a chemistry, a sense of energy coming from the audience, and the questions are just so invigorating. Steve Roberts said that when he left the stage Monday night, he has never spoken to an audience like this one. Most of them are just totaled out by the appearance of the place and the magnitude. Georgie Anne Geyer said, "I have never enjoyed a lecture more than the one I had here." She's going to come back on her own.

JR: Do most of them say to you, "Dr. Bratton I'd like an invitation again sometime?"

DB: I wouldn't say most of them, but a high number of them say that. For the average lecturer who hasn't been here before, they don't know what to expect. They arrive the evening before and they leave the afternoon after their lecture, so they get just a little taste of this place. That's very frustrating for some of them. That's why they say they really want to come back here.

JR: What are some of the moments you remember on stage? You've introduced so many speakers in 16 years, including some who made you sit there and really listen.

DB: The greatest moment on the Chautauqua lecture platform in my 16 years here was David McCullough's lecture on Chautauqua. It was a masterpiece of a lecture and it was so beautifully stated about this place. Doris Kearns Goodwin was great, too. Roger Rosenblatt and she have become good friends. That's one of the things I am so grateful for.

JR: Is the opportunity easier for you to get well known speakers now because of the previous history of this place?

DB: A lot of people want to come here. Jane Goodall's appearance here was by her initiative, not ours.

JR: She made the offer?

DB: Her office made the offer. Her office called and said, "We've heard from some of her key supporters about Chautauqua and all that it does. Ms. Goodall wants to come." That's a perfect example of your point.

JR: You said on stage that the audience was the biggest morning lecture audience in your 16 years.

DB: In my 16 years! And I haven't had the time to look back beyond that. I'm sure it's one of the biggest in history. That was 5,200 people we had there that morning. The only other time since I've been here that we had 5,000 people was one of Justice O'Connor's lectures.

JR: Thank you, Dr. Daniel Bratton.

Jim Remembers…The Other Jimmy Roselli and Broadcasting from Disney World

I once did the show from Disney World in Lake Buena Vista, Florida, near Orlando. The park doesn't open until 9 o'clock, so before that, they set me up at an outdoor studio where people entered the park. A banner on the front of my broadcast table said "Jim Roselle - WJTN". People were coming up to me and asking, "Are you going to sing for us?"

"I'm not *that* Jimmy Roselli," I said. "I hope you're not disappointed." Jimmy Roselli had been a popular vocalist, a crooner and a contemporary of Frank Sinatra and Dean Martin. He had recorded a lot of top hit albums and was wildly popular, too, though for some reason he's less well remembered today.

I wanted to call Jimmy Roselli and interview him. I thought: "Jim Roselle interviews Jimmy Roselli" would've made a great program. But it never happened.

I was at Disney World for one week with my engineer in 1990. We did my regular morning show from six in the morning until noon. Disney had a feature called *Morning Men*. Broadcasters could send in an application to do a remote show, direct from the park. That gave Disney a lot of publicity.

Our morning show in Jamestown, I think, got consideration – even though we were competing against some of the big national stations – because Michael Eisner was president of the Walt Disney Company at the time and his wife, Jane Breckenridge, was a Jamestown girl. It's just possible that connection helped us get our Morning Man spot at Disney World.

There were always two stations there at a time. When I was there, two guys, co-hosts, from Baltimore were doing their morning show, too. I was on microphone alone, though, because that's how I did my show.

After we got off the air at noon every day we had all of Disney World to explore and enjoy for ourselves. I had brought my daughter, Mary Jane and her husband, from Denver because Kathy couldn't come that year. Mary Jane was about 26 at the time and her son, Michael, was about two or three. Our sponsors at WJTN, once again, paid for the entire trip.

The next year, 1991, they gave me a return visit so I brought Kathy and her 6-year-old grandson, Ryan, for that trip. We also brought our granddaughter Michelle that year.

I had great guests on my Disney World shows. I had Mickey Mouse, people from the Main Street parade, and just regular folks visiting Disney World walking past our wonderful outdoor studio. The manager of one of the Disney restaurants came from a family who lived at Chautauqua Institution so, naturally, we had him on too.

Disney also had a contest for people who could write in and request the privilege of marching in the Main Street parade down the middle of the Magic Kingdom. A family from Jamestown had won it and came down, too.

Jim Remembers... London

Professor Bob Scharmann taught theater in the Jamestown Community College Drama Department. He asked me to join him and his students on a theater tour in London and do live broadcasts from there, as I had previously done from Disney World. We went to London for seven days during the students' Christmas vacation.

Once again, I learned that's what this town is about. WJTN got sponsors to pay for the overseas phone calls and all the trip expenses. The schedule had been planned by Bob long before our arrival in London. He had arranged for theater in the evenings, to go to plays he wanted students to see. We saw a musical version of *Gone with the Wind* with horses on stage and Atlanta burning in the background. The technology was amazing. The thing that shocked me, though – I had seen the movie with Clark Gable – was the fellow who played Rhett Butler. He had the most nasal voice you could imagine. Here I am, waiting for Clark Gable's voice to come out and the actor practically squeaked. That's not Rhett Butler!

The *British Broadcasting Corporation* (*BBC*) had not been included in the agenda. I did that on my own. While the group followed their schedule and visited the Tower of London, I called the *BBC*.

"Hello. I'm from America. I'm here with a college group, and I'm in radio in Jamestown, New York. I would love the opportunity to visit the *BBC*. I have carried many of your reports."

"Where are you staying?" A pleasant voice asked.

"The Tavistock Hotel."

"Let me switch you to another department." My call rang through to another line.

"Hello. What is it you would like?" Another pleasant voice asked.

"Hello. I'm from America, visiting London with a group of college students and I'm in radio in Jamestown, New York. I'm calling to request an opportunity to visit the *BBC*, since I have carried many of your reports on my radio station, WJTN."

"Just a moment, please. I must switch you to another department." The third time someone took my call it was a gentleman.

"Hello. My name is Jim Roselle. I'm a radio broadcaster at WJTN in Jamestown, New York. I am here in London with a group of college students. My curiosity is such that I would like an opportunity to visit the *BBC*. We do carry many of your reports."

"Where are you staying?" It must've been an important question, but didn't seem terribly responsive to my request.

"The Tavistock Hotel."

"Let me call you back. What is your room number?" I told him.

"Thank you." He hung up. All I could do now was sit in my room and wait.

In the hallway outside my door, I heard the group gathering for their trip to the Tower of London. They hadn't left yet, but I knew they would soon. I waited a little longer, weighing my options. But the phone remained silent. Coat in hand, I reached for the doorknob. That's when the phone finally rang.

"Mr. Roselle?" The caller pronounced my name the French way, as if it rhymed with mademoiselle and gazelle. "Can you be here tomorrow morning at 11 o'clock?"

"Yes."

"We'd be delighted to see you. We have another gentleman from America who will be here. He is in radio, too, in Wilkes-Barre, Pennsylvania. We have a tour planned for you."

They gave us a marvelous excursion through their complex. For lunch, they took us to the Commissary, which was actually quite a big restaurant inside the *BBC* building. While we ate, our tour guide pointed out actors and directors – even a few who had won Emmys – sitting at nearby tables. Then I was given an opportunity to sit with the manager of the *BBC*. I recorded the interview. I mentioned a few names of American sports celebrities, but with the exception of Casius Clay – Mohammed Ali – he said he didn't know who any of them were. But he did know the most popular American TV westerns. He especially liked *Bonanza*. Westerns were a big hit everywhere.

Then we went to *Radio 4*, the *BBC*'s news channel, and we sat in on a news broadcast. I saw something I had never seen in a radio studio. A gentleman was there whose only job seemed to be his stopwatch. He timed every item. Any political comment or political guest would mandate an opportunity for exactly equal air time for the opposing party or person. They didn't have to use it, but it had to be offered.

Then it was time for a live report from a correspondent in the field. The news man announced the cutaway and heard…Silence! Dead air and static. That was all. "Due to technical difficulties…"

They were very nice and accommodated us in every way they could. It was really quite a privilege.

Chapter 10

Tarzan's Real Jane and Lucy's Dad

Jim Roselle has often found that the most unusual people have the most interesting stories to tell, and even more important, a way of seeing things that will broaden everybody's outlook when they simply stop, look and listen.

What makes us human, I think, is an ability to ask questions, a consequence of our sophisticated spoken language…[but] I think we're still in a muddle with our language, because once you get words and a spoken language it gets harder to communicate.

Jane Goodall

You cannot get through a single day without having an impact on the world around you. What you do makes a difference, and you have to decide what kind of difference you want to make.

Jane Goodall

I wanted to explore problems where we didn't have answers. In fact, where we didn't even know the right questions to ask.

Donald Johansson

Jane Goodall
The Dame Sounds Off

Dame Jane Morris, DBE [Dame Commander, Most Excellent Order of the British Empire], best known simply as Jane Goodall, is the founder and director of research at the *Jane Goodall Institute of Wildlife Education and Conservation*, headquartered in Vienna, Virginia. Her life's work is focused on her 45-year study of family and social interactions among wild chimpanzees in the Gombe Stream National Park in the United Republic of Tanzania in East Africa.

Jane Goodall teaches Jim a word or two in "Chimp"

Jane's passion, her mission to save the planet's most noble and human-like creatures from extinction, primarily chimpanzees and the other apes – along with other wildlife – made her one of the few guest speakers at Chautauqua Institution who requested her own invitation to speak. She came to this citadel of intellectual and humanitarian thinking to present her cause to an audience who knew how to change the world.

Her request, of course, was enthusiastically honored. Jane, in turn, accepted Jim Roselle's invitation to share some of her experiences with his WJTN audience.

A Conversation with Jane Goodall

Jim Roselle: Jane Goodall, welcome to the WJTN microphone here at Chautauqua Institution. I see you've been with our audience autographing a lot of your books. Is your right hand in good shape?
Jane Goodall: My right hand is in pretty good shape except where a chimp bit the end of my thumb off.

JR: Can you give us a chimp hoot?
JG: Sure! [Jane gives out a loud, lively and entirely believable rendition of chimp hoots and screeches to appreciative applause and laughter from Jim and the audience.]
That means, "Hello! Hi everybody." (More laughter)
JR: You know, Jane Goodall, I agonized over whether or not I was going to ask that question this morning. But I finally got enough courage to do it. I thank you very much.
Let me go back now to a day of discovery - I think that's what you call it - the day you were in hiding and watching the chimpanzees. And you watched one that you eventually called David Graybeard. You watched that chimpanzee using a tool. Would you describe that day for us?
JG: It was a time that I was very concerned that the chimps kept running away and, although I knew, given time, that I could learn all about them, the money was running out. I knew I couldn't get more money until I began to see some exciting things.
This was the breakthrough day when I saw this dark shape squatting on one of these sort of orange colored termite mounds and I could see his hand with a piece of grass. I could see him picking pieces of grass and pushing them down into a termite hole and then putting them in his mouth. I couldn't exactly see what he was doing.
Subsequently, I was able to see that the termites were biting on the grass and he was picking them off with his lips. I also saw him picking a leafy twig and stripping the leaves off for the same purpose, which is the beginning of tool-making.
The reason this was the breakthrough is because at that time we thought that only humans made tools. Dr. Leaky said, "Now we must redefine man, redefine tool or accept chimpanzees as humans." On that one observation we got money from *National Geographic* to carry on.
JR: That was in day-to-day discovery. How did you spend your days after that? When did you get up, where did you hide yourself and how many chimps did you observe? How did you take notes and what was the day like when you finished? Can you reflect on that for us?
JG: Well, all the days were different. They all involved getting up at 5:30, getting up into the mountains before it was light. If I knew there was a fruiting tree, then I would sit where I could see that fruiting tree with my binoculars. Otherwise, I went to this beautiful peak and, again with my binoculars, just waited and waited to see if I could see some chimps.
I would see them moving about below me. Gradually I would see that they were getting used to me. Some days it was a lot of walking, crossing two or three valleys because you heard the chimps calling far beyond. No day ended until it was nearly dark and only then would we go down from the mountains, back into my little camp, my tent - this was after my mother left and I was on my own - and cooked a very simple meal because there wasn't any money to waste on food. Then I filled everything into my journal every day.
JR: The cook is important in your life isn't he? I saw a picture of the cook standing over your bed and you were in the throes of a serious illness, malaria, at the time. He was watching over you and you were having delirious moments. Was that about a 10 day period?
JG: Yes. My mother was there as well and she was even sicker than me. We didn't have any medication. We were told, for some reason, there was no malaria. I don't know why the doctor told us that. She nearly died. The cook was very worried. He kept wanting to take us into Kigoma [capital of the

Kigoma Region in Tanzania on the eastern shore of Lake Tanganyika] but we were too sick so we just said, "No, we'll stay here."

JR: And your mother lived to be 94. Recently you said, "I keep up the email, I watch videos, but I have to leave the place I love in order to save it."

JG: I am now spending about 300 days a year traveling to spread awareness, to share the knowledge I've been so privileged to acquire out in the forest. I also raise money for the *Jane Goodall Institute* so we can keep these programs going. We are caring for orphaned chimps whose mothers have been shot, working with the local people so that we can improve their lives. Then they in turn can help us save the chimps and also develop a program for young people called Roots & Shoots around the world.

JR: Can we get into your private life a little bit, and your romance? Your first marriage was to a photographer from the *National Geographic*.

JG: Yes, Hugo was sent by the *National Geographic* to make a film. It all seemed wonderful. It was very romantic. He was a Dutch Baron, he was good-looking and it was a good marriage for a while. We had a son. But sadly, it ended. My ex-husband is now living in the compound which I share with my son in Dar es Salaam, Tanzania, so we're all pretty much together again. In Arabic, Dar es Salaam means "abode of peace". It's quite ironic.

JR: Where do you make your home today?

JG: Airplanes mostly, it seems. But I have two homes. One is in England where I grew up and one in Dar es Salaam, the house of my second husband who died. That's where I have my son and my grandchildren and now my ex-husband.

JR: How can people follow your work?

JG: We have a website, http://www.janegoodall.org/, where people can find stories and videos of our work, learn of our research and future plans and even sign up and become members.

JR: Thank you for sharing your time with me, and I also say thank you to that chimp that said, "Hi!" a few minutes ago.

JG: You're most welcome.

Donald Johansson
I Love the Oldest Lady in the World

Donald Johansson is an American paleoanthropologist who, while working in the Afar Triangle region of Hadar, Ethiopia, on November 24, 1974, discovered the fossil of a 3 million year old female. She was far too old for the *Cold Case Files*, but Johansson's detective work revealed that she was definitely a human-like being, now known to scientists as a *hominid australopithecine*. The world has come to know her as "Lucy."

In his ongoing quest to understand the deepest origins of modern humans, a saga in which Johansson sees Lucy as an important ancestor, he also established the *Institute of Human Origins* in 1981.

As different as the lifestyles and life's work are, comparing Johansson to Roselle - a paleoanthropologist to a radio broadcaster - few of Jim's radio guests over the years have ever so closely paralleled Jim's life story in its essential events and wisdoms as Donald Johansson.

The parallel themes of their lives include recognizing and acting on the good fortune of being in the right place at the right time. Also, both men credit the heroic dedication of their families and a special kind of community that helped them become who they were. The ancient African landscape and the modern American cityscape, it appears, both held the power to create a singular kind of humanity.

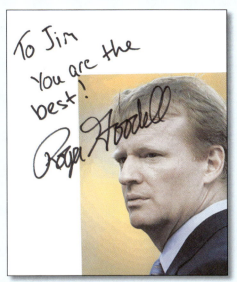
NFL Commissioner Roger Goodell

Political humorist Mark Russell

On the air with Arkansas Governor Bill Clinton

First Lady and U.S. Secretary of State, Hillary Clinton

Joseph Roselle 1875-1945

Josephine Roselle 1888-1971

Phil Roselle, Jim's brother

Jim's brother Ross Roselle and his wife Nancy

Jim's brother Joe Roselle and his wife Lois (deceased)

Jim with his sisters (left): Anna Roselle Paterniti, Grace Roselle Morrison, Sara Roselle Messina

Jim and Kathy Roselle

Jim's son Jim Roselle and his daughter Ariel

Jim's stepson Thomas Nalbone and wife Iva

Jim's stepson Philip Nalbone

Grandson Julian Nalbone-Decker

(front left & right): granddaughters Catherine Piccone & Michele Altepeter;

(second row): grandson Michael Piccone; daughter Mary Jane Piccone; daughter Julie D'Angelo; great grandson Mason Altepeter; Michael Altepeter, Michele's husband

Jim's grandson Ryan Eggleston

Jim with stepdaughter, Annette Lundsten with (left): grandsons Matthew Lundsten & Andrew Eggleston

Jim's grandson, Ricci John D'Angelo and wife Wendy with great granddaughter Olivia

(left) Kathy Roselle, Irna Morgan, Jim and "Tom as in Morgan"

An early remote broadcast from WJTN's mobil studio at the Goodyear shop on 3rd Street in downtown Jamestown

Jim with grandson Michael Piccone and Wyoming Congressman Alan Simpson

President of Chautauqua Institution, Tom Becker on the air with Jim

Jim Roselle Grand Marshall, Jamestown Holiday Parade

Jim with Lee Ann Meriwether, 1955 Miss America

Raising money for charity, Jim and Frewsburg Postmaster Dempsey Knight

On the air up in the air...Sky Jam 1987

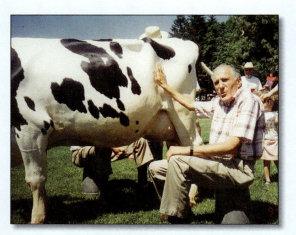

Sherman Days, Jim meets another fan!

St. Lawrence Sigma Pi brothers (left): Mike Tornatore, Nick Commisso,
Fulton Sandler, Bill McKever, Bill Lehren

When Donald Johansson spoke about the love of his life, a 3.2 million year old female of a slightly sub-human species, Jim was reminded of another conversation about longevity and a famous old man. He was sharing a Cup of Happiness one Chautauqua morning with one of the 20th Century's most famous scientists.

Jim Remembers… Don't Live too Long

Freeman Dyson, the great physicist, was a guest with whom I felt I was simply not in the same league. He is a *Fellow of the Royal Society*, a highly awarded theoretical physicist and mathematician, also known for his work in astronomy and nuclear engineering. None of those subjects are part of the broadcasting curriculum at St. Lawrence University.

Jim and physicist, Freeman Dyson take a moment to enjoy the ironies of a long life

The first time we met for an interview I tiptoed through the tulips trying to be as conversant as I could with topics in modern science. A couple of listeners I talked to later thanked me, though, for not getting too scientific. Naturally, I couldn't have done that anyway but I did have a good time with him. I wouldn't call it an ideal interview, but he seemed pleased enough with the conversation. He even came back for a second interview on another visit to Chautauqua Institution.

During our first interview I thought it would be interesting to get his perspective on perhaps the most famous scientist of all time, Albert Einstein. I had learned that Freeman Dyson and Einstein had had some professional contact over the years, though apparently they had not collaborated closely.

"What do you think of Albert Einstein?" I asked. Dyson repeated my question as if there was something he had to think about before answering.

"Well, Jim," he said, "Albert Einstein was an SOB."

Oops! I changed my line of questioning. The rest of that first interview went along much better.

Science is a subject I love to talk about, though. I love to talk about our universe. I look up at the stars in the night sky and I have to ask myself, what's it all about? What's up there? How did this all come about, and why does the universe have the rhythms that it has? You just can't help it… I kind of think everyone feels the same way… The science of it all fascinates me; though I wonder if we won't eventually find God at the end of all that reasoning.

The second time I had Freeman Dyson as a guest I posed a question about longevity because he was also well up in age.

"What do you project as a possible maximum age that humans could reach?"

"The way it's going right now," he said, "100 will not be a surprise. A century could become the norm and 120 might not be impossible."

In the audience that day was a fellow who had coffee with me every morning. His name is Mark and he was more than 80 years old. At air time he would come and sit with me, waiting to see my guest. He was especially interested in hearing Freeman Dyson.

When Dyson said 120, I turned to Mark.

"One hundred twenty years, Mark. How would you like that?"

"Are you kidding? I'd be married to the same woman for 95 years!"

Freeman Dyson laughed as hard as anyone else. The greatest minds on the planet, after all, are just regular people, like the rest of us.

A Conversation with Donald Johansson

Jim Roselle: Welcome to Chautauqua, Donald Johansson.
Donald Johansson: Good morning to you and good morning to everybody here.

JR: You were in the local paper this morning regarding your talk to the Chautauqua Women's Club.
DJ: They all felt so much younger when I told them that the love of my life was 3.2 million years old.

JR: Donald Johansson, you said, and I read, that you were ready to leave a dig site - you were heading for your Land Rover - and you looked over your shoulder and suddenly saw a bone.
DJ: I saw a little piece of elbow.

JR: A little piece of elbow. You just noticed it. You suddenly stopped, and then what else happened?
DJ: You can imagine - it was 110° in the middle of the day - all I was thinking about was going and taking a swim in the river even though there are crocodiles.

I was walking from the field back toward my car. I always look at the ground when I walk anywhere, especially when I'm on a hunt. I'm always hoping, always grasping onto the possibility I might find something. I looked over my right shoulder, fortunately, rather than my left. If I had looked to my left I would have missed her.

And there on the ground was a little, 2-inch long piece of bone that my training told me was an arm bone that allowed you to flex at the elbow, called the ulna. I knew from the shape of it, the anatomy of it, that it had to have come from a human ancestor. I kneeled down to look at it and then looked up the slope. And there was a fragment of skull, a piece of jaw, a piece of pelvis, and that's what led to Lucy.

JR: Donald Johansson, a moment ago, before we went on the air, we were talking about a dog somebody was walking by here. You said it was a dog that changed your life. Am I right?
DJ: That's exactly right. When I was nine years old I was walking home from school and there was an older guy, I think he must've been 45 or so. He was walking a dog. I've always loved dogs and this dog, Buster, introduced him to me. I was only about eight or nine years old so he was ancient to me. Now that I'm 66 I have a little perspective on what age is all about. We started to talk and eventually I learned he was an anthropologist [social/cultural anthropologist, Dr. Paul Lazer] who taught at the Hartford Theological Seminary]. Buster kept us friends over the years and led me to Dr. Lazer's library at the age of 13. That place sparked my interest in understanding the origins of humankind.

JR: Did you play the game of thinking what - if not for that dog - would Donald Johansson be today?
DJ: Isn't life wonderful? You can ask any person listening, sitting around here, to sketch out their life from here on out and you know they, we all, will be 100% wrong. We never know what's out there, but my view is that we have to be open to everything at all times. Seize the opportunity and appreciate this remarkable opportunity we have as a living human being.

JR: How dramatically did it change your life after Lucy's discovery?
DJ: It was the pivotal moment in my life. Here I was, a graduate student coming out of the University of Chicago with my PhD in August, 1974, and I remember the last thing I said to my PhD committee.

"What are you going to do now?" they asked me.

"I'm going to Africa to find something."

And once Lucy came into my life, for the last 35 years we have been inseparable. She has led me to more wonderful places like Chautauqua than I could've ever imagined. She has really become so much a part of who I am.

JR: Donald Johansson, your mother is your hero, without question.

DJ: Well, she certainly is. Without my mother and without her strength and her guidance - my dad passed away when I was two years old - as a single mother, she raised me and never faltered. She was always there to encourage and support me and be a model for success and a model for living a wonderful life. She lived to see my success. She died in 1990 at the age of 88. She was thrilled with my success and it was such a wonderful reward for both of us that I have been successful in my career.

JR: When you stop and think of the impact that people made in your life - again we go back to the dog and Paul Laser - and then we go to a professor named Clark Howell [the late University of Chicago professor who is often called the father of modern paleoanthropology].

DJ: I called him on the telephone one day and…

JR: Wait a minute. How does this young student dare to call a man of his reputation on the phone and ask for an appointment?

DJ: As my mother said, "You know he's never going to come knocking on your door to ask you if you want to go to Africa. If you want to go to Africa and talk to him, it's up to you to make the call." And I did.

JR: And he was gracious enough to accept and make the appointment with you?

DJ: He was so gracious; he invited me to his office at the University of Chicago. We sat down and talked.

"What did you like to do?" he asked.

"I'd like to go to Africa and find fossils."

"A lot of us would like to do that. Now what do you really want to do?"

"I really want to study with you," I said.

"Come here for a couple of semesters." That was a powerful expression of acceptance and confidence. I was offered a fellowship at the University of Chicago.

JR: What would it be like if you made a whole picture of Lucy? How old would she look and what size would she be and what weight, and so on?

DJ: Those are interesting questions. If we turned around and saw her walking across the commons here, we would be struck by the fact that she was walking pretty much upright, like us, on two legs.

She would have long, gangly arms which are a hangover from the time her ancestors were living in the trees. She would've only been about 3 ½ feet tall as an adult. We know she was an adult because her wisdom teeth are erupted. She probably would have been fairly hairy. She would've had a projecting face, and a brain the size of a grapefruit. She would look very much like the ape that stood up.

JR: We didn't get to how you named her Lucy, yet. You are a *Beatles* fan.

DJ: I am a *Beatles* fan and I listen to their music . On that expedition in 1974, when Lucy was discovered, I had a girlfriend on the expedition with me, her name was Pamela. We were celebrating the discovery with the other members of our team. *Lucy In the Sky with Diamonds* was playing.

I said I thought it was a female skeleton because of its diminutive size.

"Well, if you think it's a female, why don't you call her Lucy?" Pamela said.

"I'm a University of Chicago professor! We don't give cute little names to our fossils."

Well, it was too late. Once it was uttered, it was in the air, even the next morning at breakfast.

"Do you think you will go back to the Lucy site?"

"Do you think you will find more of Lucy's skull?"

"How old do you think Lucy was when she died?"

And from that very moment she started to take on a personality. She was Lucy.

JR: It's a very good thing you looked over your left shoulder. When I stop and think about it, it's like I have often said: You never know what moment is going to dramatically change your life.

DJ: I think, as a species and as an individual, we have to seize each and every opportunity. We have to be prepared for change, prepared for success, prepared for failure. We have to believe in ourselves, we have to believe in our dreams. We have to have a dream - every one of us.

JR: I have asked this question of many of my guests over many years. It fascinates me to play the "If Game". If you had a dinner table ready for special guests, and you could invite anybody living or dead to that table for dinner, name three or four whom you would invite.

DJ: I would invite my father, whom I never knew. He died when I was two years old. Of course, I would love to have met Charles Darwin, and I would love to have met some of my other heroes like Alexander von Humboldt who explored South America for five years, wrote 30 volumes on South America and lived to be in his 90s. He was an extraordinary man. The cold Humboldt Current, running northward along the west coast of South America, was named for him. I would certainly love to have met Ludwig von Beethoven, one of my great heroes.

Music is a great part of my life. I wish I had learned to play an instrument. I haven't, and I'm starting to take singing lessons this summer, finally.

JR: Donald Johansson, we'd love to hear that someday, and thank you for the pleasure of your company on this day.

DJ: Well, thank you so much. Wonderful to be on your program.

Chapter 11

Tales from the Golden Age of Radio

WJTN *started its broadcast life in 1924 only four years after the world's first commercial radio station, KDKA, was licensed and went on the air in Pittsburgh, Pennsylvania, a mere 120 miles south of Jamestown.*

There's only one interview technique that matters... Do your homework so you can listen to the answers and react to them and ask follow-ups. Do your homework, prepare.

Jim Lehrer

In the beginning, some of the music on WOCL was live

The Necessary Local Connection

The call letters of WJTN were originally WOCL, standing for *We're On Chautauqua Lake*. Today, WJTN is the news/talk component of a five-station broadcast cluster operating as Media One Group, LLC, in Jamestown, New York: WKSN-AM (Oldies), WHUG-FM (Country), WQFX-FM (Rock), WWSE-FM (Classical) and WJTN-AM (News/Talk).

The Golden Age of Radio is generally thought of as spanning the 1930s and 40s, an age when radio's reach and community impact grew and thrived. Radio brought the world into people's living rooms and it brought listeners into a wider world.

Jim Roselle exploited and polished the fine arts of radio's Golden Age as few broadcasters have done. He continued to advance his station's listenership, commercial success and community-building well into the 21st Century. In addition, WJTN's geographic location, a self-sufficient "media island", lies outside the signal radius of the big city stations with a population of 1 million+. Jamestown is not flooded by big city news, entertainment and commerce. In such locations across the country, these "small market" stations provide special opportunities for broadcasters.

Jim Embrescia, owner of Media 1 Group, congratulates Jim on his years of broadcasting excellence

World-wide networking and satellite program delivery have, by many accounts, almost driven local radio into extinction. This appears to have happened, according to many media critics, in spite of the Federal Communication Commission's historic mandate requiring every radio station to serve its "community-of-license" with local news, information and regionally needed services.

"I hope people who read this - people with broadcasting influence in their community – see how much they can achieve," Jim says, "by bringing broadcasting at its best – local people and programming

– back to their communities and hometowns. This is especially true for the small market stations like Jamestown across the country."

First: Wake the Town and Tell the People
1. Why Every Morning Starts with a Cup of Happiness

People often ask me where my signature Cup of Happiness came from. Well, it certainly wasn't planned.

It so happened that I had the morning show at 8:15 every day. I used to take over for Doc Webster, Dennis Webster's father, after his shift. He opened up at 5 o'clock in the morning and ended at 8:15. That's when I would take his microphone and work 'till noon.

But then Doc Webster passed away. After about a year and a half, the station decided that I should replace the man who had been temporarily filling in for Doc and open up the early morning show at 6 o'clock. Whenever an opportunity came about for a certain spot on the schedule, I always asked myself, "How I can relate with the audience at that time? How can I welcome them to the show?"

I figured just about everybody turns to a cup of coffee first thing in the morning. So I decided to simply welcome them into the day with me. I was going to say, "Enjoy my…" I quickly decided while I was talking not to call it a cup of coffee…I said, "…my Cup of Happiness." So there it was, just a spur of the moment inspiration. That's what it's been ever since. It is, quite literally, a Cup of Happiness.

2. The Start of *The Times of Your Life*

Jim with long-time friend and co-host of The Times of Your Life, Russ Diethrick

The Times of Your Life program, from 10:00 to 11:00 every Saturday morning, is just a couple of friends, Jim and Russ, who get together to talk about life. They interview interesting people and discuss their favorite topics, simply beginning their conversation with something like, "Tell us about *The Times of Your Life*."

Russ Diethrick, Jim's co-host, is a successful local banker, and past Commissioner of Parks and Recreation in Jamestown. He knows that Jim understands people and appreciates their successes and their adventures. He never plays "one-upsmanship" with them, attempting to match them with his own exploits. He is never jealous of their accomplishments. Jim is a humble man. Russ is fond of saying, "Roselle is spelled with an 'e' not an 'i' because there is no 'I' in Roselle."

Jim Remembers… A Great Idea

A fellow named Ron Paige, a local guy and a kind of promoter, a salesman of sorts, came to me one day when I was talking to my friend, Russ Diethrick. He said, "Look, you two guys, I've got an idea for a show you should do. You two are legends in this town because of all the ways you are involved in the community… Why don't you get together and do a show? We'll call it *The Times of Your Life*. You'll talk to people, get their stories. People will love it."

So, naturally, Russ and I thought it was a great idea. We've been doing it ever since.
Russ understands my philosophy, and I think he thinks about things the same way I do; everybody is a story. Everybody. There are no two people alike. Each one has a different chemistry, a different outlook and different ideas, and especially, they have different adventures. I am as delighted to interview

the man collecting garbage as I am delighted to interview a president. I get as much joy out of each one. Because we are all a story, every one of us.

The Times of Your Life is a kind of Chautauqua interview done in Jamestown during the ten months when Chautauqua Institution is closed, sometimes with our own hometown folks and sometimes by phone or in person with nationally known authors, celebrities, politicians and others.

Second: On the Air
1. My Style of Interview

I work very hard to prepare for every interview and I treat every day at work as if it's the first day of a new job, with excitement. I know I can always discover new things I've never seen or heard before.

Before I meet my guests, I read books written by the authors I talk to. I study the newspaper to find events relevant to my guests. Then I study what's been reported about what they do and what they think. I do not typically prepare a list of questions or a script, though. I simply allow the conversation to flow naturally, as if we're just sitting at a table, having a cup of coffee and talking over whatever is happening that day. I guess that's why I've been called the "Mayor of Bestor Plaza". A guest's answers can be serious, really funny or even shocking. I want my guests to feel like I'm a good listener, and frequently, after an interview, that is what they say.

Once in a while, after an interview is over and the microphone is off, they actually ask me, "How did I do?" They are usually people with something to say and they want to be heard.

Sometimes I disagree with a guest, but I don't usually say so. I don't try to get into a fight with them. I just let that guide me into questions that help them explain their position. My listeners should make up their own minds.

There are times when I suspect a guest has ideas or plans that they just aren't quite ready to tell the public, so I try to lead them in that direction, just a little bit, and then listen carefully. The interview with Bill Clinton, for instance, was fascinating. He was still the governor of Arkansas then. What I decided to listen for were hints that he would go farther and for a sense that there was something deeper. When I asked him for a report card on America, his answer sounded like he'd been thinking about a lot more than Arkansas. A month later, he received the Democratic nomination to run for President of the United States.

Many times, an answer takes us in an unexpected direction and that's always interesting. That's why I don't have a set format or make up a lot of questions before my interviews. Only once in a rare while can something throw me off my stride. If I'm too focused on the next question on my list, I'll miss the answer to the last one, and maybe miss a golden opportunity.

When a guest knows a lot more about their special area than I do, I like to sort of break the ice with something personal or some humor, which is better if it comes from them. Like the time I asked Jane Goodall what a chimpanzee sounds like. She hooted long and loud like a chimp, got everybody in the audience laughing and then showed me where one particular chimp had bitten off the tip of her thumb.

Then there are guests like Margaret Meade. I looked into the deeper issues with people like her. She is an anthropologist who is seeking into the deeper human matters, like questions about what really makes us human and how we came to be who we are.

Mostly, I play a little game in my mind. I try to imagine what would make this interview interesting for my listeners, what are the things they might not know? Sometimes it only takes a single, simple question to start a guest off on a long and interesting tale. A listener once thanked me for bringing "inside stuff" into her living room.

There are a couple of questions I like to ask people, too. One is: "If you could be a fly on the wall anywhere, anytime in history, where would that be?" One fellow said he'd love to be a fly on the wall when General Eisenhower decided on the D-Day invasion. He knew he'd lose thousands of men, but he knew he had to do it, too. "That must have been an interesting conversation with his officers," he said.

The other way I like to rouse a guest's thinking is to have him or her give three of four names of people, anyone from all of history, they would love to invite for dinner.

Once in a while a guest will turn it around and ask me the same question.

So, the three people I would invite to dinner would include Jesus Christ. I mean what kind of a man was he really, to talk to, I mean? Why did he leave such a legacy? Jesus was Tim Russert's first choice for a guest too. And of course I'd want to have dinner with my parents again.

If I could change my wish just a little, I'd make it my whole family. Just to sit around the dinner table with everyone there, just one more time. That would be it.

But, as I said, once in a while something does throw me off my stride.

2. The Day the Transmitter Died

I was at my usual place, outdoors on Bestor Plaza, ready with my microphone. I was going to talk to the guy who literally brought down President Richard Nixon, Leon Jaworski – the Special Prosecutor for Watergate.

Leon Jaworski, the nicest man who ever brought down a president

And there he was, heading right toward me along the brick walkway. Suddenly I was getting nervous, I mean really upset.

"Oh my God! Mr. Jaworski, our transmitter just blew. It's our tube or whatever. But I've called the station and I told them to please hurry. I hope they'll be here soon."

"Take your time," he said. "You've got a nice spot here; I'll just sit and watch. This is a very nice studio. Look at the Plaza, the people walking around. You can almost imagine Judy Garland, you know, Dorothy and her dog, Toto, walking down the yellow brick road in front of us here."

It's the atmosphere there that captivates my guests. They see my studio – really just a table and a microphone – a sort of sidewalk café where you can sit among the people strolling through the Plaza while doing a show.

He said, "I'm not in a hurry." It was close to 9:30, and he wasn't scheduled to be on stage at the Amphitheater until10:45.

Sometimes, I like to remind myself of a quote from Hamilton Jordan's book, *Crisis: The Last Year of the Carter Presidency* [Putnam, 1982]. Jordan had been Chief of Staff to President Carter. He wrote, "I believe there really is no such thing as a bad day."

The transmitter got fixed a few minutes later, and it all worked out, so I guess Hamilton was right.

3. How Radio Creates a Community

The thing that pleases me the most is, after I've had a guest for the first time, they come back again two or three years later. I'm pleased that they want to be interviewed again. That gives me pleasure because I find they have learned that I don't work for a mere small, hometown radio station. I had David McCullough, for example, three different times. The great historian gives me the pleasure of his company each time he comes. It's amazing.

The fact that these people accept the invitation is always a thrill. I figure it comes about because they trust me. They know that I'm an announcer who won't try to make them or their ideas look foolish or like they are unaware and unprepared. These people are looking for the questions that they know should be asked. My knowledge should be such that they feel confident with me. I think it means something that they have come back a second and even a third time. Look at Mark Russell; I've probably had him on the air a dozen times.

In my style of interview, I take much more than a 60 or 90 second sound bite. If you watch the *Today Show*, for instance, you'll see that most guests get, at most, two or three minutes. That's it. I would never invite anybody up to the studio and say, "Well, I've got two minutes with you." That's not my kind of interview.

Basically, over the years, I think that's what has made my show different. I'd like to think it's the reason that we remain popular locally, too. For instance, a lady once came to the studio who had written a Christmas Carol play and the songs for it. She was going to present it, *A Jamestown Christmas Carol*, on Friday night at the high school. I could have given her a PSA (a 30 or 60 second public service announcement), and say, "Okay, go and see *Christmas Carol* on Friday night at 7:30 at the high school." I think the audience deserves more information on the event.

If the audience can meet the person behind the scenes, they really know something about both the event and the artist or worker behind it. That helps create the local spirit that builds a community. That's also one of my favorite ways to get acquainted with people.

A lot of DJs never leave the studio. They are only "The voice in that box." But I did remotes on location and I did grand openings and anniversaries. That's why I broadcast more than 1000 remotes from one single business, Joe Caprino's Furniture Store, and so many others, too. It's a matter of getting connected with my listeners. A voice in the box can make music but it certainly cannot make a community.

That's why I begin every morning's broadcast with, "Good morning hometown Jamestown and all of its neighbors. Today is (date, month and year) which happens to be the first day of the rest of your life."

It's got to be more than music and ads.

I once heard Sid Caesar say the best thing for a comedian to know is that you make people laugh. He said, "When I hear people laugh at my jokes and routines, I realize they're happy in this moment. I have created some happiness."

He is right. He has put some joy into their day. It's not about making a lot of money or anything like that. The reward is to go out there and make them laugh or make them happy or to give them something to think about.

Third: How You Know There's an Audience Out There
1. One Million Dollars

Let me tell you about the million dollars we raised for the Heart Radiothon over 20 years in Jamestown. That's how you know there's an audience out there.

Heart Radiothon with the goal of $25,000

I have been asked whether anybody else could have seen the opportunities I took advantage of. Could I spot the right ones better than somebody else in my situation?

That's a hard question to answer, really. I do enjoy the excitement of a new challenge. I just think of it as a new opportunity to do something different, a chance to see what my kind of job can accomplish.

For instance, the local Heart Association made me the Chairman of the Heart Radiothon. In 20 years, we raised somewhere between $750,000 and $1 million. That had challenged me on the subject of how to get an audience involved.

When I look back, I realize we had a pretty good audience. When you have a small town, like Jamestown, you start out with a small goal like raising $2500 in 36 hours. We went on the air from Friday morning at 6 o'clock till Saturday night at 6 o'clock. I wondered how many people would be calling after midnight. Well, we picked up almost $5000. The organizers got all excited and said the goal next year will be $7500. So I said. "Okay, let's go."

The next year, we built a jail at the mall and we wanted prisoners in our jail. So I decided to get the ministers of the community, the priests and all the other clergy, and jail them. I figured the congregations would listen and they'd want them out. We put a price tag on each one. What a ball we had that Saturday! "We've got to get $200 for your minister," I said. At

Hopalong Che-si-dice can still do an interview in jail

one point, we had four of them. We had the Rabbi, the Catholic priest and two Protestant pastors. We even had the Mayor once.

When we put the priest in jail, I interviewed him. He said, "Jim, I'm hungry, really. Is there anything we're going to have to eat in the jail?" Would you believe it? People brought spaghetti and meatballs to the mall for the poor guy.

Sometimes we put teachers in jail. We locked up school principals, too, and fraternity presidents. Then there were the presidents of the Rotary and Lions. That gave us an automatic audience of all their club members. We once imprisoned a teacher named Mrs. Malarkey, the wife of a local dentist. Students in her class came marching down the center of the mall with signs, "Free Our Teacher!" And "We Want Mrs. Malarkey!!" They wanted people to pay to get their teacher out of jail. Some of her husband's patients got involved, too. I guess we had sort of put her whole family in jail.

We changed things up, too. People started calling and saying, "I'd give you 20 bucks to keep that guy in there." The more popular they were, the more fun people had with it. We "kidnapped" the postmaster out of Frewsburg. What a job he did for us. He must've raised $2000 all by himself.

That was the power of the microphone and the power of radio at that time, and it was another way of meeting my audience. I remember a lady who walked in with at least eight women with her, all under care for mental challenges. Each woman was holding a dollar bill in her hand, and was asked to bring her dollar to me, one at a time. Imagine accepting a dollar bill from somebody with a severe neurological handicap. It brought tears to my eyes. They came back for many years.

The Cancer Society turned the tables on everybody. They dressed me up as the Italian Hopalong Cassidy and put me, Hopalong *Che-si-dice* (it means something like *"What's up?* in Italian), in jail and raised money to get me out. That worked great, too.

The people were never just an audience for these events, they were individuals who truly cared about their community. Radio, at its best, can turn listeners into participants. I made friends with so many of them.

The Radiothons really let me know there is an audience out there.

2. A Fair Trade?

We wanted to come up with a way to get people to drink more instant coffee for one of our advertisers. Instant was sort of new on the market, or at least the Taster's Choice company thought they had really improved their version of it, and they were trying to make it more of a mainstream product.

I figured that if people didn't have a pot to perk their ground coffee in, maybe they'd appreciate the instant more.

It was a gamble, but I said we'd trade a jar of Taster's Choice for every coffee pot a listener brought in. By the end of the day's promotion, the floor of the Hotel Jamestown's lobby, downstairs from our broadcast studio, was littered and stacked with coffee pots. We had at least 150 by the time we took this picture.

That's how you know there's an audience out there.

Left: *WJTN's Taster's Choice Coffee Pot Hoard*

3. Only a Thousand Cups?

One particular local fast food restaurant in town gave me another chance to prove there was an audience out there. The manager had never bought any air time before, but on this occasion he agreed to try it. He had an idea and he set the stage for us.

"I'll tell you what we're going to do," he said. "I will give you a promotion and only you are going to have it. Nobody else. I'm not going to put any ads in the paper, either. Here's the pitch: Anybody who comes in on this particular morning will get a nice cup when they buy their first cup of coffee. Then we'll fill it the second time for free." He bought the promo from 8:15 until 10:30, the breakfast hour.

"We should start at 6 o'clock," I told him. "There's an early morning audience that goes to work in the plants around here. I'll do the remote right from your restaurant." It was part of a chain with three locations in Jamestown. I told my listeners, "Go to the one that's convenient for you."

"Do you think we can get to 1,000 cups?" The manager asked, still a little doubtful.

"Sure," I said. I thought that was a lot, too. But I wasn't going to admit it.

By the time the promo was over, in just 4 1/2 hours of one single day, we did 1,800 cups, that's 400 cups every hour.

And that's how you know there is an audience out there.

4. Free Gas!

Then there was the gasoline company that dared us to give away free gas to the first driver who stopped in at their gas station and mentioned WJTN. We won that dare.

One day the company's regional manager was in town for a remote I was doing at one of their stations.

"How do you know anybody is listening to you?"

"I don't know, really," I said, "but I've been working at WJTN for a few years now, and I know we've got something going here."

"Can you prove anyone comes here because they heard you on the radio?"

"Okay," I said. "How about if a guy drives in and says he listens to this program? Will you give him, let's say, eight gallons of gas? For free?"

"Yes."

"Okay, ladies and gentlemen," I said into my microphone, "if you are in the vicinity and you're the first one to drive in, and you mention the show that you are listening to, you'll get eight gallons of gas for free."

It took 45 seconds.

"You rigged it!" the company rep said.

"No I didn't."

"You're kidding me."

"You want to do it again?" I challenged him. "Right now?"

"Okay, go ahead." He was a little less smug this time, but still game.

Even as I was saying it on the air, I saw a guy coming over the hill and driving right down to the station.

Fifteen seconds.

"That's enough." The give-away was over.

That's how you know there's an audience out there.

5. A Steak Dinner

One day at Caprino's Furniture Store, the RCA representative came for the day and stayed overnight for a big promotion of his products. It was called a "64 Hour Marathon".

At 3 o'clock in the morning, I was still broadcasting. The representative noticed, of course, that nobody was coming to the store at that hour. He was getting a little doubtful his sponsorship money was buying what he needed.

"How do you know anybody is listening?"

"There's an audience out there," I said. "They're hearing about the values. Maybe when they shop tomorrow they will come in. We figure that they've got the information, and they may come down and buy something."

"But can you tell me they're listening right now? I'll tell you what; I will buy you a steak dinner if you get 10 phone calls."

"Do you really want to do that?"

"Yes."

"Okay." The song ended and I opened the microphone.

"Ladies and gentlemen, I just had an offer from the RCA representative who is here with me tonight. He said that if you call and let him know you're listening to the broadcast he will be delighted to buy me a steak dinner if I get 10 calls. But please," I added, "don't call twice. I want 10 different calls."

I had barely finished speaking and the calls started to come. I counted 10.

"Thank you very much," I told my audience. But the phones didn't stop ringing. We lost count but there were at least 15 or 20. I'd won my bet.

And that's how you know there's an audience out there.

6. A Bright, Red Line

Sometimes you know people are listening when they share fond memories with you.

One 4th of July many years ago I accepted an offer from a friend to do a broadcast from his airplane over Chautauqua Lake at sunset. There are about a dozen towns and settlements around the 40-mile shoreline, but most of it is privately owned. On the 4th of July we have a tradition that brings everyone, towns and waterfront homeowners, together around the lake. Everybody looks forward to the memorable shoreline view of the event, but few people have seen it from the air.

At a pre-set time, around dusk, everybody lights red flares on their property at the water's edge. Wherever you are, you can see the glowing, red necklace ringing the shoreline as dusk fades into night.

Not long ago, a local businessman, Randy Sweeney, the Chautauqua Region Community Foundation's executive director, told me he still remembers the night his father called the whole family together around the radio.

"OK, everybody," I had said into my microphone from the cockpit of the airplane, with my engineer, Herb Nicklaus, crammed into a back seat with the transmitter on his lap, "Light your flares!"

As I watched, it was like seeing someone with a red marker pen outline the lake. I described it as well as I could for my listeners. It was certainly memorable for me, but when a listener remembers it fondly from so many years ago, then you know there's an audience out there really listening to you.

7. Carduni Sandwich: The Media Rage

It's a scrambled egg sandwich with burdock in it, better known in Italian as *carduni,* or maybe for a Sicilian*, garduni*. It's not a sandwich that any kind of Italian cookbook is likely to have in it, though. Here's how it came about:

My mother would go for a walk around the neighborhood and see this burdock growing in people's gardens. Around Memorial Day the burdock is best. She would go up to the house and ask the people if she could pick it because they looked at it as a weed. So they said, "Sure!" So I used to hold the bag for her, and she'd put it in the bag, and we'd go around, particularly down Washington Street—there was a lot of farmland down there.

Jim and Vince Joy, Jr. assure you a burdock is not a weed, it's carduni!

It took a lot of work to prepare carduni. You had to clean it, strip it, you know, pull all the strings off, and boil it. Then you beat an egg, and you put cheese with it, and maybe you doll it up a little bit with the spices or maybe some bacon or whatever you want to put in there. It was an economical dish because it cost nothing. Now people have favorite spots they won't reveal because they want to go there every year and get it for themselves.

The story of how carduni sandwiches got on the radio started when I was doing a remote broadcast at the Super Duper Market. This guy was just standing there listening to me. He looked like he had something he wanted to say.

"So you're a Giants baseball fan," he said.

"Yeah, I have been since I was little."

"Well I'm a Pirates fan," he said with a little challenge in his voice.

"Okay," I said. "That's nice."

"Well, they are playing this weekend. They're playing a three-game series."

"Okay." I wondered where he was going with this.

"You want to make a bet?" My first thought was, I didn't want to bet money on the radio. I thought he was going say, "You want to bet five bucks? Or something like that." So I said, "Okay, I'll take your wager, but I'm not going to bet any money."

"What do you want to bet?"

Now my mind was running. "I'll bet you a carduni sandwich." That's all I said.

He blinked and looked at me. "What in the world is a carduni sandwich?"

"Don't worry about it," I said. "But if you lose you're going to have to find somebody to make you a carduni sandwich. If I lose I'll get you a carduni sandwich."

And that's how the whole thing came about. I left it at that.

When I got back to the studio, the receptionist said, "We've had some calls. Is there such a thing as a carduni sandwich?"

"Yes!"

"What is it? The people are asking."

But the funny thing was, and I knew this, the Italian ladies who were listening knew all about it. That's when they started bringing me the burdock. The next day, somebody came up to the station with the bag full of burdock. I took it home to my sister. I said, "Hey Anna, look what we've got. She says, "Good. Thanks." The next day I get another and I bring it home and my sister says, "Okay, that's nice." But by the third time she says, "Thanks, but this is hard work. I think I have enough now." I went on the air and said, "Thank you very much. That's enough."

But then people started to make the sandwiches and bring me even more. Mrs. Guiffrida, Mrs. Brucalleri, Mrs. Loverme, they were all bringing me sandwiches. They were hot off the griddle and they were good. Then the churches picked it up on their festivals. Pretty soon one of the churches sold 1500 carduni sandwiches as a fund raiser.

Pat Carr at Lakeview Gardens still brings me a dish full of carduni every May. Tony Marra from Falconer, when I am at a market doing a remote, brings me a bag full of carduni sandwiches every year.

Before all that, nobody outside the Italian community knew what a carduni sandwich was. After the carduni sandwiches became famous, Kathy [Jim's wife] had a carduni party at the studio. She figured it would be a great opportunity to get some listeners who are totally confused and set up a party to make them and taste them. Two hundred people showed up. Charlie Vullo and his wife, local restaurateurs, did all the work; he made all the sandwiches.

That whole thing was just an idea off the top of my head in a casual conversation, but it became a big symbol of some kind for me, for WJTN, and for Jamestown.

Just recently at one of McDonald's restaurants in Jamestown where I meet with some of my old Boys Club buddies for breakfast sometimes, somebody brought out two huge platters. One was filled with carduni sandwiches and the other with mustard greens. Carl Scarpinio, the retired teacher, said "Okay Roselle, we've got to split it."

People used to ask me how many people listen to my program in the morning. I would say, "I have no idea."

But when you get a reaction like that you realize there's an audience out there.

8. The Carduni Sandwich * and Other Family Favorites

Cardoons, or *carduni*, are burdock, a common weed for some gardeners but a staple vegetable and table delight for many Italians and for lots of other folks who wish they were. The burdock is a member of the thistle family. It is related to the artichoke. The Month of May is carduni picking time.

Ingredients:
2 lbs. burdock
4 large eggs (beaten)
Salt, freshly ground pepper (to taste)
3 tbsp. grated Parmesan cheese
Flour (add until batter is smooth, not runny)

Directions: Peel the strings from the internal stalks which are most tender. Cut into 2" pieces. Boil in a large pot until tender (30 – 40 minutes). Don't let them get too soft. Al dente is good. Drain well. Add burdock all at once to the batter. Fry by spoonfuls in extra virgin olive oil until golden brown on both sides.

* Thanks to Anna Roselle Paterniti, Jim's sister, for this delicious traditional recipe.

Serve while still hot as a side dish or sandwich on Italian bread. You'll wonder why the ancient Italian nobility left this delight to the peasants. *Godere!* Enjoy!

Spingi:

A Favorite Italian Dessert: Jims' sisters, Sara and Anna, made Spingi for Christmas festivities. Spingi are similar to fried donuts and very light.

Ingredients:
1 cup water
¼ cup butter
1 cup flour
5 eggs
1 tsp. whiskey

Directions: Place water and butter in saucepan. Cook to a boil. Add flour, stirring rapidly, until mixture leaves sides of pan. Let cool, add eggs one at a time, beating until well mixed. Add whiskey. Drop spoonfuls into hot grease until well browned, roll in honey and sprinkle with powdered sugar.

Cannoli: Another traditional Italian pastry dessert made by Sara and Anna was cannoli. They consist of tube-shaped shells of fried pastry dough, filled with a sweet creamery ricotta cheese filling. Some people fill the pastry tubes with a custard filling, chopped semi-sweet chocolate pieces, colored candies, and cherries are often included. Whenever Jim attends a St. Joseph Table, cannoli is one of his first choices.

Mashed Potatoes and the Tuesday Night Dinners: Sara and Anna worked together as a team during the holiday seasons making cookies and home cooked dinners. Each Tuesday night dinner was special, and given a full holiday approach. One of the favorite dishes at each meal was the mashed potatoes.

Ingredients:
5 lbs potatoes
1 stick butter
Salt & Pepper
1 tsp. sugar
2 tbsp. sour cream
Warm milk (add to desired consistency)

Directions: Whip with electric beater.

Spaghetti Sauce

Ingredients:
2 tbsp. olive oil
1 medium onion chopped (½ cup)
½ cup green bell pepper chopped
1 large garlic clove chopped
1 8 oz. can tomato sauce
1 16 oz. can whole tomatoes

1 tbsp. fresh basil chopped (1 tsp. dried)
½ tsp. oregano
¼ tsp. salt
¼ tsp. fennel
1/8 tsp. pepper
1 tbsp. sugar
1 tbsp. red wine

Directions: Cook onion, pepper and garlic in olive oil approximately 3 minutes. Stir in remaining ingredients, breaking up tomatoes. Cover and simmer with meatballs and spare ribs.

Meatballs

Ingredients:
1 ½ lb. ground chuck roast
3 eggs
¾ cup homemade bread crumbs
Salt & pepper
1 ½ cups Romano cheese

Directions: Add cold water just enough to be able to roll balls. Fry in olive oil until brown. Add meatballs to sauce and cook about 1 hour. Brown 2 pork spare ribs and add to sauce.

Jim always anticipated Sunday dinner. His mother made roast chicken with mashed potatoes. She would smile and say, *"Mangia e ti crescere forte!"* - "Eat and you'll grow strong!" The other days of the week, dinner was usually pasta with various sauces and toppings.

9. World Headquarters

Jim has heard from listeners who have locked in every preset on their car radios to 1240-AM, WJTN. Others keep a radio in every room of their homes set to 1240 and turned on. From making beds to washing up the breakfast dishes to loading the washing machine and even in the shower, Jim's been told by listeners, "I never miss a word." A local farmer even says he keeps Jim tuned in out in the barn to keep him company while he is milking his cows.

The Internet has now given radio an even greater reach. *The Jim Roselle Show*, like almost everything else that is broadcast today, is available anywhere in the world on a computer or a smart phone with an Internet connection. Jim regularly gets calls from Jamestown's snow birds – local folks who escape the region's usual 10 to 12 feet of wintertime snowfall – who listen to WJTN in the Carolinas, in Florida and anyplace else they happen to roam far from home. When he can, he delights in putting them on the air so he can give hometown listeners a weather report from sunny climates and tropical beaches.

Friends have suggested he add another line to the sign outside his studio door. The Dew Drop Inn could use another line: *World Headquarters – The Jim Roselle Show*.

Jim knows he has an audience out there.

Fourth: The Cookout Shows
1. Get Out of the Studio!

I discovered that for a story or a radio show to work, you've got to have a hook in it. That's what people will latch on to. It grabs you, it tugs at you.

Where other DJs are locked into their studios, their broadcast boxes, we went out on the road with our cookouts. That was the hook. It was probably the best way to get acquainted with our audience.

WJTN had started what they called *The Cookout* on Tuesday nights. Listeners had to send in a card saying they would like to win a backyard cookout. The weekly winner of a drawing could invite five couples to join their family at home for a cookout in their back yard. We would put the whole thing on for them.

We brought hot dogs and hamburgers, potato chips, baked beans, potato salad, Pepsi-Cola, pizza, Genesee beer and a dessert of some sort. The idea for the show was as simple as that. We counted on about 15 people, and we brought everything. The grill was from the local Jamesway store. The winners not only got the cookout and all the food we brought but kept the brand-new grill, too.

So we set up the grill, cooked the hot dogs and hamburgers, fed everybody and had a good time on the show. We would say to our audience, "Hello, we're here at the Smith residence, and we're with some wonderful friends. We just enjoyed these great hot dogs cooked on their new Jamesway grill. Then we always sang, "Hail, Hail the Gangs All Here, what the heck do we care?" Back in those days we wouldn't sing "… What the *hell* do we care?" You couldn't say that on the air. After a while we changed it to "Hail, Hail the Gangs All Here, at the WJTN Cookout." We just carried on a half-hour chat over dinner and interviewed the winners and all the guests on the air. Of course, after The Cookout show was over, we all stayed around and just got to know each other. The people who were there as guests would then go home and write a card of their own. They wanted to win a cookout at their home and return the favor. It's like winning twice. What a way to get to know your audience!

We started *The Cookout Show* in the 1960s and kept it up for about 20 years. We went to backyards everywhere WJTN's signal reached, all over Chautauqua County's 1500 square miles and 150,000 people. It was so popular we started to run it in the wintertime, too, inside the people's homes. We wondered about their privacy, but we found out they loved it. We were company. They even wanted us to use their kitchens.

Later, we started recording the programs so we would play them back on the air the next day. A person whose home had hosted the cookout one day could hear themselves on the air the next. That was very popular, too.

2. Bagpipes?

At first, I did all of the cookouts with Jack Dunigan. Eventually, however, the people back in the studio noticed how much fun it was. They wanted to get in on it. Though I shared the duties, I did more than 50 percent of the cookouts over the program's entire run.

Jack was quite the accomplished musician. I asked him to bring his guitar to our very first indoor cookout. It seemed like it would be fun to have some live music to flavor the show a little bit. I'll never forget it. We were at 15 Meadow Lane in Jamestown, the home of the Butts family.

As we started to set up, the guests began showing up. One of them, a fellow named Al, came dressed in a wonderful, authentic Scottish kilt. He had a bagpipe under his arm, too.

"Jack," I said, "you're not going to have to play your guitar."

That's the kind of show that got me involved with my audience. I was not just a voice in a box. That's what the Golden Age of Radio was like for me.

3. Washing Up

Kathy Roselle, adds, "I was often in charge of setting up the picnic. One day, I was setting out the paper plates on the paper tablecloth – which WJTN always supplied – when the hostess, whose home was one of the biggest and finest in Jamestown, stopped me."

"What are you doing?"
"I thought I would just get things going so when all your guests come, we will be…"
"Oh no!" our shocked hostess interrupted. "I do *not* use paper products. Use these." She turned and walked across the room in a way that made it plain I was to follow. She showed me an ornate cabinet bedecked in fine china and the place where her sterling silver was stored. That was probably WJTN's only cookout served on fine linen.

That was also the only cookout where I had to wash all the dishes. I didn't drop any of them."

4. Luxury: Optional

On another occasion, Kathy recalls, "I went with Jim to the home of someone who was clearly quite poor. The gentleman didn't even own a working stove. All he had was a small toaster oven. So I, without ever letting on that there was anything unusual, cut all the pizzas into small pieces and toasted two at a time. That cookout turned out to be as big a success as any of the others had been.

Then there was a time the broadcast crew was already at the home but none of their equipment made it past the front porch. 'That's the messiest house I've ever seen,' one of the crew told me while hurriedly leaving the scene. 'I think I got bugs just walking in.' He looked like he wanted to scratch an itch someplace.

We left the food on the porch but that WJTN Cookout just never happened. It was a one-time-only event and it was certainly not typical of our Jamestown audience. It may have simply been someone who was disabled and still too proud to ask for help. At least we left them a good meal."

Fifth: Broadcasting Colleagues at WJTN

My colleagues have been superb in the support and encouragement they gave me, especially when I was a rookie; I was green.

I remember when they gave me the full-time job. My first duty was to stand behind Doc Webster as he was introducing Paul Harvey and cutting in and out of local commercials during the show. Paul Harvey was Mr. "The Rest of the Story". So many people enjoyed him over the years. He had a 15 minute slot in our 1 o'clock show time.

I stood there watching Doc Webster introduce Paul Harvey on the *ABC Network*. When he had to take a break for a commercial, Paul Harvey used to say his queue, "Page 2." When he said that, it was my turn to clip him off and put my own commercial in – a one minute commercial. I had exactly one minute to get that commercial in and then get back to *ABC*. It sounds simple, but it has to be done very exactly, and I was new. I kept saying to myself, "Will I be able to do that? Will I time it right?" It felt like a challenge. That was the start.

Everybody was encouraging and supportive. They were great to work with. They were fun. I really wish more people would look at their jobs as being enjoyable, even if it is serious work. If you can go to work and take that attitude, you've got it made.

I was made an "Honorary Scandinavian", too. In addition to the big Italian population of Jamestown, we had a lot of Swedish people. As a matter of fact, the Swedish population dates back to the 1800s. They were very important to Jamestown's early commercial growth and success. We broadcast the *Swedish Hour* every week, with a wonderful host named Gerald Heglund, a retired high school art teacher. Once in a while, if he could not come in, he let me substitute on his program. I was Jim Roselleson for the hour.

Pete Hubbell was the son of legendary Buffalo-area broadcaster, Ralph Hubbell. Pete's smooth voice and easy delivery became a signature feature of the Chautauqua County sports scene from 1967 when he joined WJTN until his 1998 retirement. And what a joy Pete was to work with. We worked the Babe Ruth World Series together, a regular and highly attended event in Jamestown.

Merrill Rosen

Then there was Russ Diethrick; what a supporter. Russ is called "Mr. Baseball" in this region. He is a long time community leader and faithful booster of our teams. He was honored by having the Jamestown Jammers baseball stadium and ballpark named for him. He is the most authentic, genuine man in the community. He deserves a round of applause, whether he's on the air at the moment or not.

I work with Dennis Webster every day. Over the years I worked with Melva Webber, *Opinion Please* host; Larry Saracki, WJTN's AM Sales Manager; Merrill Rosen, the General Manager, now retired after more than 50 amazingly successful years; and Jack Dunigan... Remember his sign off? "I'm done-a-gain." Then there's John Mahoney who went on to become a noted newscaster in Cleveland, Ohio. Ray Hall certainly comes to mind, too. He did *The Hall Closet* for many years, a popular, eclectic mix of local current events, commentary, his own and his listeners' opinions. Terry Frank, the WJTN News Director, always chats with me about newsworthy events and people after the 11:00 local and national news.

Melva Webber

Our greatest graduate at WJTN, by the way, was Marshall Shontz. His professional name was Rex Marshall. He went to the *ABC Network*. He did Pepsodent commercials, Reynolds Aluminum commercials and live commercials on the *Tonight Show* with Johnny Carson. Then he bought a radio station in New Hampshire.

But there are so many more and I don't want to leave anybody out. There is Dan Warren, who works on one of our sister stations, WHUG. His son Matt, a wonderful young man, worked with me on the air through his college years and after graduation. He also works with me at Chautauqua Institution.

Hap Hazard

Hap Hazard started at WJTN about the same time I did. He won innumerable awards for his newscasts over his 40 years with us. Aside from his professionalism and wide-ranging knowledge, we all especially enjoyed his quick wit and sense of humor.

Kathy Roselle, my wife, started working as the AM Traffic Manager at WJTN in 1971 and continued in that position until 2004. "I'll be forever blessed that Si Goldman hired Kathy," Jim says today. "That might have been the best move he ever made, as far as I'm concerned," he adds with a wink and a smile.

Kathy has her own explanation of the longevity of so many employees. "It just feels like home here. We all wanted it to succeed and we were proud of what we were doing. We were pleased with the events we could be a part of." More than 40 years later, long after Kathy stopped working for WJTN, she says it still feels that way every time she enters the building.

The WJTN Dew Drop Inn can drop in anywhere Jim finds an air-worthy event or personality he can get his microphone to. He can always be found at the right place at the right time.

Chapter 12

Sports

Sports, athletic games and competitions, have apparently been a nearly universal passion throughout human history. Some say sporting events are merely the instinctive territoriality of war reduced to a game that crowns winners and lets the losers walk away to fight another day, a pastime where enemies remain friends. Jim has had a lifelong fascination and personal connection to sports. He understands athletes and admires their competitive spirit, especially when it coexists with strong community spirit.

The one thing I would hope would go on my tombstone is, 'I made my parents proud.' I've spent my life following my passion.
Roger Goodell

I always talk to kids. Sometimes hearing it from a different voice helps.
Clark 'Special K' Kellogg

Roger Goodell
NFL Commissioner, Grown Up Now

Jim Roselle has always been a sports fan, as a player, a spectator and a broadcaster. He knows the players, the statistics, the rules of the games and, usually, the odds on the best matchups.

Jim's first play-by-play broadcast was hometown high school football. He broadcast bowling scores, won foul shooting contests, earned a city-wide ping-pong championship, and has been a life-long, avid golfer. He loves sports

Most of all, though, Jim is a fan of good sportsmanship, fair play and the character building power of sports for young players. In his interview with National Football League Commissioner, Roger Goodell, Jim probes his feelings on player character and ethics.

Jim came to know Goodell when Roger was a high school student who swept up around Jim's Chautauqua Institution broadcast studio every morning and brought him his morning Cup of Happiness. This interview became as much a reunion of old friends as a radio interview.

National Football League players are remarkably muscular, extraordinarily agile and totally intimidating physically. Today's average NFL player weighs in at nearly 250 pounds and three from the 2012 season tipped the scales at 350.

Jim Roselle is not quite so fearsome an athlete, with the heft of a mere 9-stone – that's just a little south of 130 pounds – but he once earned the distinction of losing a college football game, as quarterback, to one of America's greatest athletes by just a few paltry touchdowns.

Jim Remembers...The Shot Heard 'Round the World

At St. Lawrence University we had a touch football league. You had to touch the guy with two hands to down the ball. No tackling allowed.

Believe it or not, this little Sicilian boy was quarterback for the St. Lawrence University, Sigma Pi Fraternity football team. We were going to play the dorm team on one day. We got to the field, and here came this team and their quarterback. He was six feet and two inches of muscle. I watched them warm up for the game. He was hurling that pigskin 40 yards. I was barely making 15.

So we played the game, and we got whipped 35 to zip. That game was in my senior year, 1949.

That quarterback, a multi-sport, athletic threat, had also been playing baseball while he was at St. Lawrence, but not for the university. He had been playing for the Jersey City Giants, a farm club for the New York Giants.

Now, fast forward two years. It's 1951. By then that fellow had graduated and moved up from the Jersey City farm club to the big league team. The Giants are playing the Brooklyn Dodgers in a one-game playoff to determine who would go to the World Series that year.

Baseball fans who can look back that far will remember this game very well. In the bottom of the ninth, the Giants were losing 3 to 1. That's when that touch football quarterback, a guy named Bobby Thompson, lofted the home run ball that won it all for the Giants.

It was called "The Shot Heard 'Round the World" and Bobby Thompson was "The Man".

A Conversation with NFL Commissioner Roger Goodell

Jim Roselle: Good morning Roger. Have you always had a love of football? I hear you always wanted to be in the NFL organization.

Roger Goodell: It was a passion I had, along with a great admiration for Pete Rozelle who was then Commissioner. I just wanted to work for him. When people ask if I really dreamed of being a Commissioner, I say, "I did." At first, I was just happy being part of the NFL and moving toward my goal. It's been a great story for me and a great opportunity.

JR: I brought this book by Michael MacCambridge just because of the title, *America's Game: The Epic Story of How Pro Football Captured a Nation* [Anchor Books, 2005]. I have grown up with the saying that baseball is the national pastime, Roger. Can they claim that today?

RG: We call football America's Game. The title of the book is actually fitting. I don't really spend a lot of time focusing on the other sports, though I'm a huge fan of all sports. I think that football has never been more successful or popular. I have often said to our owners, though, that there are two things we have to do: avoid complacency and not assume our success is going to continue.

What made this game great is the people who built it and who contributed so much to it. We have to continue to make the right decisions, continue to recognize where we came from and keep our eye on the great things that we have ahead of us.

JR: From a marketing standpoint, you have done an outstanding job. The NFL is such a remarkable brand name today. Where do you go from this point?

RG: I always say we can get better. We can go from good to great. Good is the issue that people have to overcome to get better.

Good is not good enough, in my opinion. I think we can be great. The NFL can continue to expand its horizons, not only here domestically but also internationally in a way that will make America's Game popular around the world.

JR: Are you looking at foreign teams?

RG: We had a foreign league. We had six teams over in Europe and it was not as successful as we'd wanted because it wasn't the real NFL. Last year [2007] we put a game in London. It was a regular season game between the Miami Dolphins and the New York Giants. It sold out 92,000 seats. They said we could have sold the stadium out 10 different times.

It was that popular so we're going back again [2008] with the Chargers and the Saints. We sold 45,000 tickets in 30 minutes. There is obviously a great deal of interest. It is certainly something that we will look at, at some point.

[The NFL Europe football league operated in Europe between 1991 and 2007. As of spring, 2014, however, Commissioner Goodell had not promoted the idea of a Super Bowl crossing the Atlantic or the return of the league to continental Europe. Wembley Stadium in London has hosted games every year since. In 2014, three NFL games are slated to be played at Wembley, one each in September, October and November.]

JR: There's a historic game that really put the NFL on the map and made America aware of pro football. I bet you can tell me the game I'm talking about.

RG: That was the Giants and the Colts, the September 28, 1958, championship game. It was a key moment in the history of the NFL. I think it vaulted professional football to another level.

JR: There were 45 million television viewers for that game! That game had everything. It even had a little bit of violence in it. Did America go for the brutality of the game?

RG: I don't think so. That 1958 championship game was so exciting - similar to what we see in Super Bowls today – you just can't script something like that. It's the ultimate reality TV. It's great athletes, it's the strategies, it's the physical contact. I think there are so many things that attract people to football and that's what makes it great. NFL Super Bowl games have been some of the most watched TV programs in history.

JR: What do you do when you realize some players with great talent aren't giving football the best image possible? And you know what I mean by that.

RG: I do, and it's a big issue for me. It is clear so many of our players are doing great things in their communities. I am so proud of what they do. Young men coming out of college are contributing back into their communities in ways that make me very proud.

I think, in the end, you have a few guys who do things that I am not proud of, things that don't reflect well on the NFL. That gets a lot of media attention, and rightly so. That's not to blame the media, though. That's just the world we live in now.

We have to understand our responsibilities. So I preach to our players, "Understand that you have a responsibility when you come into the league. It's a privilege to play here. It's not a right. While you're here, represent the league in a positive way. If you make mistakes you better learn from the mistakes."

I spend an awful lot of time talking to the guys about repeat offenders. Those are the guys who get most of the headlines. They don't seem to be learning. If they can't do it properly, then they will have to play somewhere else.

JR: There's a rule regarding the use of drugs. Is there testing for drugs?

RG: We have an in-depth testing program that tests all of our players for performance-enhancing drugs - steroids in particular - but other forms of performance-enhancing drugs, too. We also test for street drugs. It's a very, very in-depth program.

It has been widely acclaimed and it is very effective. We continue to upgrade that and have a testing program on an ongoing basis to make sure that we stay up with technology. It has been quite effective.

JR: As a fan there is one rule I would like changed.

RG: Okay Jim. We will let you be Commissioner for the next 15 minutes.

JR: Well, thank you Roger. I don't like sudden death. In overtime I don't like the flip of a coin to say who gets possession of the ball and who could win it on that possession. I think there ought to be a time period in which both teams have an opportunity.

RG: I do understand that. I don't believe the coin flip does determine it, though. When you go into a game, your job is to win the game in regulation. And if you know that you may not get the ball because of the coin flip, you will do everything you can to win the game in regulation, which is what their job is.

I think it makes the end of our regulation game time more exciting. Our statistics show that it is roughly 50-50 whether the team to get the ball in sudden death scores first or not. But that is an issue we hear from a lot of fans and we will continue to evaluate it.

JR: You know what Sunday afternoon football did to America. Did you ever believe Monday Night Football would be one of the top-rated shows in television?

RG: I did, just because I'm such a passionate football fan. But I don't think many people expected that it would continue on as many years as it has and at the kind of levels that it has. We are very proud of that franchise and we think it has been a great thing for football.

JR: Well, to wrap this up, Roger Goodell, I know you have a love affair with your hometown and you have a love affair with Chautauqua. What do they mean to you?

RG: As you know, we spent our childhood here. We spent every summer at Chautauqua, and there is no better place in the world. I consider it home and I always talk about that when somebody asks me where I come from. I talk about the Chautauqua-Jamestown region.

It had such a profound influence on me and my brothers and my family. We like to talk about our cousins and our friends from Chautauqua. We still stay in touch. It's just a unique and wonderful place.

JR: Roger Goodell, I thank you. Let's give him a nice round of applause.

Clark Kellogg
The March Madness Man

Clark "Special K" Kellogg grew up in the city of East Cleveland, Ohio. In high school he scored 51 points in one single, state final basketball game, a record that still stands for all Ohio high schools.

In 1996, Clark earned his marketing degree from Ohio State University and after graduation he starred in the National Basketball Association. In 2010, Ohio Governor Ted Strickland appointed Kellogg to the board of trustees of Ohio State. He is currently the vice president of player relations for the Indiana Pacers. Kellogg is also the lead college basketball analyst for *CBS TV Sports*.

Jim and Clark Kellogg on the air

In talking with Clark Kellogg, Jim learned they had both converted a physical disability from a stumbling block into a stepping stone. Clark's disability came during his professional playing career. Jim's, on the other hand, had been his since birth. Clark and Jim, however, had both discovered that limitations are merely opportunities in disguise.

Clark Kellogg's professional life revolves around basketball, but he and Jim are both passionate fans of all sports. Jim has been an avid golfer all his life, so it was not surprising when the conversation turned from basketball to golf. It's a game in which Jim holds a unique distinction which few people, professional or amateur, may ever achieve… or even challenge.

Jim Remembers… My 6-Mile Golf Hole

My career began in sportscasting because I was a passionate fan of everything in sports. Few people, however, can claim a feat in any game as remarkable as the 6-Mile Golf Hole, tee-to-green, that I played with Pete Hubble, WJTN's Sports Director, one warm and sunny day in July way back in the early days of my career.

It was probably the longest hole ever played anywhere – certainly in Chautauqua County – with an awful lot of roughs and hazards on the way to the cup. We were only using putters, but we played through all the way.

Play on the first (and last) hole – the single hole in play – in that marathon match – we billed as Goofy Golf – lasted seven hours. At that pace, a regulation 18 holes would have taken more than two weeks to fill up a scorecard.

The idea for our head-to-head matchup was hatched, like so many other great plans, over a couple of cups of coffee one morning. We were at the radio station. We were just talking about golf. "Why don't you tee off right here," somebody said. "We can end up at Maplehurst Country Club." Wacky memories like that are probably among the many reasons I still call my morning cup of steaming Joe, "A Cup of Happiness."

We teed off at the door of my WJTN broadcast studio in the Hotel Jamestown and putted our way to the elevator, down one floor and out to the hotel lobby, then down the staircase and outside onto West 3rd Street. The "green" was still a mile and a half of sidewalks, streets and storefronts ahead of us, and just then we were also 100 feet above the Erie Lackawanna railroad tracks on the Third Street bridge. Eventually, we reached Fairmount Avenue which stretched far out of town and into the countryside.

Two golfers and a caddy

Fans, spectators and gawkers clicked off snapshots and rolled home movie film while we putted our way along Fairmount. We were accompanied by a police escort ordered out especially for the day by Police Chief John Palladino. About four miles west on Fairmount, we putted onto Big Tree Road in Lakewood. The last half-mile finally took us from the concrete and asphalt hazards and the front lawn roughs onto a well kept green with a cup and a flag at Maplehurst.

By club regulation, we had to borrow caddies there to carry our one-club bags until we finally putted into the hole.

After that hard-fought match Pete Hubble admitted, "We had hit a few cars and lost about 24 golf balls in the fields, but we had a lot of fun."

Our game had lasted seven hours, but it could have gone faster if we hadn't stopped a few times along the "course" for some refreshments and a few words with spectators.

We declared that day – as it's been done on every course since the game was played on Scotland's old course at St Andrews way back in the 16th Century – the player who holed his ball in the fewest strokes: The Winner.

The final score card showed Hubble at 196 and me at 228. Par had never been set for our specific course, naturally, but I had to admit Hubble won. On the other hand, I could always claim he only came in "next to last." I, meanwhile, had putted my way all the way up to second place!

I was amazed they let us do it, but we had a lot of people along the way who cheered us on. That is what radio was about in those days. "A little creativity made it much better than just taking a microphone someplace to do a show."

That 6-Mile Golf Hole was a milestone in my early career.

A Conversation with Clark Kellogg

Jim Roselle: It's a privilege to have you as a guest on our broadcast. We've seen you for many years on TV analyzing those March Madness games.

Clark Kellogg: I prepare for that all basketball season long. Basically, adrenaline keeps me going during those three weeks in March. We're on the air of an awful lot. As a matter fact, my wife and kids get tired of seeing me from that box. They would much rather have me under the roof with them, on occasion, in March. But we manage to deal with it.

"Ability may get you to the top, but it takes character to keep you there."

– John Wooden

JR: Through all of the analysis, have you picked the winners at times?

CK: I've had some winners, though probably only about 50/50. I like to think I've been better, but that's a pretty good record, considering that it's actually hard to predict sports outcomes.

JR: You have a fabulous resume in the world basketball. Ohio State All-American, Indiana Pacers' rookie of the year and more. Great honors have come your way. You left basketball long before you wanted to.

CK: Knee injuries forced me to cut my playing career short. My left knee was kind of bad. I was 26 years old but the doctors told me my knee looked like it should belong to a much older person. That doesn't work for NBA basketball. It was disheartening, disappointing, but I got a chance to stay involved in the game as a broadcaster. I didn't necessarily plan on that happening but as God unfolded that opportunity, I've stepped into it. By now, I've been talking about college and pro-basketball for over two decades and they can't seem to get rid of me. I'm going to try to hang around for a while.

JR: Somebody told me to ask you what your golf handicap is.

CK: (laughing) I am floating right around 11 or 12 right now. I feel like I am headed in a real good direction this season. Once I get to start playing, that is. I've only played four times so far this summer.

JR: Can you play in the celebrity tournaments?

CK: On occasion. Three, four, and five a year is typically what I do during the off-season.

JR: I have to ask, what has Tiger Woods done for golf and sports? [This conversation predated Woods' well publicized personal problems.]

CK: I don't even know if I can quantify it. When you consider his success, the types of fans, younger fans, minority fans whom he has been able to touch and impact by how he plays. It's not only what he does, but how he goes about it. His determination, his focus and all the things that you want to see in somebody who enjoys success. He has been able to reach a point that very few athletes have been able to reach. Especially in the game of golf, which in many cases has had limited access in urban areas for minority populations. It's great to see the kind of fans who come out now and the programs that have been started through his foundation. There's his First Tee [Junior Golf Program Teaching Life Skills], for instance. He tries to make golf more accessible so kids can gain valuable lessons through participation in golf.

JR: People sometimes say he's from a different planet. But is winning everything? Is it winning or else?

CK: It shouldn't be, and I don't think it is. Clearly, in our culture, you would get that impression. That's one of the things that concerns and disturbs me in sports. There's too much emphasis on winning instead of developing and growing through participation in sports.

JR: Well, what about the fact that if you are not a winning coach you lose your job? You could be the greatest teacher.

CK: I agree whole heartedly. The business aspect is so enamored with winning that the teaching and development of young people is sometimes not enough for men and women to keep their jobs. The stakes are that high.

JR: Are parents putting too much pressure on their kids?

CK: It's one of the most disheartening things I see, and not just in athletics. It could be in the arts or any extracurricular or academic topic. Some of it is our cultural push to accelerate development and to be over concerned about winning.

There's nothing as challenging and encouraging as exposing kids to different things so they get a handle on what their giftedness and passions are. The focus can't be solely on the end result. It has to be on the development. That's what sports can do when it's done right.

JR: Did you ever think there would be this kind of money in sports?

CK: I am blown away. It is mind-boggling. The salaries in professional sports, football, basketball and major league baseball are a function of the TV rights and the fees they pay. Advertisers want to take advantage of the eyeballs that are attracted to sports, and that's how the circle works.

JR: What about drugs in the world of sports?

CK: It's disheartening. It speaks to the integrity of both the games and the individuals playing in the games. And it goes back to the point you made earlier about winning at all costs. Folks feel they need to do illegal things that are damaging to their body to gain some competitive advantage. Drug and alcohol abuse permeates our society and destroys lives, families and communities.

JR: Just where has sports made its biggest impact in our culture?

CK: Sports is an area where those who participate, as a player, coach, referee, umpire or official, learn the inherent values in sports that lead to being productive and successful in other areas. The teamwork, the discipline, the adversity you work through, are all part of what we go through in life.

Sports has a way of crystallizing that. That's where sports have impacted our culture, especially in the enjoyment aspect of it. There is a benefit to what I call "Splenda moments," those sweeteners that God gives us in life. Sports is one of those things.

JR: You seem to talk a lot about God.

CK: My personal relationship with God, through Christ, is the driving force and foundation of my life. I became a Christian in 1986, and that, to me, is really who I am and what I am about. God created us to know Him and honor and worship Him. We are created in His image and that, to me, is foundational to all that I am. That's the starting point and that will be the end as well at some point.

JR: That's a very good note to end on, Clark Kellogg. Let's give Clark a nice round of applause.

CK: Thank you much, Jim. I appreciate it.

Jim McCusker
Hometown Gridiron Great

James Brian "Jim" McCusker is a Jamestown native and former professional football defensive tackle. He played in the National Football League for five years and in the American Football League for one year. In the NFL draft, Jim was a second round draft pick to play for the Chicago Cardinals in 1958, after graduation from the University of Pittsburgh.

Jim played for the Philadelphia Eagles from 1959 to 1962, and 1960 was a banner season. That year he started in every game and helped the Eagles beat the Green Bay Packers 17 to 13 in the NFL championship game. He then played for the Cleveland Browns in 1963 and for the New York Jets in the American Football League in 1964. In his six years of professional football, Jim played in 83 games and started in 26. He also retrieved the football for his team with four recovered fumbles during his career.

During his NFL years with the Eagles, Jim played with a number of Hall of Famers, including Chuck Bednarik, Sonny Jurgensen, Norm Van Brocklin and Tommy McDonald. During his single season with the Cleveland Browns, Jim played with all-time great, Jim Brown.

McCusker was inducted into the Chautauqua Sports Hall of Fame, headquartered in his hometown of Jamestown, New York, in 1982.

Jim with Jim McCusker

In retirement, Jim returned to his hometown where, with his wife Mary, he now owns a popular, downtown restaurant and bar called "The Pub".

Jim Roselle and his co-host, Russ Diethrick, along with their friend, Randy Anderson, president of the Chautauqua Sports Hall of Fame, welcomed Jim and Mary McCusker to *The Times of Your Life*.

A Conversation with Jim McCusker

Jim Roselle: Good morning, Russ Diethrick.
Russ Diethrick: Good morning, Jim Roselle. It's great to meet you here at the Super Bowl.

JR: Well, we feel super about the fact that we've got a super guy who's coming along here soon for a great conversation. This is a moment for us on *The Times of Your Life* to talk about a fabulous career and a great guy, a great citizen of our community, Jim McCusker. Do I introduce you, Jim, as Jim McCusker of the National and American Football Leagues (NFL and AFL) or as Jim McCusker of The Pub?

Jim McCusker: Just call me Jim McCusker.

JR: Randy Anderson, let me first thank you for making the arrangements for this interview.

Randy Anderson: You're welcome Jim. I want to thank Jim McCusker and his wife Mary for being a part of this.

JR: Jim McCusker, you hold what everybody aims for in professional football, a championship ring from a championship game. But we want to go back, don't we Russ, to the very beginning of your interest in the game of football. When did that start?

JMcC: I wanted to play right from the time I was at Washington Junior High School here in Jamestown. I had a great coach, Harold Rumans. I started playing there and then moved on to the high school. I loved the game and was not about to quit.

RD: Who are some of the other fellows you played with in high school?

JMcC: There was Roger Bartleson, a lineman; Dickie Pollino, Al Marucci, Buddy Bender, and quite a few others.

JR: When did the idea occur to you that you might be able to get a football scholarship?

JMcC: That came to me in my senior year in high school when the colleges started contacting me.

JR: Were you considering any other possibilities besides Pittsburgh?

JMcC: Sure. There was Syracuse and most all of the colleges you could think of. They contacted me and wanted me to come out to see them.

JR: Did you agonize over one school or the other, or did you immediately know?

JMcC: I didn't really agonize over it. I talked to my dad, mainly, and set my mind on the University of Pittsburgh. My sister followed me to Pittsburgh, by the way. She went to nursing school there. I'm glad I made my decision.

JR: What is the difference between wearing a football uniform at the high school level and at the college level?

JMcC: Everything is expanded in college. Anything from the number of players, to where you eat, to the different cities you go to, to the restaurants. It all expands.

RA: Back to your high school career. Who was Jamestown high school playing in those days? I assume it wasn't the suburban Buffalo schools, like we are playing these days.

JMcC: We played Elmira, New York, and we did play a couple of Buffalo teams, maybe Kenmore and Niagara Falls.

JR: Did Jamestown have a winning or undefeated season when you are playing?

JMcC: We were not undefeated but we had a very good team. We had our nemesis, too. That was Warren, Pennsylvania. I can't believe we don't play them anymore. No matter who else had a good team, we had to really worry about them. Warren always got up for that game.

JR: In your first year at the University of Pittsburg, what was it like to meet other ballplayers coming from all parts of the country?

JMcC: You're just a pea in the pod. All of a sudden, you are in an army and you don't know anybody, but it evens itself out. Your friends at first are the other freshmen. It's no different from anyone else who goes into college. You just keep working along. Sometimes you just have to let them know who you are (all laugh).

RA: You've got to establish your territory quickly. How long did it take you become comfortable that you could play at that level?

JMcC: I was comfortable by the end of my freshman season. In my second year, I had to go out and go after the position, which I did. I became a starter in my sophomore year.

RA: Did you play both sides of the ball in high school and college?

JMcC: Yes I did. I wouldn't like to not play both sides.

JR: Our guest is Jim McCusker, who started as an offensive lineman at Jamestown high school, named a Western New York high school All-Star two times, went on to the University of Pittsburgh, considered one of the Panthers greatest linemen, named on the Associated Press All-Star team three times and a United International All-Star twice. You played in the East-West Shrine game, which was the college All-Stars Senior bowl, against the champion Detroit Lions. What's it like to know you're going to play against the pros as a college player?

JMcC: We were completely hyped up. We wanted to beat them. That's all that was on our mind. We didn't care how we did it, we just wanted to win. We had to get the points on the board.

JR: What was the final score in that game?

JMcC: (Laughing) I don't remember, but the main thing is that we won.

JR: You beat the Lions! That doesn't happen often. And eventually, you went on to play for seven years in the NFL.

RD: What was it like when you stepped out on the field for the very first NFL game and looked into the stands around you?

JMcC: Nervous. I wanted to head back to the bathroom, and you know what I'm talking about. I wanted to be sure my uniform was on straight and right side out, too.

RD: But after that first snap, that was it, wasn't it?

JMcC: Right. Once I got into the game my mind was focused.

RA: You were drafted by the Chicago Cardinals right out of Pitt. How did you feel about being selected by the Cardinals?

JMcC: To be truthful, I didn't want to be with the Cardinals, but I could not help that. I would rather have been with the Steelers.

JR: We hear about the big money in football today, Jim. What kind of a signing bonus did you get from the Cardinals?

JMcC: I signed for $8500. (All laugh) And that was tops. That was good money. They also gave me a $5000 bonus just to make sure I didn't go to Canada. A lot of the guys are going to Canada in those days.

RD: What was your first autograph request in the NFL like?

JMcC: It was great. It was some little guy, and not too many girls.

RA: You played one year in Chicago and then you got traded to Philadelphia. Were you pleased to be traded to Philadelphia?

JMcC: Yes I was, without question. We weren't going anywhere as a team in Chicago. Actually, what happened there was that the Chicago coach left, and they brought in this fellow from the Canadian League. He had been a big gun up there. He and I just never got along. He dug into me one too many times. We had words a number of times and luckily I got traded to Philadelphia.

JR: How many years did you stay in Philadelphia?

JMcC: Five years.

JR: 1960 was your championship year.

JMcC: After the head coach of the Eagles retired, they promoted Nick Skorich from line coach to head coach. That put unbelievable pressure on him. If you are not winning, which was the case at that time, things got worse and worse. One day he called me into his office and wanted me to tell him what was wrong. So, I told him what was wrong: it was him. I told him it was his attitude, he tore people apart on the field and he did it during the game. I said, "These guys aren't going to take this stuff, so consequently they are not playing for you." He did not want to hear that so I got traded to Cleveland.

RA: I'm starting to see a pattern here, Jim.

JMcC: Well, you know, I'm Irish. What can you do?

JR: What was the highest salary you received during your years in the NFL?

JMcC: $22,500, and I had been on a championship team that had done very well.

JR: At that time, did that seem like a big paycheck?

JMcC: No it did not, not at all. But I loved the game and I loved playing in the NFL and naturally the notoriety was an ego thing. It was a good living back then, though.

JR: Now we have to go back to that day, December 26 in 1960. You were playing the heavily favored Green Bay Packers. What was the pep talk like by your head coach in the dressing room prior to going on the field?

JMcC: If you knew Buck Shaw, you know he never would swear and he would never raised his voice. It was always, "Son of a buck, you guys!" (All laugh) He said, "Son of a buck, you guys, we're up against these guys." That would be his last word as we were going out the door. You could not have found a better coach or gentleman.

JR: At half-time in that game, the Eagles were trailing 13 to 0. Norm Van Brocklin rallied the team in the final quarter, highlighted by a 5 yard touchdown run by Ted Dean with only 5 minutes and 20 seconds remaining. It's a storybook ending. What was that play called in the huddle?

JMcC: I don't remember the numbers, but I sure knew where the play was going. I can still tell you that.

JR: What was your assignment on that play?

JMcC: Most of the time I was playing against a defensive end named Bill Quinlan, a very good defensive back. Fuzzy Thurston was on the inside, the defensive tackle. We were up against two very good guys, but, you know, statues fall. So we blew them out and we went in.

JR: I think I have a description of the play where Ted Dean scored. It says right here that he was a rookie and he had grown up in Philadelphia. You said that you ran a play around your end. Then you said: "I hit the defensive end, threw him off balance, and Billy Ray Barnes finished him off." The crowd must've gone wild after that touchdown.

JMcC: They sure did. We had a great crowd. Philadelphia has tremendous fans.

JR: To finish the story of that particular play, after Billy Ray Barnes took care of that defensive end, you had to proceed and pick up the middle linebacker, one of the great players of the day for the Green Bay Packers, and you had to put him out of action. That was Ray Nitschke.

JMcC: If you are an NFL player, you have heard of Ray Nitschke. He's a very good friend, too. It's too bad I can't tell you what he said. (All laugh)

RA: I bet it wasn't, "Son of a buck."

JR: What was it like to get a championship ring and put it on your hand?

JMcC: It was terrific. It was the epitome of what I was doing. There's nothing even close to it.

JR: When did the decision come about that you were going to leave football?

JMcC: I went from Philadelphia to Cleveland and then to the New York Jets. I just decided that was enough. I didn't really see the Jets going anywhere, though that's exactly what happened. I decided that enough was enough. I had played my seven years and I just didn't feel like going back and just playing for eight or 10 years.

JR: When did you decide to come back home?

JMcC: When I decided I was through, I wondered what I wanted to do next. I decided to come back to Jamestown and open up this pub and see how it would go in the Jamestown area. So I came back to do what I have done. I wanted it on Main Street amongst the three big banks. I wanted walk-in traffic. It all worked out and it's been a great ride.

JR: You had visited many restaurants in Philadelphia, hadn't you? You said one or two of them impressed you with the way they designed their places and with the atmosphere they created. You brought back that kind of atmosphere to The Pub.

JMcC: That's exactly right. I wanted a narrow dimension, not a big, wide room. I had an idea for the shape of the bar and the steam table and all that sort of thing.

RA: You opened that in 1965 and here we are more than 45 years later. Did you ever think you would be in it this long, Jim?

JMcC: No, I would never have thought that when I started. I just wanted it to be successful, that's all. I didn't know how long it would be there.

JR: We have a beautiful young lady sitting in the other room. Her name is Mary McCusker. So, put football aside for a moment, and let's talk romance here. (All laugh) Where did you meet Mary?

JMcC: Right here in Jamestown. Her father, at the time, owned the building that I put The Pub in. I saw her getting out of a car one day, and I said, "Who is that?" Somebody said, "That's Mary," and that was the start.

JR: Well, we are delighted to have her here. We all know Mary very well, and what a good cook she is, and we enjoy going there as often as possible to enjoy her wonderful sauce with all the meals.

JR: Back to football. The game is being criticized today for its violence, for those head-on tackles and those line drive hits with a helmet used as a weapon.

JMcC: It has always been there and it is always going to be there. Suppose the other team gets ahead of you and now you're lined up for the kickoff. You're madder than hell. You were ahead the whole game and now maybe you've got 10 minutes left, so you pick on whatever guy you are supposed to get. You don't block him. You run right through him. That's what happens. More than one time I did that. The collisions are there, that's a part of the game itself. I don't know how to answer any other way. Wilson came out with a different helmet, a rubber helmet that's all rubber on the inside. It was hard to understand each other and the play calls because the sound was very muffled, so it didn't go over very well.

JR: I'd like to go back to that championship game. I have a note here that on Green Bay's final drive, Bart Starr threw a pass over the middle to Jim Taylor who was wrapped up by the middle linebacker, Chuck Bednarik, another future Eagles Hall of Famer, on the 9 yard line. With that tackle, the championship belonged to the Eagles. You and your teammates earned $5800 for that victory. Did that check seem big to you?

JMcC: I'm sure it did!

JR: You played with a great quarterback, Norm Van Brocklin. When you look at the roster of quarterbacks today, who do you admire today for the way he plays the game?

JMcC: The first thing I want to tell you is that the quarterback really is the difference. As far as I'm concerned, as a line man, the offensive tackle, I had to take care of that guy. Sonny Jurgensen was a great passer but he just didn't have the generalship. Being the general, taking charge of the team, is what's important. As for the guys today, I don't know.

JR: [Jim asks to have the microphone moved a little bit closer to Mary] Mary, please talk to us for just a moment. Good morning.

Mary McCusker: Good morning.

JR: Just give us a thought or two about being married to an NFL champion football player.

MMcC: Well, I never think of him as that. (All laugh) He's been great, but that has nothing to do with it.

JR: But isn't it wonderful to realize how proud the town is of your husband?

MMcC: Absolutely! I'm pretty proud of him myself.

JMcC: Wow! I don't hear that very often. (All laugh even longer and louder)

JR: Well, if you would remember how many years you were married, that might help.

MMcC: That's right! [Mary turns to her husband and shakes her finger] 35 years, Mister. (Laughing continues) You better remember that, McCusker. It's going to be a long ride home.

RD: That's beginning to sound like a halftime talk.

JR: I guess it is going to be a long ride home.

MMcC: You got that right.

JR: Jim McCusker, thank you so much.

JMcC: I enjoyed it very much.

JR: We will see you at The Pub.

JMcC: Okay, partner.

JR: Thanks to Randy Anderson and my good friend, Russ Diethrick. This is *The Times of Your Life*.

Sharon Robinson
Jackie's Daughter – Dad's lessons

Jackie Robinson

Sharon Robinson's father was the baseball legend, Jack Roosevelt "Jackie" Robinson, the first African-American to break the baseball color line, ending racial segregation in Major League Baseball. His major league playing debut was on April 15, 1947, with the Brooklyn Dodgers.

Sharon is now vice chairman of the Jackie Robinson Foundation and the educational consultant for Major League Baseball (MLB). Sharon is also an acclaimed author and now manages *Breaking Barriers:*

In Sports, In Life. The program is a baseball-themed character education curriculum distributed nationally to help empower students to face life's challenges. In its first 17 years, it has reached more than 22 million students and nearly 3 million educators.

Sharon Robinson has said, "Inspired by the high expectations and stellar examples of my heroes and "sheroes", I strive for excellence as an educator, writer, and parent."

Sharon Robinson has dedicated her career to her father's philosophy of life

Before signing on with MLB, Sharon's 20-year career as a nurse-midwife and educator gave her a deep understanding and appreciation of the value of making a child's early years a springboard to a successful life.

Jim's love of baseball and the Jamestown Boys Club came together one day when he and his friends got to witness one of baseball's most memorable events. In the pantheon of great moments in baseball, it probably does not quite equal Jackie Robinson's first day on a major league baseball diamond, but perhaps it does rate in the top 10.

Jim Remembers… The End of Joe DiMaggio's Hitting Streak

The story starts at the Boys Club. We had Friday night movies in those days, and the kids sat around on the gym floor to watch.

When the Club opened in 1939, Mr. Clemments, the club director, got a few of us together.
"How would you boys like to run a candy stand on Friday nights? You can sell candy before the movie."
"Okay!"
"So here's what you do. You go down to Jacobson's store and buy the candy. Buy what you think you need." We bought Baby Ruths, Butterfingers, Mallow Cups, Snickers or whatever the popular bars of the day were. So there we were, selling candy bars on Friday nights.

After so many Friday nights - I don't know how many anymore - Mr. Clemments came to our meeting - we called ourselves the JBC Club inside the Boys Club, it stood for Justice, Behavior and Courtesy - and he said, "You boys have made a neat profit. You've got a little pot of money here. What would you like to do with it?"

The other guys spoke up quickly. They said, "Can we go to a ballgame, a major-league game?" Mr. Clemments found out that they were Yankee fans; I was the only Giants fan. He looked at the schedule to see when the Yankees would come to Cleveland, because that's the closest city that would be possible for us to get to. We couldn't go all the way to New York City, naturally.

He promised to talk to the board of directors so he could arrange rides for us. Some of the board would have to be willing to use their cars. We thought that would be wonderful. Later, he came back and said, "Well, boys, we've got enough cars and the game that you want to see. The Yankees will play against Cleveland on July 21. We'll see a ballgame and the Yankees."

He even thought maybe there was a possibility that before game time we could go talk to the players in the dugout. We were all excited, naturally. There were four or five cars and each car had three or four kids in it.

Finally we were on our way with the cars following one another. Then one of the cars got a flat tire. We all stopped to get it fixed. That lost time prevented us from going down into the dugout; it was too late and the infield practice was over. We did get good seats along the third base line, though.

That was the night that Joe DiMaggio's hitting streak of 56 games stopped while the largest crowd of the 1941 baseball season – nearly 68,000 people in Municipal Stadium – looked on.

The first time DiMaggio came to bat, he hit a screamer down the third base line. Ken Keltner made a spectacular backhanded stop. He threw Joe out at first by a half a step. Joe drew a walk in his second at bat. He hit another ball to Ken Keltner in the seventh-inning, maybe not as good, but still a hard smash down the line. Keltner made another stop and got him out.

Then, the most dramatic moment came. His team had saved a last at-bat for Joe in the seventh inning. He was 0 for 3 with a fourth inning walk in the mix. In order for him to get to bat, the Yankees had to start a rally to get men on base. DiMaggio wasn't in the top three that would definitely get to bat, but they loaded the bases for Joe to come to the plate.

Sixty-eight thousand people stood up. They realized this was it. This was the moment. Will he save the streak? Or won't he? He hit a ground ball to Cleveland shortstop, Lou Boudreau. Boudreau turned it into a double play from Ray Mack at second to Lester Grimes at first. The inning was over and so were Joe's chances.

The Yankees won the game but Joe DiMaggio's streak was broken. We were there to see it.

Following that game, he hit safely in the next 15 straight games. If not for this one game, he would've had a 70-game hitting streak. The closest anybody has come since then was a 44-game hitting streak by Pete Rose. DiMaggio never bunted to get on, just trying to save it. He always hit away, and he had to wait until his last at bat of a game, sometimes. I don't think DiMaggio's record of 56 will ever be broken. Today's platoon system probably means that one has very little chance of being broken.

Less well known but just as amazing was DiMaggio's 1933 61 game hitting streak as an 18-year-old rookie with the San Francisco Seals in the Pacific Coast League.

There's one more remarkable story to follow up on that day long ago in Cleveland. It was 60 years later, in 2001, when we, the Boys Club alumni, went to another game in Cleveland with some of the current club kids. We were at the ballpark early, about 11:30. Game time was 1 o'clock, so we just sat down on a big concrete flower pot to watch the people for a while. Some of them were wearing Yankee baseball caps, others wore Indian baseball caps and almost every other kind. People were just walking around and we were just observing.

For some strange reason a guy came directly at us, right over to where we were sitting, Frank and Gabe and Sam and I. The guy just looked at us.

"Hi," we said.

"You guys ever hear of Ken Keltner?"

"Sir, what did you say?" We looked at each other.

"You guys ever hear of Ken Keltner? You know what he did?"

"Sir, you may not believe this, but we were right here. We were at that game."

We told him the story about being Boys Club members and about our trip to Cleveland.

I'll always wonder why in the world he had stopped to tell us that. It's just another example of being in the right place at the right time and meeting the right people.

A Conversation with Sharon Robinson

Jim Roselle: It was a historic moment in 1947 when Branch Rickey made the decision to take your father from Montréal and put him on the Brooklyn Dodgers team. Did your mom or your dad ever talk about that first day he walked out of the dugout, the Dodger dugout, to go on the field?

Sharon Robinson: My dad was very humble. He did not come home and talk about his feats. He didn't brag about his baseball days - neither the pain of it nor the glory of it.

It wasn't until just about when I was going to lose my dad, when we were at the World Series game in Cincinnati. Dad was pretty disabled by diabetes, and they were honoring him there for the 25th anniversary.

I just wanted to know everything. I asked him, "Dad, what was it like? Were the black people sitting or standing when you came onto the field? How did you feel?" That particular day was so important to me because it was painful to think of my dad out there on the field all by himself.

JR: I had Roy Wilkins on this program. I asked, "Mr. Wilkins, if you could put one thing into a time capsule that would be opened 100 years from today, what would you put in?" He answered, "A picture of Pee-Wee Reese with his arms around Jackie Robinson." Does that say something?

SR: The Pee Wee Reese and Jackie Robinson story is an important moment in baseball history, but more important than hugging him - and no one really knows what was said between them, Pee Wee Reese and my father don't even remember - was that someone from leadership, someone from the South who represented the "other side", stepped across and said, "I'm willing to play with you. We are teammates."

It was a pivotal moment for the Dodgers as well as for the other teams. They sent a huge message.

JR: You have said your dad never raised his voice at home. He could come home from a game totally frustrated from a game where he was separated from the whites, but he never came home in anger.

SR: It's pretty amazing. He played golf all of his life. It was the game he loved. He would say to me, "Sharon that's why I like to play golf. There I am, swinging as hard as I can, and I'm hitting a little white ball." I'd say he had ways to defuse his anger.

Also my mother talks about being on the way home from the games and talking about what went on purposely so that he wasn't bringing that home.

JR: I think you've met Jack Voelker [Director of Recreation and Youth Services for Chautauqua Institution]. You and he are here today for the Boys and Girls Club and the Young Readers, right?

SR: One of the things I love is talking with kids and adults at the same time. All my writings and all my talks are designed to stimulate discussion between kids and adults.

JR: For your dad, family was very important, wasn't it? In the final months of his life, as his diabetes and heart problems were taking their toll on his health, did he hold out hope that things would improve and he would be around for a much longer time with his family?

SR: My dad was very much a positive thinker, so he had a lot of hope, certainly. In the last few months my dad got to the point where he was essentially blind. He had partial vision in one eye. One of our last trips as a family in terms of vacation was to Jamaica. My dad's doctor had said to him, "You should have a drink." But he was very moral about this drinking and smoking thing. He just didn't do it. The doctor, however, had said, "Every night you must have one drink."

On this vacation my father just started this regimen of having one drink a night. He had us fix him vodka and orange juice. He would swallow it down quick because it was his "medicine."

He left for vacation a little bit early because he got a call from his doctor who said that they want to try a laser treatment for a detached retina, although he was only starting to go blind. He left us before the vacation was over and flew back to New York. Then we came back as a family because he was nervous about the surgery.

It was early in the development of that kind of surgery and it actually made him more blind. That was very disappointing to him because seeing was so important. He was also becoming less mobile in his legs by then. The important thing was that he got up every single day to go to work.

It was the 25th anniversary of his breaking the color barrier so there were lots of public ceremonies. The public ceremonies meant our family came together. That way he was being celebrated by baseball plus getting his family there from all over, along with very close friends, who came to acknowledge him. So he had this amazing final year.

A few days before he died we were at this World Series game. It was at a time when our family had begun spending less time together. It seemed everybody had something they had to do. But he said, "Just trust me. Come to this." So we all met and we had this wonderful weekend together.

I went back to Howard University and he called me the next morning.

"I just called to tell you I love you," he said. Apparently he made a call like that to a number of his really special people. Although my dad had always expressed his love in lots of ways, he wasn't one to send love letters. He didn't say things like "I love you" every day. That was a little unusual.

He died a couple of days later. I think he had had a kind of premonition.

JR: Was your father happy with the way Hollywood made the movie, "*The Jackie Robinson Story*"?

SR: Well, he played himself. He couldn't hate that. I think he is pretty happy with the production. That story was about the first year. My mother wanted it to go beyond the first year and show his commitment to social change after his baseball years and long after he had retired from baseball.

JR: How did your dad react to being one of the most noted people in the world? President Eisenhower had invited him to the White House, and he went to so many affairs where he met famous people.

SR: That's what I loved about him. He enjoyed it but he still remained true to himself, very committed. He was meeting presidents but he was still going to 125th St. where he got a kind of nourishment from walking the streets and hanging out. It was his neighborhood. It was home for him.

He helped to form Freedom National Bank which could bring some economic development to Harlem, a poor black community at that point. It was a struggling community with no options for getting loans to rebuild the community. My father just remained himself and he fought really hard to do that.

JR: How do you react when somebody knows you are Sharon Robinson, and you are Jackie Robinson's daughter?

SR: I am very proud. I had incredible parents and I love the way they raised us. They raised us to care about the world, social change and family. We have a legacy in the family that makes us strong. We are a family that can overcome whatever personal obstacles enter our lives. I am very proud.

My father also was very respectful of individual rights. During a period when I needed to separate from my family and find out who Sharon was, I think he respected that. He gave me the space, and for that I am very thankful.

When he moved us to Connecticut, which was isolating in many ways because it was an all-white community, we lived on six acres surrounded by woods. He did that so we could have some privacy as a family. That taught me a lot. Now, I cherish privacy, and it's why I live in the Virgin Islands part time.

I got up in time to see the sunrise this morning and it was incredible over the beautiful lake [Chautauqua Lake], but I have a sign up at my house that says, "My favorite time is just before dawn. That's the time I can be who I am before somebody tells me who I am supposed to be." I always cherish my early mornings before I come and do things like radio interviews.

JR: I could spend all morning with you, Sharon Robinson. We are thankful that your dad gave us sports fans, and gave America, so many thrills on the baseball field. I think we are learning more of what a gentleman and what a crusader and what a man he was because of his fight for dignity. We are all learning a great lesson from it, believe me.

SR: Thank you so much. Thank you for having me here at Chautauqua Institution.

One more baseball story deserves mention…

Jim Remembers… The Men's Room Interview

The Crystal Ballroom in the Hotel Jamestown once occupied the other half of the second floor, directly across the hall from WJTN.

I could open the door to leave the studio and walk right into the Crystal Ballroom. That's what made it so easy have access to all the sports stars. All I had to do was go over and get them and bring them into the studio. I was the gopher boy for News Director Max Robinson. "Go get Rocky Graziano," he would tell me. "Go get Joe Louis; go get Ezra Charles; or go get whoever else is there." Stars were frequently in Jamestown for a sports banquet or some other big event.

Jamestown was, and still is, a wonderful minor league baseball town. The original team, the Falcons, was in the PONY (Pennsylvania, Ontario and New York) League for many years. Today they are the Jamestown Jammers.

One year, Dick Williams, the manager of the Red Sox, accepted an invitation to deliver a talk at the Town Club, an exclusive, Jamestown members-only dinner club established in 1929. During his major league career Williams had played left field and third base, worked as a manager, a coach and front office consultant for Major League Baseball. He had also led his teams to three American League pennants, one National League pennant, and two triumphant World Series campaigns.

I was doing WJTN's play-by-play for the Jamestown Falcons when Williams accepted the invitation. I was not going to miss this golden opportunity to meet and interview one of baseball's greats.

A Quiet Place to Talk

When Dick Williams came to town, I grabbed my recorder and went to interview him. It was lunch hour when I got there, well before his speech. The dining room was busy and very noisy, so we decided to go to the upstairs another dining room, but that was busy too; there was a banquet going on.

"We've got to find a better spot, Dick," I said, "a spot where we can talk."
"I don't know where to go," I said. I was afraid my opportunity for a great interview was slipping away.
"Let's use the men's room," Dick said.
"Well… okay," I said, surprised. I guess I was willing to take even an oddball suggestion seriously at that point. It did not occur to me until years later that Dick might have been kidding.
So, we went to the men's room.
I put my recorder on the sink because the AC plug was there in the wall, beside the mirror. No one was in the room at the time and I started the interview.
Just then, believe it or not, Milton Battler, the manager of the Hotel Jamestown, opened the door and walked in. I was interviewing Dick Williams on tape and a moment later Milt was doing what a man's got to do right there near the sink. I was afraid my listeners would hear certain recorded sounds later on the radio that they wouldn't understand.
After he was done, I saw Milt scribbling a note. He handed it to me as he left, closing the men's room door behind him as quietly as he could.
I kept on interviewing Dick Williams. While he was answering a question, I looked at the note. It consisted of just five words: "Nobody will ever believe this."
"This story is going on the chicken and biscuit circuit with me," Dick Williams said after the interview was over. "I've just got to tell this story everywhere I go.

Chapter 13

Commenting on the World

Commentators are really interpreters. They observe people and events while they are happening and then they interpret it all for the public. They create the first traces of history yet to be written. Commentators' analyses are the stuff from which the public can create informed opinions. Uninformed or overly biased commentators are only would-be demagogues. Jim Roselle talks to commentators who have something worth saying. He establishes their believability for his listeners in simple, neighborly conversations, not by trumpeting their status or credentials. Commentators are most credible for their common humanity.

There is a future out there, if we change the way we do our politics, which could be very bright for our kids.

David R. Gergen

Parenthood offers many lessons in patience and sacrifice. But ultimately, it is a lesson in humility. The very best thing about your life is a short stage in someone else's story. And it is enough.

Michael Gerson

It is never too late to apply good sense as a corrective to stupidity.

David Ignatius

I have great faith in the intelligence of the American viewer and reader to put two and two together and come up with four.

Jim Lehrer

The scientific theory I like best is that the rings of Saturn are composed entirely of lost airline luggage.

Mark Russell

The problem with smear campaigns is that too often they work.

Mark Shields

Many people don't give a rip about politics and know as much about public affairs as they know about the topography of Pluto…We live in an anaesthetized society.

Tony Snow

David Gergen
The Presidents' Man

David Gergen worked in the White House for four presidents – Nixon, Ford, Reagan and Clinton – as an advisor, speechwriter and in other key roles. Having served in both Republican and Democratic administrations, he is a respected commentator with an objective political voice.

Gergen is currently the Professor of Public Service and Director of the Center for Public Leadership at the Harvard Kennedy School, a senior political analyst for *CNN* and was previously editor-at-large of *U.S. News and World Report*. He has landed two Peabody Awards [recognizing "distinguished and meritorious public service" by individuals, networks, and producing organizations in radio and television]. He has also been awarded 25 honorary university degrees.

Having served in the U.S. Navy for three-and-a-half years as a damage control officer on a repair ship, the USS Ajax, Gergen once wrote: "Learning to control damage, it turned out, was the best possible preparation for my coming years in the White House."

Gergen wrote the New York Times bestseller, *Eyewitness to Power: The Essence of Leadership, Nixon to Clinton* [A Touchstone Book, Simon & Schuster, 2000] about his work in the Nixon, Ford, Reagan and Clinton administrations. He describes seven vital leadership traits:

- ✓ Inner mastery
- ✓ A compelling, central purpose deeply rooted in moral values
- ✓ Ability to persuade
- ✓ A talent to work within the system
- ✓ Ability to make a sure, quick start
- ✓ Strong and prudent advisors
- ✓ A passion that can inspire others to carry out a mission.

Jim has learned that no one person is so different from another that they can't find a common bond Among their experiences, no matter the level of leadership they may one day attain or their ultimate field of endeavor.

Jim Remembers…What I had in Common with Cronkite, Reagan and Gergen

At St. Lawrence they let me do the play-by-play. That's not all I learned, but that's the kind of radio I wanted to do more than anything else.

Even skill and enthusiasm, however, weren't quite enough. The extra ingredient that's needed is creativity. If you have that, then the sky's the limit. Without it, you just go home.

It was nice to hear from David Gergen that even the great ones like Walter Cronkite and Ronald Reagan had to call on that magic ingredient early in their radio careers, too. It's just one of those little connections that I enjoy discovering in my interviews, from time to time.

A Conversation with David Gergen

Jim Roselle: A round of applause to welcome David Gergen. You've honored me by making this appearance.
David Gergen: Thank you very much. It's my privilege to be here. It's idyllic here at Chautauqua.

JR: You've been commenting on the political scene.
DG: I know. Isn't it awful?

JR: Can you tell us about something on the positive side of your experiences, maybe something more personal about the men you worked with?

DG: One of the most wonderful moments I had in government was when Walter Cronkite retired and he came in to see President Reagan for his final interview at the White House. The two of them started talking about their sportscasting days. When Cronkite was sportscasting college football games, it was all done by Western Union; you weren't at the game at all. You got the ticker tape at the studio, and you announced what was happening from that alone. You called the plays and you did all the sound effects in the studio. It had to sound like you were really watching every play.

One day when Cronkite was in the middle of a football game the ticker went dead. It was a very important game, so he started making up plays. He kept both teams within the 40 yard lines so that nothing really happened. Then finally when the ticker came up again, there'd been about two touchdowns scored and he had to really speed up the action.

It turned out the same thing had happened to Reagan. He was doing baseball and the ticker went dead so he decided to have the batter foul the ball back. Reagan had his batter hit 25 foul balls in a row before that ticker finally came back.

JR: David Gergen, let's talk about the decline of America. What are you worried about?

DG: I think we have all been enormously privileged. We grew up in a country in which we could dream our dreams, as you did, and you're here now in this idyllic setting. We had an opportunity to make of ourselves what we wanted to be, to realize our dreams, a promise that is coming true especially for women in recent years.

I must tell you though, we're in danger that the next generation will be the first generation in US history that will not live as well as their parents. That's never happened before. From 1900 through the 1960s and 1970s, every generation of children went to school, on average, two years longer than their parents. Now all of that has leveled off.

Now other countries are passing us by. We're not only falling within the international ranks, but there's a sense of real deterioration within the country and a sense that the morale of the country is down. We're dispirited; the job situation is much bleaker than it has been in years.

In the 1980s, when Reagan was president, this country created over 20 million jobs. In the 1990s when Clinton was president this country created over 20 million jobs. You know how many net new jobs we've had in the last decade? Zero! Over the last three years [through 2008], all the net new jobs have been part-time and they pay on average only $19,000 per year. People can't make it with that kind of income. I believe that has a lot to do, not with the American people losing their drive, but with our politics. It is becoming broken down and not unleashing the innovative spirit of the country.

JR: How do unemployment and money come into play in electing or re-electing a president?

DG: The higher the unemployment number, obviously, the smaller the chance. But campaign contributions are important too…A billion dollars is not unheard of.

JR: Did you ever dream that kind of money would be involved in the political processes of this country?

DG: No, but there's been a gradual escalation. We've been in a spending arms race by candidates. Obama raised $750 million last time around, which was eye popping. Frankly, I thought they made a mistake by announcing a goal of one billion dollars. In hard times, it sounded almost obscene to raise that much for a campaign.

JR: Are you concerned about the recent Supreme Court Citizens United decision that says money is freedom of expression?

DG: Well, I know there are those who are deeply concerned about it. Labor unions can pour in a ton of money, and a ton of activity which amounts to money, into Democratic or Republican campaigns. To say that corporations can't spend while unions can, I think there's a certain lack of balance in that. The critical element is to make sure whatever is spent is publically identified, that there is transparency in the system so everybody knows who's bought. Both sides are engaging in interest group politics: You produce the money and we'll produce the benefits. There's a sort of an exchange that goes on; it's informal, but everybody knows what's going on.

JR: You were a speech writer for Richard Nixon. You said he had leadership qualities. You also said he had some demons.

DG: Carl Jung made the argument that we all have bright sides, the same things Lincoln called the "better angels in our nature." We also have dark sides. The struggle in life, in becoming a full human being, is to deal with your dark side; to understand, to come to grips with and master those things, the temptations, the anger or whatever it may be that one has on the dark side. If you don't get hold of that in politics, or in any leadership position—any CEO or any church leader has the same issue, whether you run a church or a synagogue—you need to deal with and address your dark side and have it under control.

In Nixon's case, he had a very, very bright side. He was the smartest strategist I've ever met. I haven't seen anybody who can parallel him in thinking about the larger strategic picture and where the world is going.

Nixon also had a very, very dark side. Once you got to know him well, and as he began to trust you, he let the veil drop and you could see into him a little bit. I began to realize he was just boiling over with resentments. Now it's been said that even paranoids have real enemies, and he did have real enemies. He invented a lot of enemies, too, and these demons inside him eventually brought him down. It was a great national tragedy from my point of view.

JR: Tell us about when you went to the White House looking for Nixon, and you found him in a bowling alley you didn't even know existed.

DG: There's the White House proper, then there's the West Wing and the living quarters and there's also a big old building next door which is the old War State Department. I love that building. I worked there for two or three presidents.

I had to bring a speech over to him about 8:30 at night. I usually took such things up to his residence and gave it to him. This evening, however, they said, "You've got to take it over to him in the bowling alley."

It's down in the catacombs of that old building, way back in there through the piping and the dark, underground hallways. I eventually found it. There were a couple of Secret Service guys outside the door. I walked in. It was pretty late at night, but Richard Nixon had his dress pants on from his suit, his wingtip shoes, white shirt with cufflinks and a tie, bowling alone.

He was extremely lonely. You just had a sense of someone being very isolated, very much not in intimate relationship with others. And I felt sympathetic for him. I realized this is sort of a fellow who is so bright and yet he has such a gnarled inside that it was difficult for him to relate.

There were times when he had a gathering with his daughters, and I had to write talking points for him to use when he was going to talk to one of them. Now his daughters loved him. Julie, in particular, has been devoted to him for all of her life, as was his wife, Patricia. He was a lonely man, though. Somebody once said, "I don't know what happened to him when he was very young, but whatever it was, it was pretty terrible." He was so bright and yet he was held back by those inner inadequacies, those demons that he just could not control.

JR: If you could have three other presidents at dinner, other than the ones you have served, what three would you love to have dinner with?

DG: The pantheon of great presidents in the minds of historians includes George Washington, Abraham Lincoln and Franklin Roosevelt. As much as I admire Washington as a leader, he spoke through deeds not words. History says he was not a great dinner companion. I would substitute Teddy Roosevelt for dinner. Teddy Roosevelt was a raconteur of the first-order. He was unbelievably well read. When he was in the White House, he averaged reading one book a day.

Owen Wister, a very good novelist of the time who wrote *The Virginian*, came in late one afternoon for dinner and gave him a copy of his book. The next morning when they sat down for breakfast Roosevelt talked to him extensively about what was in the book; he had pretty well mastered it. Roosevelt, by the way, loved it up here in Chautauqua.

JR: Let's give David Gergen a round of applause.

Mark Shields & Michael Gerson

Mark Shields, born into an Irish-Catholic family in the town of Weymouth on the Massachusetts seacoast, carries the dual distinctions of honorable service in the United States Marine Corps and graduation from Notre Dame University (class of '59). As a political columnist and commentator, he airs weekly observations and political analysis for the *PBS NewsHour*. He has been well known as an editorial writer for *The Washington Post* for 17 years and as the moderator and panelist on *CNN*'s *Capital Gang*. Shields has also taught at the University of Pennsylvania's Wharton School, Georgetown University's Graduate School of Public Policy, and served as a fellow at Harvard's Kennedy Institute of Politics.

Shields' dry humor and acerbic wit, evenly balanced by his respected critical insight, is neatly summed up in his published advice to recent presidential candidates—advice he also takes for himself: "Instead of more PowerPoint presentations, rehearsed lines of attack and hubris, how about showing us, if you have any, some genuine humility and humor? Voters would cheer, believe me." (Creators.com, Mark Shields 2012)

Michael John Gerson, often branded a neo-conservative, notably by some of the more mainstream conservatives, served as chief speechwriter and senior policy advisor for President George W. Bush from 2001 until June 2006. He is an op-ed columnist at *The Washington Post*, a policy fellow with *ONE Campaign*, a visiting fellow with the *Center for Public Justice*, a former senior fellow at the *Council on Foreign Relations* and was a member of the White House Iraq Group. In 2007, he inaugurated his twice-weekly *Washington Post* op-ed column appearing on Wednesdays and Fridays.

Jim's interview, however, did not begin with politics. He loves sports, all kinds of sports, and Notre Dame Football is very near the top of his list. That simple fact created an instant bond between Jim and Mark Shields.

Jim's experience with Notre Dame Football, however – as a radio sportscaster – was probably a little less conventional than Mark's had been during his student days.

Jim Remembers... Tiny Tim and the Notre Dame Press Pass

Tony Barone, one of my friends, made Notre Dame Football history all by himself, as a fan.

Tony had attended 175 home games in a row at Notre Dame Stadium in South Bend, Indiana. He never missed even one, starting in 1971. At the very least, that's 140,000 miles of driving from his home in Lakewood, New York, and back, not to mention all the away games he attended too. Tony Barone, Notre Dame Class of '56, even arranged to have me officially appointed as an honorary Notre Dame alumnus.

Tony wanted to take me to my first Notre Dame game. He said, "You know what? I'm going to write a letter to John Heisler [Notre Dame director of Media Relations Department]

Jim and Tony Barone

and let him know you're a sportscaster at a local radio station and see if he might possibly give you a press pass. That would mean you go to the press room after the game where the coaches give the press their comments on the game or a player who made an outstanding play in the game."

He thought I'd enjoy that. I'd have my recorder, and I could tape it as they were speaking. Tony got a reply. Mr. Heisler said, "Fine! We will have a pass available for him when he gets here."

When we got there, Tony wanted to get a parking spot for a tailgate party as soon as he could. He had a van full of everything you could imagine; he had the refreshments, folding chairs and more. After he found the spot he wanted he said, "Okay, now I'll take you over to the building where the office is. You go up and introduce yourself to the girl at the desk. She'll have a pass for you."

"I'm Mr. Roselle," I said, "and Mr. Heisler has been kind enough to give me a press pass. I'm from a radio station in Jamestown, New York."

"May I have some ID that shows you work for the station?"

"I don't have a calling card or a business card on me," I said, checking the same pockets over and over again as if something would turn up if I tried hard enough to find it. "I don't have a thing, believe me, but I can tell you word for word the letter that my friend wrote about me and I can give you word for word the response Mr. Heisler gave him. Nobody else would know that."

"Sorry, sir. I need some ID, something that connects you to the radio station." She said it over and over again, every time I tried to persuade her to give me my press pass.

"Sorry, sir. I *still* need some ID."

Finally I got her to call Mr. Heisler's office. He wasn't there, he was already at the stadium. Eventually she reached him there and they spoke for a couple of minutes. Then she put the phone down.

"Mr. Heisler would like to see you at the stadium. It's a short walk. Just go over and ask for Mr. Heisler at the gate." So I walked over there and spoke to a gentleman standing at the gate.

"I'm supposed to meet Mr. Heisler here."

"Wait a minute." He made a call. A moment later the elevator came down. Mr. Heisler stepped out and greeted me.

"I have an opportunity to see my first game here," I started my explanation all over again. "I want to thank you for the opportunity to have a press pass. The receptionist sent me over here to see you."

"Do you have some ID?" All this way and I'd gotten nowhere.

"Mr. Heisler, I basically don't have a card that guarantees I'm with WJTN."

"Gee, that's unusual." I couldn't tell whether he was skeptical or amused.

"I agree," I admitted. "I should have brought something like that with me." I started searching through my wallet again. I was looking for something with WJTN on it. And of course, as before, I didn't have anything, I just didn't. But then I had an inspiration. I knew my chances with it were slim, but at least I could try. I took my wallet out again and handed him a picture I had stuffed in amongst the dollar bills.

Jim Roselle's Press Credential: Tiny Tim at Loblaws remote with store manager, Tony Teresi

"Mr. Heisler, this I think will show you that I do a radio show and here was one of my guests."

He looked at the picture.

Tiny Tim had once made an appearance at a nightclub in Jamestown. Before his appearance they had brought him down to Loblaws, one of a chain of Loblaws grocery stores at the time, for publicity. I had been doing a remote from there. In the little photo was the manager of Loblaws with me and Tiny Tim. Mr. Heisler looked at it and just sort of rolled his eyes.

"Wait here."

He took off and I just stood there. I wondered if he had gone to get a security guard to usher me back out the gate. After way too long he came back down the elevator.

"Here's your press pass. Have a good day."

Some time later I was invited to a church to give a talk about my experiences as a radio broadcaster and I used that as one of my personal stories. Unknown to me, my colleague, Dennis Webster, recorded it. He played it on his morning show the next day. And now he plays it every time the football season comes around. It's become a tradition simply known as "The Tiny Tim Story."

A Conversation with Shields & Gerson

Jim Roselle: Mark, you and I met a few years ago, but you are not aware of it. I was at Notre Dame for a game against Pittsburgh. I went to breakfast that morning in the hotel. You were having breakfast with your wife. I said hello to you. I'm glad I had that opportunity because a good friend of mine is a man who graduated from Notre Dame in 1956, and you graduated in 1959.

Mark Shields: You are absolutely right. I can't argue with a single thing you said so far. Imagine that! I'm talking to the media and they are telling me the truth for once.

JR: I had to bring these pictures just to prove it, Mark. I had the opportunity that year to also interview the president of Notre Dame. As you know, on Saturday mornings at the bookstore they have those personalities from the past history of Notre Dame and they're all signing their books. What an opportunity it is for a loyal Notre Dame fan to get that moment with the stars.

MS: It's a very special experience, a Saturday in South Bend on the Notre Dame campus.

JR: Well, it's good to have you here, Mark Shields. Welcome to Chautauqua for the first time.

MS: Delighted to be here. It's lived up to all expectations and beyond. It's just wonderful here.

JR: Then let's welcome Michael Gerson, too. He probably thought we forgot about him. Welcome to Chautauqua, Mike.

Michael Gerson: It's great to be here. This is not my first time. I visited and gave a lecture here three years ago on the subject of religion and politics.

JR: You have written a book called *The City of Man: Religion and Politics in a New Era* [Moody Publishers, 2010].

MG: It's a theme I often write about in my column in the *Washington Post*.

JR: When we talk about religion and politics, is there too much of it in the [2012 Obama/Romney] campaign?

MG: I guess the question is whether it is the right kind. We need to talk about civility in public life, about polarization. Religious values can play either way in those debates. They can divide people or they can motivate you properly to be concerned about good and to respect the rights and views of others. So it's a two-sided coin, as usual.

JR: When you craft a speech for the president of the United States is it an intimidating process?

MG: Well, the stakes are quite high. You have an international, a national and a historical audience; it's a tightrope. I could never watch the speeches and I never went to them. Like being a playwright on opening night, it was too intimidating for me, but it was still very rewarding to feel like you have a part in history.

JR: I had an opportunity 30 years ago to interview Ted Sorensen [President Kennedy's special counsel, adviser and speechwriter]. He wrote into John F. Kennedy's inaugural speech: "My fellow Americans, ask not what your country can do for you, ask what you can do for your country." Was that the most famous quote from inaugural speech?

MG: Other than Lincoln's second inaugural? That was one of the great defining speeches in American history. But both of those speeches prove that rhetoric can change the country and shape history.

JR: I want to turn the microphone over to Mark Shields. You talk a lot about what undecided voters might do.

MS: It's interesting that over the past 30 years half the time the presidential nominee who was ahead in June lost and half the time that nominee won.

Undecided voters are really not undecided. Undecided voters have made up their mind. When you have an incumbent, whether it is a senator or governor or president who is well known, by summer more than 95% of the people already have an opinion of him. Some attitudes may be far more negative about the country's direction. They might not be bullish on a challenger, but they may be "closet supporters." They may have already made up their mind that they don't like the presidency, the direction, management or leadership. It can be tough to win the undecided back. They have to enlarge the electorate by getting the people who supporting him to vote in greater numbers, that's not a persuasion campaign, it's a mobilization election.

JR: Gentlemen, certainly you have thought about the Citizens United ruling by the Supreme Court. How is that going to impact this election?

MS: The Citizens United ruling basically took off the limits on what could be spent. As a preface, after the Watergate election of 1972, the Congress of the United States wisely established a form of public financing for presidential elections. To participate in public financing you had to limit what you spent in primaries seeking the nomination and what you could accept in contributions. You couldn't accept any private contributions in the general election.

This was a system that leveled the playing field in United States politics. Ronald Reagan ran three times under it and called it welfare for politicians. George H. W. Bush ran three times under it, George W. Bush ran two times under it.

Then along comes the Supreme Court and says, lo and behold, "Corporations are people." I don't have any corporations living next door to me. Maybe they are nice people, maybe they are good neighbors. I don't think they have children, I don't think they worry about whether or not the kids get back in by midnight or whether one of the children is sick.

So corporations became a source of unlimited money.

JR: I've got to give Mike Gerson a little time here.

MG: I do have some concerns about Citizens United as well. I would only add, though, that often these things have unintended consequences. So the main people who don't like Citizens United, in addition to those who are concerned about the role of private money in American politics, are incumbents and front-runners. They like predictable campaign finance systems. The person who is hurt most by Citizens United is the challenger during the primaries. Some people do argue that this at least introduces an anti-incumbent, anti-frontrunner element. I think it both corrupts the system and in some ways has opened the system. There are two sides to it.

JR: Now here's my Chautauqua Question. If you had an opportunity to have dinner with any living or dead president, what four presidents would you invite to dinner?

MG: You would have to put Lincoln in that category. I approach things as a former speechwriter and there are only a very few presidents in American history who had advanced because they were writers themselves. Lincoln was one of them. With the Cooper Union speech and others, he rose to national prominence because of the craft of his writing. Thomas Jefferson was in that category, too. He emerged as the writing founder. Barack Obama is in that category as well, and he would be a fascinating dinner companion. I have always been interested in the history of progressivism, so maybe I'd invite someone like Woodrow Wilson, too.

JR: How about you Mark?

MS: I would want to have dinner with Franklin Roosevelt. Winston Churchill said that being around Roosevelt was like opening a bottle of champagne; it was exhilarating all the time. I think I would include Teddy Roosevelt in that list, too, and then I would ask Lyndon Johnson where he thinks he went wrong. That would probably end the dinner party right then and there when he turned over the table, but he was just such a remarkable figure in some respects, yet there was the fatal flaw of Vietnam, and what it meant to him.

Beyond that, I'd invite Warren Harding just because I would like somebody to pick up the tab for the dinner.

JR: How about a round of applause for Mike Gerson and Mark Shields.

David Ignatius
Fiction that Tells the Truth

David R. Ignatius is an outspoken journalist. In May, 2011, three months after Egyptian President Hosni Mubarak resigned in the wake of 18 days of fierce demonstrations during the 2011 Egyptian revolution, Ignatius said: "What's needed in Egypt and the other Arab countries that have suffered from dictatorship is a sense that the rule of law will prevail, with safeguards against vindictive prosecution."

Ignatius' scholarship and accomplishments as a journalist have earned him the Legion of Honor from the French Republic, the Urbino World Press Award from the Italian Republic and an award for Lifetime Achievement presented by the International Committee for Foreign Journalism.

Ignatius once also told *Foreign Policy*, "American leaders must give up the notion that they can transform the Middle East and its culture through military force..." and "...get out of the elusive middle, step across the threshold of anger, and sit down and talk" with the leaders in the Middle East.

David Ignatius' work includes reporting, contributing and editing for such prestigious media outlets as *The Washington Monthly, The Washington Post, the Wall Street Journal* and *The International Herald Tribune* in Paris with frequent contributions to *The New York Times Magazine, The Atlantic Monthly, Foreign Affairs, The New Republic* and *Talk Magazine.* The list of other publications, leadership positions and awards, including radio and TV is, as Jim Roselle has said of many of his guests, "...so long there would be no time left for an interview if I read them all."

Ignatius has served as an adjunct lecturer at Harvard University's John F. Kennedy School of Government and is currently a senior fellow in the Future of Diplomacy Program.

He has both defended and criticized the CIA and the U.S. government's tactics and philosophy in foreign and domestic intelligence and in the use of torture as an information gathering technique. Based on deep knowledge gained in these issues he has also written many popular suspense and espionage novels.

A Conversation with David Ignatius

Jim Roselle: Good morning David Ignatius and welcome to Chautauqua. Is this your first visit here?
David Ignatius: It is, but I can tell you just by looking around that it certainly won't be my last. I wish my wife and kids could see this. It's exquisite. Just a place out of time.

JR: We hear that often. And it is a wonderful setting to hear about your latest novel. You've written eight so far, right?
DI: Yes, I have, and there's always another one in the works. I just published my eighth about a month ago called *Blood Money: A Novel of Espionage* [W. W. Norton & Company, 2011]. And then there will be another one after that. I think I'm kind of hooked on this.

JR: When does the moment come when you think your work is ready to put out there?

DI: I will give you the short version. I worked on a story as a reporter when I was covering the Middle East and Beirut that was so powerful and so raw, so close to the bone, that I really couldn't write it anymore as a factual account. To tell that story in all of its richness I had to figure out how to be a novelist. So I taught myself how to do it. That book is still in print.

JR: It is not only a novel but it is fact.

DI: The first book, although I didn't say so at the time because I was so nervous, really was as close to fact as I could make it. I had a picture of the real-life hero on my desk, and I finally put it away in the drawer because I realized that if I didn't I would just be writing a 100,000 word newspaper article which nobody would read. I decided to make it a novel instead. People still read it, I think, because it is real life, but re-imagined.

JR: *The Buffalo News* also carries your column twice a week.

DI: I'm happy to be a local columnist.

JR: You recently returned from Afghanistan. What feelings did you bring back with you?

DI: I have gone there three or four times a year for the last few years. What struck me on my last trip was that we finally have some programs that are making a difference for people. For example, Khost, a city east of Kabul along the Pakistan border, is one of the many places in Afghanistan that has no judges and no prosecutors.

If you lay a map of the districts in Afghanistan that have no law and no judges, it is the same map as the districts where the Taliban is strong. That is the only thing that they offer. They are brutal, they are usually terrorists, but they do offer quick justice for people who need it. We finally have understood that we need to get some judges in there. We've been training Afghans, helping them go to these little villages in sub-district offices to dispense justice. It's a program that just started and seems to be working. We've been fighting this war for 10 years, and we are just starting that program. I just hope it can continue.

JR: You praised the work of our Army and commanders in Afghanistan.

DI: I wrote a column that appeared on the Fourth of July; it's a good day to talk about our military. I wanted to note that our people out there doing the fighting in extremely difficult conditions in Iraq and Afghanistan, and have learned how to deal with people who are very different from Americans. They have learned how to adapt by learning from failure.

We really have made some huge mistakes. I met people who are on their sixth, seventh and in one case eighth deployment. Can you imagine that? Eight deployments in the last 10 years in these war zones. And they are great soldiers, they are smart, they have some cultural understanding. We may have blundered into these wars and broken a lot of the china, as Colin Powell said.

JR: You have interviewed Assad of Syria.

DI: I first interviewed him in 2003 and I've been back often since then. Frankly, President Bashar al-Assad is a man who never gets it done. The man knows, in his private moments and in conversations with journalists like me, what Syria needs. But either he cannot or will not make it happen. He is running out of time, not because we say so but because his own people say so.

JR: Were you aware of the revolutionary spirit of the common people in the Middle East in the spring revolution that is taking place?

DI: People in the Middle East want to write their own history. They are sick of having their history written for them by outsiders, especially by the United States.

The Arab world has the most screwed up political culture that I know. Finally, however, people want to stand up and say, "I want to control this. I am somebody. I deserve to have rights. I'm not going to be pushed around by the cop. I'm not going to be pushed around by my government." Americans know that impulse is a righteous one; it leads, over time and a lot of struggle, to good governance.

JR: What about the Israeli-Palestinian situation?

DI: The Israelis have a terrible problem. They truly desire to make peace, but they don't have a counterpart that is yet prepared to sit down with them and accept their reality and go about it. We have come right up to the edge of a treaty. I think anyone of us could name the basic elements that would be in that treaty.

We know pretty much what the borders would be. We know pretty much what the deal would have to be on Jerusalem. We know pretty much what the deal would have to be on the non-right of return for the Palestinians. It's just a question of making that happen and having the political will and the sense of momentum to make it happen.

JR: What prompted you to be a journalist?

DI: I wasn't good at anything else. I had hopes of being an economist. I went to graduate school to study economics at Cambridge University in the United Kingdom and I had one of those 'come to Jesus' moments when I knew I just wasn't going to be very good at it. I had to look for something else. I could've been an ordinary economist, but I chose another field.

JR: Being so closely associated with the scene in Washington, what bothers you the most right now about what we have heard called the "poison partisan atmosphere?"

DI: Our system is losing the ability to solve problems that the people care about. We no longer value and protect the common space in the middle where decisions are made. All the energy in our system, including the media, goes to extreme viewpoints.

I hear the president talk about compromise and conciliation and solutions… and he is just getting hammered from both parties. That is a pretty typical American political moment. I could go down a list but my basic point is, we love America and we are proud of our country, but we need to face up to the reality that our basic institutions of governance, especially the Congress, are not working.

JR: What about the technology of the day? How have the Internet, twittering and blogging affected the candidates?

DI: I would liken it to the way a strobe light lets you only see things in flashes, momentary flashes. Putting the whole thing together becomes difficult. It is fragmenting the full bundles of information. *The Washington Post,* for instance, is a bundle of things for everybody. *CBS Nightly News* used to be a bundle of information with something for everybody. *Time* and *Life* are classic examples. Those bundles are of less and less value when people can pick their own little bits out of the information stream and say, "Well, I don't need the whole thing; I just want the stuff that I'm interested in." They don't accept a challenge from the opposite side.

The tradition of all reporters is to challenge what people think, to challenge their ideas, to challenge the people in power, whoever they are, Republican or Democrat. I just worry that that basic idea is changing in this digital world where you can take some bits and not others. It is skewing the country further and further into separate camps, each with its own information stream. The thing in the middle, the common thing that's bundled, the thing that allows for good governance, loses out.

JR: That brings up the question I normally conclude with. Who are your favorite heroes of the past?

DI: Before reading about Andrew Jackson I read a superb biography, *Alexander Hamilton,* written by Ron Chernow [Penguin Press, 2004]. Alexander Hamilton is in so many ways the founder who understood the essence of democracy and the threat to democracy that comes from an uninformed citizenry, which comes from the kind of mob psychology that can take over.

Hamilton was sort of the Mozart of politics and government. He created out of nothing, our banking system, most of how our executive branch runs and a lot of the basis of our legal traditions. I have never encountered a personality in history quite like Alexander Hamilton.

JR: Name another two that you would want to sit at a dinner table with.

DI: I would want to sit at the dinner table with Graham Greene. It would be an unpleasant conversation because he was a really unpleasant man. He was difficult, he was willful, he was tormented by Catholicism that he could never really carry out in his life and, as we know, he was talking about Catholicism and constantly falling in love and having affairs. As a writer, though, he had a gift for capturing moral dilemmas, how people live.

Before I start most of my novels I reread a novel by Graham Greene just to kind of get in the place where I think about the things that he was thinking of.

I would love to have dinner with Mike Shanahan. He was the coach of the Washington Redskins. I'd ask him how he screwed up so badly last year and whether we're even going to have a football team in the National Football League this year.

JR: Maybe this will surprise you. Roger Goodell, the Commissioner of the National Football League today, was once a teenager here, working at Chautauqua. Each morning he would come out and clean the debris around my studio.

DI: Then I want to say, Jim, that you have made the NFL what it is today by taking care of Roger Goodell.

JR: I'm going to end on that note. Let's give David Ignatius a nice round of applause.

Jim Remembers... NFL Commissioner Goodell - The Coffee Gopher

I had the pleasure of interviewing Roger Goodell one day at Chautauqua. Roger already knew the neighborhood pretty well; he grew up in Jamestown. The last time I had seen Roger, he was only a young lad with a summer job at Chautauqua Institution. I still remember the conversation we had on the air all those many years later.

Jim Roselle: Good to see you again, young man.
Roger Goodell: It's good to see you too. I think I was sweeping the floors last time I was here. I used to bring you coffee every morning, too.

JR: Let me share this with our audience. I hope you know, Roger, that it was your dad [United States Senator Charles Goodell, R-NY] who first inspired me to do this broadcast from Chautauqua Institution. I looked at an advanced schedule one day and saw that he was going to be a speaker. And I thought, it's time to go to Chautauqua and do a show. I came, requested permission from the management here and I've been doing it ever since. He was giving a talk that day on the abuse of government power.

RG: I'm glad he was the inspiration, but you deserve the credit for doing it. I remember sitting here and cleaning up around you while you worked. It's amazing where life takes you.

On the air with Jim Lehrer

Jim Lehrer
Dean of Moderators

James Charles "Jim" Lehrer is possibly best known for his long-time partnership with Robert MacNeil on *The MacNeil/Lehrer Report* and as the "Dean of Moderators" for 12 televised U.S. presidential campaign debates. He is also the executive editor and a former anchor on the *PBS NewsHour*. He has also published many fiction and non-fiction books based on his news work and his fascination with history and politics.

Lehrer could not be blamed for quoting Dorothy in the Land of Oz; "It sure doesn't look like Kansas anymore." He was born in Wichita, Kansas but graduated from high school and college in Texas and journalism school in Missouri. That may have inspired him to seek a bigger world beyond Kansas, as he then joined the United States Marine Corps. He later claimed it was those experiences which taught him to look beyond himself and connect with all the world's people.

Numerous journalism awards and honors have come Lehrer's way including several Emmys, the Peabody, the William Allen White Foundation Award for Journalistic Merit, the University of Missouri School of Journalism (his alma mater) Medal of Honor, and an honorary Doctor of Journalism degree from McDaniel College.

Jim Roselle, always drawn by the personal as much as the professional qualities of his guests, learned that Jim Lehrer is a hobbyist of a rarified kind; he is a bus enthusiast.

Lehrer's father, a bus driver, also briefly ran a bus company. In college, Lehrer worked as a ticket agent at the Trailways Bus Company terminal in Victoria, Texas. He collects bus memorabilia of all sorts today and supports bus museums in California and Pennsylvania.

When Jim Roselle engages his guest, Jim Lehrer, for this interview, he brings motivations and methods in campaigning into sharp focus. Jim Roselle himself was once courted by the political community in his own Chautauqua County to run for elected office. Probably in no other way could he have come to grips with some of the key personal issues every politician must face.

Jim Remembers… I Was an Almost Ran

I never take sides in political campaigns. I'm a broadcaster and people have to trust that I'm neutral, that I report both sides fairly.

At one time, I did think of running. The Democratic Party okayed it; they said they would endorse me. I was going to run for the Chautauqua County Legislature. As I began to think about a campaign, I realized I just wanted the experience so I could understand how it works. I wanted to get in there and find out why there are differences deciding on things you either want or don't want in the budget. I especially wanted to know where the pressures come from. I thought that experience would give me more information so I could be more credible in my reporting on election night.

I talked it over with some trusted friends. They said, "Jim if you go on the air representing a particular party your image will change. It will not be for the better. The people at the other end of the political spectrum will start thinking you are spinning your news or slanting your comments every day. It will change the way they listen to you. Right now they accept whatever you do and that's the way it should stay."

People only think I am a Democrat because I always report on election night from the Democratic headquarters. That is only a tradition, though. When we started doing that the other newscaster would not go to the Democratic headquarters. He wanted to a report from the Republican side. We just started doing it that way and have done it that way ever since. That doesn't necessarily mean I'm a Democrat, or a Republican, either, for that matter. I won't be seen as neutral unless I keep that sort of private.

My friends also reminded me that I do the early morning radio show. Many of the committee meetings run well past midnight. Some people also call meetings whenever they think there is something urgent, regardless of whether or not is the regularly scheduled meeting night. Regardless of the night, sometimes I wouldn't get home until 1 o'clock in the morning. I'd still have to get up at 5:30 am for the day's radio program.

I decided not to change my image just because all I wanted was the experience. I also know I wouldn't want to get involved with people who take rigid positions and wouldn't budge. That would be hard and probably against my nature. I have that so-called naïve attitude; you take an office like that and do what's best for the people no matter what party you are with. I think some people would also say I'm too compassionate for people who don't have much.

A Conversation with Jim Lehrer

Jim Roselle: This is the week that we are supposed to become well-informed voters at Chautauqua Institution. Have you found it true so far that we are?

Jim Lehrer: Most of the people who come to Chautauqua are already pretty well informed, or they wouldn't be coming here. Chautauqua is an informed place.

JR: Let's deal with what is on the mind of every American today; the election year. We have just seen a brutal primary campaign season. The nation is, I think, asking "Isn't politics better than this?"

JL: That's exactly what they're saying and hoping it is…and they are realizing that it isn't right now. I don't think the politics of the United States of America, at this point is matching the expectations most people have. There is a lot of rhetoric. There is a lot of questioning; "Hey, wait a minute. We're supposed to work together. We're supposed to get from here to there regardless of what our differences may be. We still get things done. We still govern, whether it's at the local level or the national level or the international level and there are a few things falling through the cracks and a few dots not being connected." People are aware of that. They don't understand what's going on. I understand why they don't understand.

JR: Do you feel, at times, that some people want to ask the candidates a "gotcha question"?

JL: Absolutely! To me, there is no excuse for that. I think gotcha questions are for another line of work. Gotcha questions are aimed at showing off how really brilliant the moderator or the questioner is. They're hoping somebody says, "Oh that's a really great question, boy that's terrific, you really got him or her or whatever." So I say, "Hey Billy Bob, that's not what this is really all about. This is about the candidates and what the candidates are showing or not showing. It isn't about the moderator or the person asking the questions. It is so easy to show off."

I have all kinds of little rules for moderators.

1.) Do not see it as an audition for a better job.

2.) If you want to draw attention to yourself, go get on the top of a flagpole and sit on it. Do not do so at a presidential debate. That's not what this is about.

3.) This is not about you. Sit in front of a mirror and say, "This is not about me. This is not about me. This is not about me. It's about Sally Sue and Billy Bob."

JR: You have written about your experience as a moderator of 11 presidential debates. What gave you the idea to title it *Tension City: Inside the Presidential Debates* [Random House, 2012]?

JL: I remembered something that George H. W. Bush had said in an interview about the debates seven or eight years after he had left the White House. I asked him some not so hard-hitting questions like, "What was it like, Mr. President?" He said, "Oh Jim, those high visibility things, they are Tension City." My editor and I had been struggling to find a title, so I called him and suggested Tension City. "You're on!" He said. I'm glad it turned out that way because tension really is what it's all about for the folks who are involved.

JR: This is July 4, Independence Day, the birthday of America. What if the founding fathers were here today to look at what government is like today. What do you think they would feel?

JL: I think they would be pretty pleased. They believed that a real, functioning democracy is going to be messy, not a pretty sight. They thought about order and chaos. Order came with monarchs and dictatorships. Chaos came with a democracy. They bought into the idea and formed a government and set out a constitution that encouraged dissent, loud noises and loud speeches and off-the-wall ideas and times like now. They knew it wasn't going to be pleasant.

For instance, they decided to set aside the slavery issue in order for there to be a union. They knew there were things coming that they didn't resolve because they could not resolve them. They felt they had to make the ultimate compromise. Today people say we shouldn't compromise. If it wasn't for compromise we wouldn't be sitting here talking about the Fourth of July and Independence Day. There would be no United States of America if they held rigidly to their positions.

JR: You had 30+ years as a *PBS News Hour* host. Was it agonizing for you to give up that program?

JL: No. Fortunately it was all my decision when to do it and how to do it. It helps in these situations when you're the boss so I worked it out and I decided how I wanted to do it. I've been in daily journalism for 50 years, going back to my newspaper days. Deadlines were an intimate part of my body and soul, and I'm used to them; I thrive on them. It's just a natural part of my life. I realized, though, that was enough. No problem.

JR: I'll ask you the Chautauqua Question. It's about the wonderful dinner you're going to have with four people, either living or dead. Who would you choose to have dinner with?

JL: Winston Churchill, Thomas Jefferson, JD Salinger, (laughing) if he would show up, and I don't know who the fourth would be… I'll get back to the fourth.

JR: What would you ask JD Salinger?

JL: Where have you been? Why did you quit writing? My only experience is that writers write. So what happened? I would be curious to talk to him about that.

JR: What quote from Winston Churchill have you often used?

JL: It's the one about fighting the Nazis on the beaches "…we shall defend our island, whatever the cost may be. We shall fight on the beaches, we shall fight on the landing grounds, we shall fight in the fields and in the streets, we shall fight in the hills; we shall never surrender…"

What I admire about Winston Churchill is that he was a man of his own habits and his own mind and his mind went everywhere. He was a terrific writer and a terrific speaker. He annoyed a lot of people because he had very strong opinions and he expressed them strongly. But he was a man of action, a man of involvement. When something had to be done, he was there. When there was something that had to be debated, he was there. I admire him for all that.

JR: Of all the possibilities you have had in your career, which will you choose to top the list of the assignment you liked best?

JL: The one I've had for 37 years. I can't imagine doing anything better or different that would be better than being involved in a leadership position of a nightly news program whose journalistic standards were the highest with highly qualified people and able to practice the kind of journalism we want to practice in an atmosphere of complete freedom and independence. There have been people looking over our shoulder, but nobody could say, "Hey, don't do that. Don't cover that." Anybody could say anything they wanted to after the fact, but nobody has ever tried to influence anything we've done. There are not many people who have practiced journalism as long as I have who can say that.

Journalism is little boy and little girl work. It's all about the sirens. We're sitting on the porch here in Chautauqua and if we suddenly hear a siren you're going to want to know, and I'm going to want to know, is that a fire truck? Is that an ambulance? Is that a police car? And where is it going? We're going to want to get out and go and find out. And that is the same about war and all kinds of other things all over the world. Journalists are the little boys and the little girls that get to go and follow the fire engine, and get to go follow the siren. That's what I've done for these 50 years and I am a very fortunate person.

JR: Jim Lehrer, I can't thank you enough for the second opportunity to talk with you.

JL: Thank you.

Mark Russell

Commentators *commentate*, Mark Russell might say. But even if they only *comment*, Mark Russell does that too, frequently, and to the amusement and (quasi-) enlightenment of Americans from coast-to-coast from his piano keyboard/bully-pulpit/headquarters in Washington, DC and almost every place else where he can…especially at Chautauqua Institution encamped in front of his old friend Jim Roselle's

Jim and Mark step into the sidewalk studio

ever present microphone. Jim thinks that his interviews turn out to be warm-ups for Mark's performances at the Institution's Amphitheater and for the TV cameras.

Then one day in July 2010 Mark even turned the broadcast tables on Jim. He commandeered the microphone before airtime and began to spar with the audience. Jim had little recourse but to admit the obvious…

More Banter with Mark Russell

Jim Roselle: Welcome to the Mark Russell show here on WJTN radio.

Mark Russell: That has a ring to it, doesn't it? And today's guest: Jim Roselle.

JR: Do you want to interview me?
MR: Yes I do. How long have you been at the station?
JR: 46 years.
MR: That's enough. Now, ask me something.
JR: Ah… this is program number 29…
MR: (interrupting) A guy goes to the doctor.
   "What's your problem?" The doctor asks.
   "I can't urinate."
   "How old are you?"
   "92."
   "You have urinated enough. Go home."
JR: Are you telling me I've been here long enough? And I can go home?
MR: A guy goes to the doctor and he examines the numbers in the doctor's bill.
   "I can't pay," the patient says.
   "Why?"
   "I'm broke."
   The doctor says, "That's a pre-existing condition."
JR: Let's talk about another interesting issue. It is a very touchy, sensitive issue: sexual harassment.
MR: It was Gloria Steinem who really confused everybody a while ago when she wrote an op-ed piece in the *New York Times* that gave a lot of people the impression that she was saying that men in the workplace should be given, if you will, a free grope, a free shot. Then how do you know if it's the first one for a guy, is there a bulletin board for that? I must've been out of the loop that day that Gloria Steinem changed the rules.

And so, what she seems to be saying is, "One grope and you are just a guy. Two gropes, you are a predator, three gropes you could be President of the United States." Now, I have no opinions on this but—I have to go home tonight—if a feminist sees a Republican groping, that feminist is going to say, "Aha! That's sexual harassment." But if she sees a Democrat groping, she would say, "Well, you know, at a certain angle that could be the Heimlich maneuver."

Jim and Mark at it again

A year later, in August 2011, the tables got themselves turned "right side 'round again" but the commentative shenanigans, of course, were back.

Jim Roselle: Welcome to the *Jim Roselle Show* from Bestor Plaza.
Mark Russell: And a cup of coffee too. Wasn't that your old slogan?

JR: It still is. But it's not a cup of *coffee*. It's a Cup of *Happiness*.
MR: Where I come from a cup of happiness has a head on it.
JR: Ladies and gentlemen in the radio audience, just moments ago, before we came on the air, we sang Happy Birthday to Mark Russell. But I want to do it one more time because I want this to be recorded. Are you ready? [Jim signals "Go!" The audience sings Happy Birthday.]
MR: That was wonderful. Thank you. I'm 79. You had to ask? That was much better than before we went on the air. That was embarrassing (audience laughs) and at a place so musically attuned as Chautauqua Institution. I was shocked, but this time was very nice. I don't feel 79. I've got to tell you, I feel about 84.
JR: Mark. A big surprise: you retired.
MR: Well it's not the kind of retirement you think of at Chautauqua. For me there is no golf or tennis or anything like that. My kind of retirement is where your career becomes a hobby. So I do that for my own amusement. There is the cliché, "spending more time with the grandchildren." But now I have seven grandchildren and the youngest one is my last chance to do all of the old grandfatherly shtick that the older ones are so bored with. And my children said there aren't going to be any more grandchildren. So this is it. For me this is the last chance. So the day he was born, he was just a few hours old, I thought, "Nothing is old to him. Any old joke is new to this child." None of the old corny stuff where you put your head around the corner and then you make believe you're strangling yourself, he's going to see it for the first time. I'm holding him now and he's just hours old, so I told him a joke. He yawned and pooped and went back to sleep. [Mark points toward the audience and says, "Just like that fellow over there."]
JR: The big question today is where is Gaddafi? [Dictatorial ruler of Libya for the preceding 42 years.]
MR: Muammar al-Gaddafi has been overthrown in Libya, as you know, or as Michelle Bachmann said, "The Bolivian people are now much better off." (Audience laughs) No, she didn't say that. But Gaddafi is missing. This is an all points bulletin now from WJTN, or has the station been sold while we're talking? No? Okay then this is an all points bulletin to all of your listeners. If you see Gaddafi, please drop him off in Lockerbie, Scotland. But nobody knows where he is. He could be at an ATM machine trying to get his frozen assets or you could look for him in Iran, and see if he is in bed with Ahmadinejad. Or he might be writing a book or co-authoring a book with Egypt's Hosni Mubarak. They could title it: *"Hanging Together".*
JR: Can I go back one more time…
MR: You're not going to ask everybody to sing Happy Birthday again, are you?
JR: I want you to expand on how tough the decision was to retire.
MR: It was easy. I always warn people here not to mistake a standing ovation for applause. It's really a call of nature here. The other thing I tell them is that you never really know you're going over with the audience until all the women put down their needlepoint… Or the men put down their needlepoint. I decided—I hate the word retire—on taking some time off until Herman Cain is elected President of the United States. And what a moment that would be: the first black president to follow the first black president [as some had called President Bill Clinton].
JR: How is Obama doing?

MR: He's doing his best, which could be part of the problem I suppose. This is not terribly original, but everybody is giving Obama the same advice, and most of it is coming from Democrats, ironically. What Obama has got to do is take charge, and lead, and take the bull by the horns, and step up to the plate, and ask himself the question: "What would Hillary do?" And then others say, "Well, he's got to do what Franklin Delano Roosevelt did back in the Great Depression in the 1930s. He's got to establish a big federal project of fixing cities and roads and build bridges like Roosevelt did and invading France and packing the Supreme Court and having a mistress named Lucy. That's what he's got to do."

JR: Really, Mark Russell, what's the root of our problem?

MR: Jim… I'm going to be like your more serious guests here… I'm so glad you asked that question. Jim, what's the question again? Oh yes, the root of our problems… And I really mean this folks… I think all of the problems in the United States today, the root causes, go back to the time that we established men's suffrage. This country was doing great until we gave the vote to men and started electing male presidents. I mentioned Hillary moments ago and a lot of women, I call them recovering Hillary supporters in rehab, are still bitter over the fact that she didn't get the Democratic nomination, so that's why Obama gave her the most prestigious job in the cabinet—Secretary of State. And she is getting good marks for that. Bill is kind of on his own back here in the States. He took his dog to the veterinarian the other day and the vet said, "You want to have him neutered?" And the dog said, "Yes!"

JR: I'm going to get this laughter as long as I can, Mark. But really, the Tea Party?

MR: Can you imagine being a fly on the wall at Tea Party Headquarters during that embarrassing session about raising the debt ceiling? Here they are, the Tea Party:

> "What are we going to do?"
> "Well, unless we raise the debt ceiling the Social Security checks won't go out and we wind up screwing the seniors. So what we do is, we raise the debt ceiling, we cut Social Security and then we can screw the seniors at the same time." Or they will say, "Unless we raise the debt ceiling the stock market is going to go down the toilet."
>
> So they did, and it did. As we all go swirling down, down, down the drain with the Tidy Bowl man in his little boat. It was during that debt ceiling thing, and that was embarrassing, we heard, "The balanced budget amendment, back by no particular popular demand, like a bunch of alcoholics trying to vote on whether to stop drinking or not. So the rhetoric during the debt ceiling, sounded like this:
>
> "This is not a game." And then they accuse their opponents of moving the goal post.
> "My way or the highway." You know the ones who say my way or the highway are the same ones who vote to cut the budget for highways and transportation. And then what it wound up as was this little group of 12, six House and six Senate members, a super-Congress. By the way the words super and Congress should never be in the same sentence. And so there were 12 members, not to be confused with the 12 Apostles who only had one Judas. Now while all of this was going on, at the same time the report came out saying the Apple Company has more money than the US Treasury. So when Obama says, "We need jobs," he's talking about Steve [Jobs. Apple Computer's founder.]

JR: Speaking of marriage, Mark Russell…

MR: I'm spoken for.

JR: Same-sex marriages.

MR: In New York, the deciding vote was the senator from Buffalo. I went to high school with his father. Dick Grisanti's son was one of the voters there. So the New York State Senate okayed same-sex marriages making it possible for Donald Trump to be engaged to himself.

JR: Mark Russell, I have to take a moment to express my deepest thanks for the appearances you have made on my broadcast.

MR: Thank you.

JR: This man has given me an interview a year for the past, what would it be, at least…

MR: 56 years. Calvin Coolidge had just been elected, I think. It's a pleasure. I mean it. You're the best, you really are the best. When there's an author on the show, this guy has read the book. Most of them, your colleagues, you know what they do? They bend the book back, and then they rub it on the floor and get some dirt on it so the author will think that he's read his wonderful book.

JR: By the way I did the favor you wanted me to do.

MR: What's that?

JR: I took Ira Cooperman [one of Jim's "Breakfast Gang"] to see the house you lived in on Lakeview Avenue in Jamestown.

MR: Upstairs, 34 Lakewood. The rent was $45 a month. I've got to go back there because the souvenir store wants some more memorabilia.

JR: Then I took him by Sixth and Main where your dad ran a gas station.

MR: Yes he did. It was a Mobil station. It wasn't one of those combination gas stations and convenience stores. It was a Mobil station and there was a Catholic Church across the street. My father used to tell customers every morning the priest comes across the street and blesses the tires that were for sale.

My mother worked at Clarke Hardware. They bought a piano from Swanson which we still have in the family. My daughter has got it. And they paid about $150, on-time payments, for which they still have the payment book. So there are a lot of memories for me here in Jamestown. We only lived here for a year but when I first played the Amphitheater [at Chautauqua Institution] in 1979 somebody said, "He grew up in Jamestown, born and raised in Jamestown." This man (Mark points at Jim) started even before radio was invented. He used to walk through downtown Jamestown with a megaphone announcing "10 o'clock and all's well."

JR: I'm not sure the audience is aware that your brother is a piano player.

MR: He's a very good piano player, better than I am. He's in about his 30th year at the Mayflower Hotel in Washington DC. I had a lot of piano lessons, too, about seven or eight years. He had one year from a nun in Kenmore, New York. He is just a brilliant, brilliant pianist.

JR: Are you going to miss the business now that you're retired?

MR: I'll miss the money. But it's still a hobby. It's like doing a crossword puzzle. I'll try to keep the brain going and try to write a song once in a while. And this is the largest audience I have had in a year. We have family reunions and they say, "Ah well, look at the time." But really, this is a nice turnout and I really appreciate all of you very much.

JR: Let's give Mark a thunderous round of applause (audience applauds long and loud). When you stop and think of it, do you realize how much laughter you have given millions of people?

MR: Dozens, dozens, some nights, dozens. Some nights they used to sit there in the audience and say, "What the hell is he talking about?"

JR: Not anymore, Mark. They know what you're talking about, and we thank you sincerely for what you have contributed to our life. Thank you very much. One more round of applause. Happy Birthday to Mark Russell.

Tony Snow
Telling Inconvenient Truths

Robert Anthony "Tony" Snow was a political commentator, the host of the syndicated television program, *The Tony Snow Show*, a syndicated print columnist, radio program host, and the third White

House Press Secretary under President George W. Bush from May 2006 until he resigned in September 2007 due to serious health concerns. He died in July, 2008. He had also worked in the administration of President George H. W. Bush as Chief Speechwriter and Deputy Assistant of Media Affairs. Most of Snow's political commentary and actions were carried on within a conservative political philosophy.

Tony Snow (1955-2008)

Tony Snow, a Kentucky native, was also an avid musician, playing the guitar, saxophone, trombone, piccolo and flute. He performed publically with a number of rock bands. Broadly educated in philosophy and economics, he also once taught high school physics.

In June 2000, Tony Snow was Jim's guest on Bestor Plaza. Their conversation had begun with talk of particular topics in the politics of the day, but then their thoughts turned to more general ideas that still animate the political dialog today.

A Brief Conversation with Tony Snow

Jim Roselle: Are you saving some of your stuff for the lecture platform?
Tony Snow: I've got this egghead kind of lecture. I think I am just kind of thrown to talk that way when I talk politics.

JR: How do you feel, Tony, on the topic of money in politics?
TS: I think it is overrated if you take a look at, for instance, what we spend on potato chips, it's far more than we spent on every American political race in the last 20 years.
What I'm more worried about is mediocrity in politics. You've got people, politicians, right now who get their beliefs from pollsters and focus groups. That, to me, is crazy. You've got to have people who say, "Here's what I believe. Take it or leave it. If you don't like it, don't vote for me."
I would much prefer to see a candidate who knew his own mind and heart, or her own mind and heart, than somebody who calls in pollsters every day and asks, "What shall we do today? What word should we use?" That gives you the kind of politics that careens from issue to issue and it doesn't give people the sanity and security of knowing that they have somebody at the helm who knows what they believe and also will be reliable in a crunch.

Jim and Tony move on to wade through some of the less noted intricacies of the upcoming 1999/2000 Bush/Gore presidential election and then on to some peculiarities of that contest in which Tony throws light on the kind of dynamics that can apply to both past and future elections.

JR: Tony Snow, Al Gore seems to be having some trouble trying to get some rhythm in his campaign. It seems to have stalled and some of it even seems to have gone backward. Tell us what's happened.
TS: Al Gore's got a unique problem. It's very difficult as a vice president to run for president. You've got to get out of the shadow of the president. But normally what you do is throw both arms around the person who brought you there and hope that that will carry you to victory. That's what George Bush did in 1988. The read my lips, no new taxes stuff was his way of saying, "I'm Reagan's guy."
Gore has to find a way to take credit for peace and prosperity without having to get personally attached with Clinton. It's a very weird dance. Nobody has ever had to do it. It's more complicated by the

fact that only twice in American history has someone gone from the vice presidency to the presidency by an election.

Gore has to figure out how to become his own man. He has to somehow stand away from the Clinton scandal. None of this stuff sticks on Bill Clinton and all of it sticks on Al Gore. He's like a duck in an oil spill. It is a terrible mess for him. And that is the definition of the problem.

He says, "No, no, no! I'm a new Al Gore." People will say either he's a phony or an opportunist, or a backstabber. Or they'll say he was a coward for eight years and never spoke up. It's a very, very tough position.

Now, having said that, I have to add that Gore is a hard worker. I think he is a harder worker in terms of the day-to-day nuts and bolts of politics than George W. Bush. He is feverishly ambitious. You've got to be crazy ambitious to be president anyway. So he's got that working on his side. He's got to work very hard in debates and his people all want to win. So right now you've got George W. Bush enjoying leads virtually everywhere but New York where he is getting creamed. He's going to get creamed there, in the end. That won't change.

JR: The interesting thing that was said the other day was that Al Gore would consider Jesse Ventura as a running mate. (All laugh)

TS: Why would you have as a running mate a guy who writes a book saying he doesn't wear underwear? (Laughing continues). I left you speechless on that one, didn't I?

JR: No. I was trying to think of a comeback. I was going to ask you, "Is it Boxers or briefs?"

TS: What he is not wearing, I don't want to know.

Jamestoon

by Gary Peters

Chapter 14

The Plane Left without Him

It has been said we all live on borrowed time, and perhaps we do live years beyond those we can hope for in a dangerous world. A near-miss on a wintery road, recovery from a deadly disease or survival on the battlefield often leave us grateful, possibly for divine intervention, instead of merely proud of the accomplishment in a situation that may have been beyond our control. In his youth, Jim Roselle experienced one of those close calls with death which may have prepared him better than anything else for a guest whose brush with catastrophe altered his life forever.

I saw the smoking hole where I should have died. That's where I got my life back.

Rev. Dr. Steve Scheibner
American Airlines Pilot

Steve Scheibner
In My Seat

One Saturday morning in the autumn of 2011, on the 10th anniversary of the 9/11 attacks, Jim and his *Times of Your Life* co-host, Russ Diethrick, reached out by phone to Steve Scheibner at his home in Georgetown, Maine.

Scheibner, a 20-year veteran pilot with American Airlines, had been the scheduled co-pilot for American Airlines flight 11, a Boeing 767, which was the first of the four planes commandeered by al-Qaeda terrorists. They crashed it into the North Tower of New York City's World Trade Center killing all 92 aboard and about 1,600 office workers, visitors and rescue workers in one of New York City's most iconic skyscrapers.

Steve should have been the first officer on that flight, but another pilot had bumped him and took the trip instead. It was a "near miss" that forever changed, not only the course of Steve Scheibner's life, but thousands of people across the nation who have since heard his inspirational message, watched the video or read his book titled *In My Seat* [by Megan Ann Scheibner, BookBaby, 2012].

Jim and Russ had heard Steve speak to a packed hall at the nearby Lakewood Baptist Church a few weeks earlier and wanted to bring his story to the WJTN audience.

Life threatening dangers, Jim knew from his own experience, can arrive with frightening speed, unexpected and deadly. Survival is never guaranteed, but after a near miss with a near-death event, never again taken for granted.

The danger that just missed Steve Scheibner had come from the air, and so had the violence that just missed Jim many years earlier. For both men, the events also prompted similar responses: Josephine Roselle's *"Grazie a Dio!"* and Steve Scheibner's "Thank God!"

Jim Remembers… A Big Wind in Brooklyn Square

My neighborhood was a safe place. That means when there's a sudden danger you don't expect it…you don't even see it coming. Then, when you find out it missed you, you are very thankful… almost as thankful as the pilot who missed his plane.

I was in the big gang on Franklin Street. We were all a few years older than the kids in the little gang. We did let them play with us sometimes, but we never let the little kids go to the theater with us.

One Sunday afternoon, we walked from Franklin Street down to the Roosevelt Theater – later known as the Park Theater – in Brooklyn Square. It cost $.10 for kids to go to the theater then. I don't remember what we went to see, but by the time the movie was over it was a warm Sunday evening, and we went right next door to Johnny's Lunch for a dog and a Coke. Johnny's Lunch, by the way, is still around, though they moved across town a long time ago. It is now run by Dianne, the daughter of the founder, Johnny Colera, and her husband, Gus Calamungi. They invited me do their 50th, 60th and 70th anniversary radio shows from there, and they expect me to do their 80th in a couple of years.

The weather that Sunday evening had looked like rain was coming, but we had no idea of what was already roaring toward us from just beyond the hill. The time was almost 9:30, late twilight, on June 10, 1945.

We sat in those old, high backed wooden booths just talking and enjoying our food. Then we heard the crash of glass. We just thought somebody had slammed the door too hard. Then we heard it again, only much louder. That one was the whole glass storefront to the dining room. Somebody yelled, "Duck!" So we lowered our heads and got under the table and waited. That's when we heard the wind roaring and the driven rain pounding on the roof and hammering the walls.

Soon it quieted down again. It was over. We went to the front of the store and looked out. Sparking wires were hanging down from the telephone poles and lying in puddles across the sidewalk and in the street. Everything was in shambles. It looked look a war zone.

That's when we realized a tornado had just passed through. Those things just never happened here, only out West or someplace, but not here in Jamestown, New York.

We couldn't go home the same way we came. We had to take a different path. We went uphill, not back along Harrison Street where all the damage was. The whole fourth floor of the Maddox Table Company had been sheared right off the top of the building. The fourth floor was now scattered up and down the street, nothing more than wreckage and dangerous debris. And that was only a little bit of the destruction we saw until daylight.

I went home and told my family all about it. All they could say was, *"Dio benedica!"* God bless. They figured it was best that we were in Johnny's lunch just then and not walking home when it happened. That was a pretty lucky hotdog.

The next morning, on Monday, I took a walk down through that area with a member of the Boys Club Board of Directors, Dan Lincoln, to see the damage. We realized how fortunate it was that nobody got killed. They found part of the Veterans Memorial scattered from there all the way up the hill beyond town. If that tornado had hit the restaurant, we might not be here today. It had touched down at the corner of Palmer and Hallock Streets, less than a mile from Johnny's Lunch, and then that twister blew its way right through downtown only yards from where we had sat the night before.

That was a close call with death. All I can say about it today is, *"Grazie a Dio!"* Thank God!

A Conversation with Steve Scheibner

The Times of Your Life begins with its usual Saturday Morning sign-on: "Good morning, I'm Jim Roselle... and I'm Russ Diethrick. Welcome to *The Times of Your Life.*"

Jim Roselle: We got acquainted with Steve Scheibner about a month ago at the Lakewood Baptist Church, and he was kind enough to accept our invitation to be a guest on our broadcast today. We thank you for that, Steve.
Steve Scheibner: Thank you for the invite, Jim and Russ. I appreciate being here.
Russ Diethrick: Tell us about your responsibilities in September of 2001 at American Airlines.

SS: Every flight has two pilots, a captain and a first officer. I serve as the first officer, what most people call the co-pilot. Both seats have to be occupied for the flight to go.

I am what American Airlines calls a "reserve" pilot which means I am on call for any pilot who, for whatever reason, is missing from a flight. When that happens, I have to bid the open seat. There was a list of eight or nine of us on reserve at American.

On September 10, 2001, I was available to go flying on September 11.

RD: When did they finally make the assignment?

SS: In those days they made the assignments at 3 o'clock in the afternoon. So 3 o'clock on the 10th, I went to my computer to login and see what I was going to do the next day, if anything. There was only one flight open, American Airlines flight 11, [the daily transcontinental flight from Boston's Logan International Airport to Los Angeles International Airport].

On 9/11 there was only one reserve pilot available to go flying, and that was me.

I had the crew schedulers pencil my name in. For a small, 30-minute window of opportunity, according to our contract, they also make that flight available to any senior pilot who might want it. That's the only time they can bump a reserve pilot who has signed up for an open seat.

And that's exactly what happened to me on September 10, 2001.

RD: All of your life was affected in that 30-minute window. How many flights do you have in a month, generally?

SS: Typically, I will fly 3 to 4 times a month. The idea is to use them as little as possible by keeping the entire system operating as efficiently as possible.

JR: Steve, now we realize that 24 hours later the tragic event happened in New York City. Where were you, and what was your emotional state at that moment?

SS: The afternoon of the 10th came and went. It's very, very rare that somebody bumps a reserve pilot. It has only happened to me three times in 20 years. I went out to my car, got my traveling suitcase exchanged my dirty laundry for clean laundry, and put the bag back in my car.

"I'm going to Los Angeles tomorrow," I said to my wife. I was just waiting for the phone to ring to confirm it, but the phone never rang. That was unusual.

A senior line-holding pilot by the name of Tom McGinnis, who was celebrating his birthday with his wife and his children, was just looking to pick up an extra trip. During that 30-minute window he called in, saw my name penciled in and asked if he was "legal" to bump me off of the trip. They said yes, and he did. That's why I didn't get my confirmation call.

The next day, Tom showed up for work and departed on time for Los Angeles. At 23,000 feet Tom engaged the autopilot to take them the rest of the way. Everything was just as routine as routine could be.

At that moment, a fellow by the name of Mohammed Atta on that airplane had sinister intent in his heart. There is no other way to express what happened next. At that moment, all hell broke loose on that airplane.

JR: And on the 11th?

SS: On the morning of the 11th, having realized that the assignment was not for me, I put my Navy uniform on and drove the 7 miles to the base where I was working on a project. Then, like everyone else around the world when the news broke, I began to watch what happened unfold on the TV.

It still didn't occur to me that was my flight, even though I heard that it had been flight 11 out of Boston. I knew the crew on that flight because Boston is a very small base. I was concerned for the families, the pilots and flight attendants because those people are my personal friends. It wasn't until later on that evening that it hit me.

I pastored a church in my neighborhood at that time and we had an impromptu prayer meeting at my house that evening. During the prayer meeting I went back to my computer to see if I could bring up the names of the crew on that flight. The media wasn't going to release those names for a few more days. I thought maybe there was a back way in at American Airlines to find out who was on that flight.

When I logged into the airline site the screen from the 10th came up, and it had the flight assignment and where my name had been penciled in. Now there was no name. All it said was: "Sequence failed continuity." That is code at American Airlines meaning that the flight never reached its destination. That is a huge understatement.

That's when it hit me that was the flight that I had packed my bags for and been bumped from.

I was overwhelmed. I just went blank inside; I didn't really know how to feel. My wife came in and watched me staring at the screen.

"What's wrong, Steve?"

"Honey, I packed my bags for Los Angeles," I said. "That was the flight that was hijacked." We just sat there in stunned silence.

JR: Have you had any other close calls?

SS: I've had a couple of near-death experiences in airplanes. I've been in combat, and I've been shot at. I've had some very close calls landing in rain so heavy that the plane began to hydroplane, just like sliding on black ice in an airplane going 130 miles an hour. We finally brought the plane to rest with about 3 feet of runway left out of 8500 feet, but that was way too close.

Those are moments when you go home and hug your wife and kids at the end of the day. Every once in a while there is a rare moment like that in aviation.

JR: Look at what Sully Sullenberger did with that plane.

SS: That's absolutely amazing. What's most amazing to me about landing that airplane in the Hudson River is that the airlines don't train for ditching at sea or on the water. The conventional wisdom was that it can't be done so they don't want to waste any time on it. A couple of times in the past that airliners have ditched in the ocean or on water, everybody died. It was a disaster.

Sully had never trained for it. His decision-making process when both engines quit at 3000 feet while climbing out of LaGuardia Airport was amazing. He took control, came up with a plan of action and executed it all in 3 ½ minutes. Meanwhile the crew in the back and air traffic control were both calling him while he was sorting through his own emotional upheaval. Sully Sullenberger ought to be Man of the Year, in my book.

JR: Well, Stephen, I would like to get to the reason you were at the Lakewood Baptist Church. I think you used the phrase that you live with more intensity now.

SS: It's a sense of urgency. Now I travel around to churches sharing the rest of the story. I talk about living like a "borrowed time believer".

There are two sorts of Christians these days that I am observing. There are "Sunday Saints" and there are "borrowed time believers". Sunday Saints are always going to be getting around to getting serious about their faith, someday, but they've kind of got God at arm's length. For a long time in my Christian life, I lived like that.

The events of September 11, 2001, showed me my own mortality. I think that is a distinct privilege. With that privilege comes an obligation. I am obligated now to live like I am living on borrowed time, which I am. I have seen my smoking hole on national TV. I know I should have died, but I did not. It has changed the course and the intensity of how I live each day of my life

In the last 10 years, I have started a church, I have grown another church, have completed two master's degrees and a doctorate degree and adopted a child. I wrote a Navy Core Values course and put about 10,000 people through that course. All of that is evidence of the fact I got hold of my life in a real way, and I'm living it every day with that sense of urgency.

RD: I hope next time I fly, you're in the cockpit, Steve.

JR: Thank you for that message, Steve Scheibner.

Chapter 15

Actors – Cinema Stars - TV Personalities

Jamestown, New York, more than most people would suspect, is a "show biz" town. This is not only because it is Lucille Ball's hometown, but because, especially in recent years, the annual Lucille Ball-Desi Arnaz Comedy Fest hosted by Jamestown has showcased dozens of the country's most famous comedians, comic headliners and the brightest, new and rising stand-up stars. Both the history and the future of American comedy are rooted in Jamestown. Just as the comedic and tragic faces of theater are depicted back-to-back, the dramatic stars of TV, stage and cinema have always received the same kind of welcome as the comics at Jim's microphone.

Luck? I don't know anything about luck. I've never banked on it and I'm afraid of people who do. Luck to me is something else: Hard work - and realizing what is opportunity and what isn't... Ability is of little account without opportunity.

Lucille Ball

I don't look on it as any great shakes of acting, it's not subtle or restrained. It isn't any of the things you like to think might apply to your acting.

Margaret Hamilton on her role as the Wicked Witch

Judy kept us all going. When she came on the set, it was as though the lights got brighter. Her freshness and vitality are things I will never forget.

Margaret Hamilton on Judy Garland

I think that you have to believe in your destiny; that you will succeed, you will meet a lot of rejection, and it is not always a straight path, there will be detours - so enjoy the view.

Michael York

Gregg Oppenheimer
I Remember Lucy

Gregg Oppenheimer, son of *I Love Lucy* creator-producer and head writer, Jess Oppenheimer, entered the entertainment world as an unwitting humorist in 1955, when his dad brought four year old Gregg to the *I Love Lucy* set. Lucille Ball looked at Gregg, knelt down on the stage and asked him, "Where did you get those big brown eyes?" Gregg replied in a perfectly innocent deadpan, "They came with the face." Lucy, they say, nearly fell off the stage laughing.

Gregg's father, Jess [Jessurun James Oppenheimer] had begun compiling a memoir, but it remained unfinished at the time of his death in 1988. In tribute, Gregg devoted several years of research to completing the unfinished work. His labor of love made him one of the world's foremost authorities on I Love Lucy and on the stars and performers connected with the show.

The memoir was titled: *Laughs, Luck...and Lucy: How I Came to Create the Most Popular Sitcom of All Time* [Syracuse University Press 1996].

Jess Oppenheimer's career had spanned the years that came to be called the Golden Age of Radio. His credits included co-producing *The Danny Kaye Show with Lucille Ball, The Debbie Reynolds Show, Bob Hope Presents the Chrysler Theatre, The United States Steel Hour,* and *Get Smart.*

Jim Roselle understood that Golden Age, too. It was a time when people, if they wanted news and entertainment from anywhere beyond their hometown borders, could only go to movies, magazines, a few newspapers and to radio. Families, in those days, would often gather around a radio in their living rooms and listen to the words and music, the ads and adventures that engaged their imaginations in ways beyond the power of tell-all-television. TV left much less to the imagination and, some would still claim, turned family time into couch potato time.

Gregg Oppenheimer's father, Jess, had produced *I Love Lucy* when Lucy came to television. Lucille Ball, however, had been on the radio long before that, most notably in her lead as Liz Cooper on *My Favorite* Husband. When radio's Golden Age began to fade in the light of TV, Lucy turned to television. Jim Roselle, on the other hand, kept riding the wave of Golden Age radio. He created a huge fan base and thousands of lasting memories across the community by broadcasting popular music in a way that both rivaled and modeled itself after his new competitor, television.

Jim Remembers... The Golden Age of Radio and the Sock Hops

I remember the Golden Age of Radio. That's when the Wednesday night sock hops came along at Midway Amusement Park on Chautauqua Lake and at St. James and Ss. Peter & Paul's recreation halls in Jamestown. Those were just about the most popular of all entertainments for young people in those days.

Dick Clark and his popular *American Bandstand* program had inspired hundreds of local bandstand shows all across the country. I had modeled mine after his, too. We were averaging 900 kids at our bandstand sock hops, and each one paid 75 cents to get in. Of course, Midway and the others benefited, too, because the kids all bought lots of refreshments there.

We weren't playing rock 'n roll, though. We were playing Glenn Miller, Tommy Dorsey, Nat King Cole, Tony Bennett and Frank Sinatra. With that lineup, we beat the other Jamestown station that only played rock 'n roll.

Herb Nicklaus, WJTN's engineer, built two sturdy cases with turntables in them. They were like two big suitcases. And they never broke down. They lasted for all the years I did the sock hops. Herb never "broke down" either. He remained the engineering genius at WJTN for 41 years.

People still remember those sock hops. A woman recently stopped me on the street to ask me about something she still remembered.

"Jim, do you remember me? I came to your sock hops at St. James." That would have been way back in 1958. "I came to the hops at Ss. Peter and Paul Church, too, and never missed one."

"I'm sorry, I don't exactly remember you," I said, trying to apologize.

"You should. You used to tease me. You always made little fun out of my name. You turned it into Ticky Tacky." She was smiling, though, so I knew it had been OK. "It was fun," she said.

"Well, yes! Now I do. I remember you very well." Her real name immediately came to mind. "Bring me up-to-date. It's only been a little more than 55 years, Ticky Tacky." We both laughed. Then I learned about her marriage and her four children and much, much more.

Those Sock Hops were more than dances; they played an important part in a lot of lives.

A Conversation with Gregg Oppenheimer

Jim Roselle: Good morning, Gregg Oppenheimer. Welcome to Chautauqua.
Gregg Oppenheimer: Good morning. I'm looking forward to getting back to Jamestown.

JR: This is a big weekend. It's the weekend of the Lucy Fest [The Lucille Ball Festival of Comedy, held every year in Jamestown, early in August near Lucy's birthday, August 6].

GO: It's just wonderful. The warmth that I feel from everybody when the town has the festival every year is just phenomenal. After so many years, Lucy is still such a beloved character and such a beloved show. It's just terrific.

JR: You are going to be a big part of it, presenting a couple of radio plays.

GO: I traced the origins of the Lucy Ricardo character to a thing my dad did before that, which was the Baby's Snooks Show starring Fanny Brice. It started on the radio in September, 1944. We'll do a bit of that.

JR: That was a wonderful show. We're proud of our own WJTN personality, Lee John, who became part of that program.

GO: This year I'm adding something else. Two years ago I wrote my own play, *I Love Lucy-The Untold Story*. I've now written a second act for that. I'm going to do one scene that commemorates the birth of Little Ricky. It is behind the scenes in the fights with the network about whether they would show a pregnant woman on television.

Back then, you couldn't do that. You couldn't even say the word "pregnant" on radio. Now, you can practically see how it happens on television.

JR: Your dad, Jess Oppenheimer, produced the comedy that Lucy and Desi presented for 155 episodes.

GO: He wrote the show, too. He and his work were wonderful influences on me. We were very close. We tended to finish each other's sentences.

JR: Didn't he think, after all those episodes, they had reached every corner of comedy they could?

GO: He tried to talk Lucy and Desi into quitting while they were ahead. He wanted them to go out on a really high note because he had taken them to Hollywood, and he had taken them to Europe. He said, "Where do we go next, the moon?"

JR: Lucille Ball was a real innovator in TV technology, wasn't she?

GO: She studied the point of view of the audience looking toward the stage and created the technique of using three cameras. Nobody had ever done that before.

The other amazing thing is that *I Love Lucy* had only three writers. Shows usually had about 18 writers, and they would do 22 shows a year. Lucy did 40 shows in 40 weeks. They were making everything up as they went along, including where to put the bleachers, whether to use chairs, where should the booth be and how to use the lights. They had no idea. They had to invent everything as they went along.

Everybody is still using the same techniques, except that it's videotape now instead of film, but other than that it pretty much looks like the *I Love Lucy* stage when you walk into any TV studio today.

The big difference is that Desi was very insistent that it should be run like a play and go to film just like that. There were very, very minimal breaks and pauses in the action except to reload film when we had to. We got out of there in 45 minutes. And now it's 3 ½ hours to tape the usual TV sitcom.

JR: What do you see in the world of comedy today?

GO: There are some great comedians out there. The problem is that you can say anything. Orson Welles once said, "The absence of limitations is the enemy of art." I think that is true. It is true of movies too. Since they can do anything with computer graphics, you don't get blown away when you see something amazing – it's probably only computer generated.

Back then, if you saw something on film, they actually had to do it. On TV, there were so many limitations to what we could do on *I Love Lucy*, what we could say and the subjects we could cover, we had to be really creative. That's why it's held up all this time. We had to be really creative or else we wouldn't last more than a few weeks.

JR: Was it true that they were concerned about the bedroom scene, that nobody ever put husband and wife in the same bed together?

GO: Actually, Lucy and Desi never were shown in bed together. They were in twin beds which were right next to each other. In the pilot, the beds were several feet apart. They moved the beds farther apart when Lucy got pregnant.

JR: If I'm correct, the episode *Lucy Goes to the Hospital* [season 2, episode 16] still remains one of the most watched television programs of all time.

GO: In terms of percentage, it is the most-watched ever, and it will never be exceeded. I can guarantee that because the audience share - the percentage of all the TV sets tuned to *I Love Lucy* that evening - was 72 percent – 44 million viewers. That is unbelievable.

JR: The *I Love Lucy* episodes literally changed the life of America on Monday nights.

GO: Department stores closed on Monday nights. The episode where she had the baby was the night before President Eisenhower's first inauguration, the first televised inauguration in the nation's history. They thought the inauguration was going to be huge, but Lucy got 15 million more people watching her.

In fact, they interrupted the pre-inaugural balls and parties in Washington DC to allow a TV set to be brought in so everybody could sit down and watch the show.

JR: You mentioned Desi's tight scheduling around the filming of the *I Love Lucy* episodes. Although those were the early days of TV, even big stars like Lucy knew radio was still king – the overlap between the rise of TV and the Golden Age of Radio was an interesting time.

I interviewed Lucy once during those days. Lucy respected radio enough to make time for the conversation. I had to respect TV enough to work around Desi's super tight filming schedule for the episode they were doing that day.

Jim Remembers… The Girl on the Telephone*

Lucille Ball and I grew up in the same hometown - Jamestown. Lucy's career had already brought her fame and fortune in the days when I was still a new broadcaster. In 1953, one of Lucy's Hollywood hits, *The Long, Long Trailer*, had arrived for screening at Jamestown's Palace Theater. Along with Lucy and Desi, the box office hit featured Marjorie Main and Keenan Wynn. I knew she'd be a great attraction for my radio audience.

For some reason, I thought it natural to just pick up a phone and call her studio in California, though in those days transcontinental calls to places like Hollywood needed live operators and a lot of planning. Fortunately, my engineer at WJTN was able to help me with that part. I pitched my idea for an interview to Lucy's publicist. Lucy accepted my invitation right away; she'd never lost touch with her hometown and never stopped loving it.

Lucy, however, was in the midst of filming an *I Love Lucy* episode. Production schedules for the show were as tight as a chorus girl's stockings; Ricky wanted scenes filmed in a single take. Weekly TV shows, especially this most popular show ever, made uncompromising demands. Lucille Ball had to call me on her lunch hour. Even her star status couldn't change that.

It was 1 o'clock out there in Hollywood, so it was 4 o'clock here. Lucy was on her lunch break, and she decided to talk to *me* instead. Can you imagine that?

"Hi Jim!" Lucy said. "What's the weather like back in Jamestown?

I think I told her it was a nice summer day, but you know, it mattered to Lucy. I think, as good as things ever got for her, you could always find a hint of a homesick girl there. We talked about her movie, all right, but we talked just as much about the people in Jamestown, like her old girlfriends, Pauline Lopus and Marian VanBlack, and lots of the places around town we both knew.

When I recall my conversation with Lucille Ball back in 1953 about *The Long, Long Trailer,* I still have the impression that Lucy felt a personal connection to one certain line in that movie.

"It's a fine thing when you come home to your home and your home is gone." She was far from home and she missed it. I could tell.

*This 1953 telephone conversation between Jim Roselle and Lucille Ball was either not recorded at the time or is lost from the WJTN archives, but still remembered in vivid detail by Jim.

Margaret Hamilton: That Wicked Witch

Margaret Hamilton
a fine lady, not a wicked witch

Margaret Brainard Hamilton (1902-1985) is best known as the Wicked Witch of the West in Metro-Goldwyn-Mayer's film, *The Wizard of Oz* [Warner Brothers, August 15, 1939]. In the film, Margaret played both Dorothy's thoroughly unpleasant Kansas neighbor, Miss Almira Gulch and the Land of Oz's Wicked Witch. After filming *Oz*, Margaret played important roles in more than a dozen Hollywood movies and performed frequently on stage.

Jim Roselle was never a wicked witch, but he was a bug-eating psychotic.

Jim Remembers… Eating Flies

The Lucille Ball Little Theater in Jamestown had just hired Frederica Woodard as their new artistic director and her husband, Dan Woodard, as technical director. When they came to town to take those positions, I invited them to the studio so I could introduce them to my audience.

Renfield catches flies

They started to follow me whenever I was on location for a remote broadcast. That usually gave them an opportunity to plug the next play, and I was always glad to put them on.

Then one day they came to the studio. The sign outside my door says, "Dew Drop Inn," so they did. But they only opened the door and threw a book at me. It was a script. They said, "See you tonight at 7 o'clock," and then they walked out. I didn't even have a chance to chat with them.

After they left, I picked up the script and looked at it. It was *Count Dracula*. They had underlined the part they wanted me to do. It was Renfield, the assistant.

When I saw the lines that I had to say, I went home and I asked my sister, Ann - I was living with her between marriages - what she thought. I didn't think I could do those lines.

She said that maybe I should go, anyway, if only as a courtesy. So I called my friend, Sam Paladino, who I happened to know was doing the Dracula part. Sam was a good friend, a very successful local businessman, a veteran stage performer and known around town as a gentle man who defined dapper in his attire and demeanor every single day.

"Sam?"

"Yeah, Jim?" I told him what had happened.

"Sam, I'm asking your advice. I just feel like I'll be unable to do Renfield."

"Show up," Sam said. "Just show up. Please do me a favor and show up."

"Okay, buddy." So I showed up.

Backstage that night they didn't pay any attention to me at all. I asked them what to do. They told me to just listen for the line right before mine, and then walk on and do what the script says. It was only a couple of lines, so I did it.

I was hoping they would tell me "Nice try," and that would be it. But what they did say was; "Show up tomorrow night."

I got the part, and it changed my life. I'm grateful I did it because it gave me an insight into theater. Since then, I go to the theater a lot. I can appreciate it because I realized what is involved. I realized what a director goes through. I learned how she educates an actor on how to do a scene, what's important, how to block, and much more. After all, when you're *not* talking, what are you supposed to do?

Well, she taught me how to catch a fly in midair and gobble it down. That's what Renfield did, so I did it, too.

Like Margaret Hamilton, my character didn't make me look too good, but it was a good character to do, and I'm glad I did it.

A Conversation with Margaret Hamilton

Jim Roselle: I feel I'm meeting somebody I've known so closely and so intimately over the years. Some people say that to me, too, because maybe I'm in their homes every day on the radio. This beautiful lady has been in my home every year, for years and years. Let's welcome the Wicked Witch.

Margaret Hamilton: Thank you. Glad to be here. But this sure isn't Kansas, is it? Though it's pretty nice here, too.

JR: Did you think at all when *Oz* was made that it would have such a long life?

MH: I think not, if not for television. That's the thing that really did it.

JR: *The Wizard Of Oz* was made in 1939. It's been repeated on television about every year ever since. I can't help picturing you riding your bicycle.

But it's amazing. Most people have greeted you here as Cora the Coffee Lady [in TV commercials as Maxwell House Coffee's General Store owner, Cora, over a period of eight years]. It's kind of a dilemma. Which do you like to be remembered by?

MH: I like Cora. I think she's a nice person. But, of course, the witch is a little more substantial in some ways because that is not going to end and Cora is, eventually.

JR: Do children who watch *Oz* recognize you?

MH: Something very nice has happened. You know, a lot of little children are very frightened of the witch, for which I have some regret. Having taught kindergarten and nursery school for six years before I went into the theater, I'm very fond of children, so it seemed sort of ironic that I should end up being thoroughly hated by most of the very young ones.

Since I've been doing Cora, the little children are told that's the lady who does the witch. They say, "No that's not the lady. She isn't green, and she doesn't have that hat." But finally, mother persuades them it is so. It has been very comforting, apparently, to a lot of them to think that I am really a perfectly nice person and can smile and be pleasant - not really a witch.

JR: How was it working with Judy Garland?

MH: She was a darling. She was 16 and really one of the dearest young people I've ever known. We were all very, very fond of her and devoted to her. Everybody was enthusiastic and excited about it because she was so excited about a lot of it.

She was also finishing her last year in high school at the same time. She would go off and study. We didn't talk a great deal because she would leave immediately and go to a little area that was screened off as a school room, and she would go on with her work. Then she would come back and do her scene and go back again. It was amazing that she could do both those things at the same time.

JR: Do you sit back on a Sunday night and watch the *Wizard of Oz* like the rest of America?

MH: I do if I'm there by my TV.

JR: How long does it take to put together a Cora Coffee Lady commercial for Maxwell House?

MH: It takes a full day to make a 27 second commercial. They are very, very particular. I think commercials are among of the hardest things actors do. They are very definite in every single move. They have to have every word exactly right. You do it over, and over, and over, and over again until you get it exactly right and exactly within 27 seconds. It can't be 26 ¼ or 26 ½ or a whole second over. A second is too long.

JR: We are just delighted to have you here at Chautauqua, and I will not think of you as a wicked witch anymore, but the nice lady who runs Cora's General Store. Is that all right with you?

MH: Yes, that's all right.

JR: It's been a delightful moment for us to have a great lady on our microphone, Margaret Hamilton.

Michael York
Synchronicity and Shakespeare

By 2014, Michael York has celebrated nearly 100 screen acting credits, almost uncountable stage and television appearances and continues to lecture internationally on the history and art of acting and on William Shakespeare's works and the authorship of plays. His many contributions to acting have earned him Britain's OBE (Order of the British Empire), France's *Arts et Lettres*, and a Hollywood Walk of Fame Star.

York grew up in England, earned an MA degree from Oxford University, and eventually became a citizen of the United States, settling in California.

Jim and Michael's conversation touched on the topic of synchronicity. They each had, over their lifetimes, encountered powerful "coincidences" that, whether orchestrated by chance, by fate or by God, moved and shaped their lives in wonderful and wholly unpredictable ways.

Michael York also revealed that he has found reasons to believe William Shakespeare is "The Playwright Who Never Was". Jim has his own story of the "Guest Who Never Showed", reflecting that the synchronicity is never assured of the right people being in the right place at the right time.

Once in a while, synchronicity becomes tragically misaligned and what might have been never comes to be.

Jim Remembers… The Guest Who Never Showed

Edgar Bergen has been gone from show business for 35 years, but his fame continues through his daughter, Candice, better known as Murphy Brown, winner of five Emmys and two Golden Globes and nominated for many more honors for her starring roles on TV and in film.

Edgar had started his career in vaudeville back when vaudeville was still a big and brassy thing on the American stage. He was a ventriloquist with a dummy named Charlie. They had already scored huge successes in show business - on stage, in the movies and on radio and TV - for 56 years by the time Jim Roselle booked him for a radio interview on WJTN and a fundraiser for the Jamestown Boys Club in October, 1978.

Edgar Bergen was much loved but less often honored than his daughter. He eventually did receive an Oscar of his own, though. The Academy made it honorary. They gave him a fine wooden clone of the golden Oscar in honor of Edgar's lumber-headed friend, Charlie McCarthy.

Edgar and Charlie had always fascinated Jim Roselle. He had also entertained WJTN's radio audience for years. Ventriloquism on the radio, of course, is an oddity. Its appeal is mostly visual, but the audience simply loved to listen to Edgar, Charlie and another of their blockheaded friends, Mortimer Snerd.

Edgar Bergen threw his voice out of Charlie McCarthy's sassy, girl-crazy mouth and pulled off stealthy *double entendres* the Federal Communications Commission of the day would have censored, had they not appeared, albeit on radio, to emanate from a wooden head with a top hat and monocle.

On one evening's show, Edgar's guest was Dale Evans, the gun-toting, hard-riding and glamorous wife of TV and film star, the cowboy, Roy Rogers.

    Charlie: "May I have a kiss good-bye?"
    Dale Evans: "Well, I can't see any harm in that!"
    Charlie: "Oh. I wish you could. A harmless kiss doesn't sound very thrilling."

Mae West was once banned from *NBC* radio for more than a decade following an even spicier (for the day) on-air chat with Charlie. She blamed Charlie, of course.

Jim Roselle knew that air time on WJTN with Edgar Bergen would be an amazing "get" for the station and his upcoming Boys Club benefit. He called Bergen's agent and, to his delight and surprise, he booked an appearance and arranged to pay his appearance fee. Adding to Jim's amazement, Edgar even tacked on an extra 45-minute show in the afternoon for the younger fans without an extra appearance fee.

The arrangements were finalized in mid-September of 1978 just after Bergen had announced his retirement, slated for the end of a two week farewell appearance at Caesar's Palace Hotel in Las Vegas. That show opened on September 27, 1978.

Sadly, only about a week before Edgar Bergen's Jamestown show, Jim learned that his promised guest had died in his sleep of kidney disease at age 75, only three days after stepping on stage for his final tour.

Jim recalls, "A listener named Brett Johnson heard the story. He felt so bad about my missed opportunity that he went out and bought me fully functional (except for Edgar's irreplaceable voice, of course) Charlie McCarthy and Mortimer Snerd dummies that still sit on a shelf in my office and watch me work every day."

Edgar Bergen's agent, loyal to his star's commitments, even to the end, called Jim and offered to replace the stricken star for Jim's benefit show with "somebody just as big", a famous opera singer.

Jim understood the radio business and he knew his audience. He respectfully declined the offer.

A Conversation with Michael York

Jim Roselle: Is this your first visit to Chautauqua?
Michael York: Yes it is, but I have heard about it so much that I am thrilled to finally make it.

JR: We are thrilled to have you, and we are delighted to display your book, *Accidentally on Purpose* [Simon & Schuster, 1991]. Why did you title it that?
MY: I wanted a sort of catch-penny title that that you would look at twice. But there was a deeply serious and philosophical intent, too. If you examine an actor's life, which is an odd thing, you find there's no blueprint. You don't join in the mailroom and see your way up a specific way to the boardroom. There is no logic behind it. If you do A, B doesn't necessarily follow. Does this all happen by accident or is there some sort of other plan?
JR: I have heard another name for it. The word is synchronicity. Have you heard about that?
MY: Absolutely. I'm a great believer in synchronicity.
JR: In other words, it is not accidental.
MY: If you like to believe someone is doing all of the traffic controlling, that's a lovely way of thinking of it. I would love to think of it that way. That it's not all anarchy, that there is, sort of, some purpose. Of course my book was written far too early. They say, "Write your life." But I think that's absurd because I hope, touch wood, I'm only halfway through. It's too soon to write it all.

But then you think, rather than wait right up until the end, when maybe the memory is unreliable, take a pause and see where you've been in order to make what lies ahead maybe more meaningful.
JR: There are so many ways to define acting. You have written, "Good acting happens when you are not entirely aware it is happening."
MY: Let me explain. It's a right brain, left brain activity, especially movie acting. On the one hand, you are being totally technical. You are moving to a mark, getting into a light, you are pretending that this camera is not there, you're being highly technical and efficient. Meanwhile the other half of the brain is forgetting all of that and just trying to be creative and inventive. I think you are both aware and not aware.

When I was in the National Theater [London], when Lawrence Olivier was running it, there was a famous production of *Othello* that he did. It was spectacular.

There was one performance where the audience was electrified, and so was the cast. The hairs were standing up on the back of the neck. It was fantastic. At the end of the performance the audience exploded into applause. The cast applauded Olivier all the way back to his dressing room only to hear the door slammed in fury.

So someone gets up courage and knocks lightly. "Larry? What's the matter? Tonight you were simply sublime. You were wonderful. You were in another realm. You were fantastic."

The door hadn't opened but we heard him shout back through it, "Yes! I know I was. But I don't know how on earth I did it, so how can I do it again?" And that is the mystery. That's why we all go to the theater. You never quite know what you're going to get.
JR: You also mentioned George Burns' brilliant observation. He said to you, "The secret of acting is sincerity. If you can fake that, you've got it made." Is that the way you still feel?
MY: Absolutely. That's it in a nutshell. He certainly made it work for him, wonderfully. You know good acting when you see it. It's hard to describe. It's something that doesn't conform to any rules.
JR: What age were you when the acting bug bit you?

MY: I was very young. It was something I loved to do as a kid. But I also loved to kick a football around and play cricket. Later, though, at Oxford, there was a chance to do every kind of drama, from experimental theater to the classics. I didn't want to go through life knowing that I could have done it but I hadn't dared. I thought I would get that out of my system, so I went into the business. Fortunately one thing led to another.

JR: I can relate to that, Michael, because I had the same feeling that if I don't try it, I will always regret it. You were offered the role in *Love Story*, weren't you? Why did you turn it down?

MY: Nobody had any idea that this little story would turn into what it became. I thought it was a little, dare I say it, overly sentimental. And I went to see Robert Evans in his office. He said, "We are doing this little movie. There is no money in it, but if it is successful, there is money at the back." That's a good way of having a profit participation in a movie. Had I taken that film I would have been so rich it would have ruined my life. But you can never tell. That's what I love about it.

You don't know how something is going to turn out. The big studio films or the other little ones where, you know, the soufflé doesn't rise. The little independent films are the ones suddenly everyone wants to see. The golden rule of Hollywood is, "No one knows anything."

JR: Tell us about working with Lawrence Olivier.

MY: I was very fortunate to work with him because he had been an idol of mine. He seemed to have encompassed everything as a role model. He was a legendary actor in all the media, from film to stage, but he was also a producer and a director. He started the National Theater Company [London, 1963].

JR: I've got to ask you about an argument that's been going on for - I don't how many years now. Did Shakespeare really write Shakespeare? It's the famous authorship question.

MY: It's a very legitimate question and it's the most interesting, unsolved detective story that we have.

I personally don't think it was the "Stratford Candidate." There is such slim evidence. He would be a man with an illiterate wife and daughter, who owned no books. Nothing is known about him and this sort of cantankerous, litigious old devil was not the genius who could empathize with everyone. The argument is, however, "Yes, but he was a genius."

As if genius covered everything. Of course, to a certain extent it does. For my money, the most plausible candidate is Edward DeVere, the 17th Earl of Oxford who was a peer of the realm, a great writer in his own right. His work is almost indistinguishable from the so-called Shakespeare or, as it should be pronounced, Shack-spur.

Shakespeare was an Elizabethan era give away for a pseudonym. His coat of arms is someone shaking a spear. Edward DeVere solves the question of the sonnets. What is that Warwickshire yokel doing writing highly erotic, charged sonnets to a peer of the realm? It's unthinkable. When you have Edward DeVere, on the other hand, who is writing these messages, it becomes sensational and everything comes into focus.

Now this is highly controversial. It's debated endlessly. I must say, though, that when it is debated Edward DeVere usually wins. One day we're going to find the smoking gun, that piece of document that will link everything together. Why didn't he come out and say he was Shakespeare? Because he couldn't.

Being an actor in that day was being a rogue and a vagabond, you had to go to the red light district amid the bearbaiting and the prostitutes to see drama. It was not respectable. It all had to be kept under wraps. In any case, it is a thrilling mystery story. [Since the date of this interview, York has co-signed a document titled *The Declaration of Reasonable Doubt About the Identity of William Shakespeare* along with nearly 3000 popular and scholarly signatories.]

JR: I thank you for that. Now I have to put in my famous "what if" question. I'm going to take you back from Day-1 of history up until now. There are four people within all that time you could invite to dinner some night. Who would you love to have sitting at your table that night?

MY: Mozart, because he's so funny and has so many vulgar jokes. Then I'd go and ask him to play and I'd be mesmerized. Of course, I'd have Shakespeare, because I'd find out who he was. And you're very welcome to come, too, Jim.

JR: Boy, am I glad I got this on tape.

MY: You'd get the best interview you've ever had. But I need some help with the fourth dinner guest [Michael turns to the audience and asks his wife for a suggestion. She calls out an answer.] OK, Great idea. Leonardo DaVinci.

JR: Michael York, thank you so much. We welcome you to Chautauqua.

MY: And thank you. Delighted to be here.

Midway Park, Maple Springs, New York

Sock Hop

St. James Church, Jamestown, New York

Chapter 16

Religious Leaders

*F*rom fundamentalist to evangelical, from new age to mystical and from every one of the world's great religions, Chautauqua Institution draws religious leaders to stimulate thinking where there are differences, to spur dialog where there is controversy and to inspire hope, optimism and deeper faith wherever it is wanted and needed. Jim Roselle, raised and nurtured in the traditional faith of his family, seeks insights and understanding among religious leaders who carry on the best Chautauqua traditions there every summer. In these interviews, Jim's open microphone invites open minds to join the inquiry and continue along their own journeys of faith.

The most powerful moral influence is example.

Huston Smith

The Gospel is about grace, and we all know that grace is about us receiving from God blessings that we don't deserve.

Tony Campolo

I experience God as the power of love.

John Shelby Spong

Religious Leaders at Chautauqua Institution

The historic roots of Chautauqua Institution are deeply planted in religion, especially in Christian education and scholarly debate concerning spiritual matters.

In 1874, when it was founded by two Methodists, Lewis Miller and John Heyl, the rustic campground was called the Chautauqua Lake Sunday School Assembly. It operated as an experimental educational program for out-of-school, vacation learning. Its success almost immediately broadened the curriculum to offer a wider range of academic subjects along with art, music and physical education.

Within its first decade the religious offerings also widened, becoming more ecumenical in spirit and practice. Chautauqua Institution's Department of Religion now presents eminent religious leaders from many faith traditions to encourage growth, debate and tolerance in both the spiritual and intellectual realms of religion. The summer's speakers, whether preachers or teachers, are drawn from across the United States and around the world.

Jim Roselle, having been raised in a sincerely religious family, and having adopted deep commitments to honesty and integrity in both personal and community matters, always makes an easy, personal connection with the religious leaders at Chautauqua. He invites them to lively conversations around the WJTN microphone.

For Jim, his personal faith tradition, like Tony Campolo's, never drew a line in the sand between sacred and secular, never set up a wall of exclusion against what some have called the "worldly pleasures". As a boy, for example, Jim was delighted to join his altar boy buddy in a musical adventure that could have skirted some tricky issues for the more puritanical among his neighbors.

Jim Remembers…A Prayer and a Song

My mother had always been serious about her faith. She was a devout Catholic, and she made sure we were, too, even down to that dime she had ready for us every Sunday. I certainly went to catechism on a regular basis.

I went to the Samuel G. Love Elementary School where we were given release time in the afternoon once a week for catechism class down at the church. We had nuns doing the teaching. They were pretty strict. But we loved the competition on learning our lessons.

I competed against Tony Lucca, the fellow whose sister married Joe Caprino. Tony was very good at knowing facts and lessons. We would compete to win the St. Joseph medals. You could win if you knew your catechism lesson well. He was pretty sharp, but I did beat him once in a while. He became an altar boy. We all thought he was going to be a priest; we were really pretty sure of it. He wanted me to be an altar boy, too, so I tried. But I had a difficult time with it. I didn't feel comfortable. I did one mass, I think, or maybe two, but I didn't stay with it. He was always very sincere about it, though.

On another occasion, Tony talked me into going into an amateur contest at the local theater. It was called Uncle Walt's Club. They had a talent show on Saturday afternoons. The rules were that you could do whatever you wanted to do and try to win five dollars. That was first prize. He talked me into going down there with him and we sang a song, *Rainbow on the River*.

> *There's a rainbow on the river,*
> *the skies are clearing . . .*
> *You'll soon be hearing a heavenly song,*
> *all the day long . . .*

That was a popular song in a 1936 movie [*Rainbow on the River*, RKO Radio Pictures] starring boy soprano, Bobby Breen. Canadian born Breen had started singing in a smoky Toronto night club at the age of four and later performed in the bawdy vaudeville houses of his day. Although we were good Catholic boys, we didn't let those associations bother us. There was nothing to take to confession about that, as far as we could tell!

Then people had to vote during the week for the best act. We got all of our cousins and everybody in the neighborhood to vote. We won first prize! Five bucks. That was my fabulous singing career.

Tony Campolo and the Prostitute's Birthday Party

During the fourth week of the 2012 Chautauqua season, the Reverend Tony Campolo was the Chaplain of the Week at the Institution, a role in which he has served on a number of previous occasions.

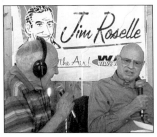

Tony Campolo and Jim on the air

Campolo is the author of about three dozen books, serves as professor emeritus of sociology at Eastern University near Philadelphia, and is a former University of Pennsylvania faculty member. He also founded and serves as president of the Evangelical Association for the Promotion of Education.

Reverend Campolo is renowned as a passionate and outspoken champion of living in the world as a socially conscious, Evangelical Christian activist caring for the poor, oppressed and forgotten and, especially, for children the world over who live in such oppressive circumstances.

During this on-air interview [one of the many conversations Jim and Tony have had over the years] they discussed the Zimmerman case in Florida in which a young black man was fatally shot by a civilian neighborhood watch officer who had received a highly controversial not guilty verdict following his trial for murder. The conversation stimulated some deep discussions and became rather serious.

Then Jim changed the direction…

Jim Roselle: I'm going to get to a lighter subject.
Reverend Tony Campolo: Yes please! I always enjoy the show, and when I leave, I'm always happy, so let's get to it. All of a sudden, here I am down in the dumps.

JR: Okay. You're going to be happy at the end of the show because I was told I have to get Reverend Campolo to tell the Birthday Party Story.
Rev. C: Okay. That'll be fun.

I went to do a speaking engagement in Honolulu. When you come from the East Coast, the time difference is such that you wake up at about 3 o'clock in the morning, and you're hungry. I went looking for something to eat.

Up on a little side street, I found this greasy spoon. I went in and saw there were no booths; there was just this row of stools in front of the counter. I sat down. Nobody was in the place. I didn't touch the menu. It was one of those plastic menus with grease piled up on it. It hadn't been cleaned up in who knows how long. I was sure that if I opened it something extraterrestrial would fall out.

Then this really big guy, no other word for it, this *fat* guy, came out of the back room, I guess it was the kitchen. He was unshaved, wearing this greasy apron and smoking a cigar. He took the cigar out of his mouth and put it down on the counter. He looked me over.

"What do you want?"
"How about a cup of coffee and a doughnut?"

He poured the coffee. Then he wiped his hands on his filthy apron and picked up the doughnut. I really hate that.

And so I was sitting there eating my dirty doughnut and drinking my coffee at 3:30 in the morning in this empty greasy spoon and the door opened. Eight or nine prostitutes came walking in, and they sat on either side of me.

"Tomorrow is my birthday," said the one right next to me to her friend. "I'm going to be 39."
"So?" her friend said. "What do you want me to do, sing happy birthday? Do you want a cake? Do you want a birthday party?"
"Look, I'm not looking for anything. I haven't had a birthday party in my whole life. I don't expect to have one now."

Well, that hit me. I waited until they left and I called Dirty Harry over.
 "Do they come in here every night?"
"Yeah," he said. "They do."
"And the one next to me?"
"Her name is Agnes."
"It's her birthday tomorrow night. What you say we decorate the place and have a birthday party for her?"
"Hey Mister, that's brilliant. Yeah, that's brilliant!" He called his wife out of the back room.
"Jan, come out here. This guy wants to throw a birthday party for Agnes." She came out, came over and grabbed my hand.
"This is lovely. You wouldn't understand this, Mister, but Agnes is one of the really good people, one of the really kind people in this city. I know you know what she does to earn a living but she's a good person and a kind person. Nobody ever does anything for her. This is going to be good."

"Can I decorate the place?" I asked.

"To your heart's content!"

"I want to bring a birthday cake."

"Oh no, the cake is my thing," Harry said. *Oh geez,* I thought, looking at his apron again.

I get there about 2:30 the next morning. I'd bought some streamers at the K-Mart and strung them across the place. I had bought poster board and made a sign: Happy Birthday Agnes. I put it behind the counter on the mirror. I had the place spruced up as best I could. Jan had done the cooking and had gotten the word out on the street.

By 3:15 every prostitute in Honolulu was in this place. It was wall to wall prostitutes. And me! About 3:30 in the morning Agnes and her friends showed up. We were all poised, we were all ready for her and when she walked in we all yelled, "Happy Birthday." We started cheering like mad.

Agnes trembled. She shook. They steadied her and got her over to the counter and sat her on a stool. Harry brought out the birthday cake, and when she saw it she started to cry. Harry just stood there with the cake in his hands.

"Okay! Knock it off, Agnes. Knock it off. Blow out the candles. Go ahead, blow out the candles."

She tried and she couldn't do it so Harry blew out the candles himself. Then he gave her the knife.

"Now come on, Agnes. Cut the cake, cut the cake." She sat there for a long moment, and then she turned to me.

"Mister, do I have to cut the cake?"

"It's your cake."

"What I would like to do is take the cake home and show it to my mother. Can I do that?" She stood up with the cake.

"Yeah, I guess so, if you want to. But wait a minute. You don't have to do it now, do you?"

"I live two doors down," she said. "Let me go and show them the cake and then I will come back. I will bring it back. I promise." She got up, pushed through the crowd and out the door. As the door swung slowly shut, there was stunned silence. Absolutely stunned silence. It was an awkward silence. I didn't know what to say, so I said the first thing that came to me.

"What do you say we pray?" It sounds weird now, looking back on it; a sociologist leading a prayer meeting with a group of prostitutes at 3:30 in the morning in a greasy spoon diner in Honolulu. It was the right thing to do, though. I prayed that Jesus would make her new again and deliver her from the dirty, filthy men who made her do the things she did.

You know how these things are. A girl 13 or 14 years old gets messed over by some filthy, stinking man and her whole self image is destroyed and it's downhill from there. She spirals downward and… She's a victim, she is not the victimizer, she is the victim.

I prayed that God would make her new because I believe in a Jesus who can invade us and transform us from within and make us into new persons. I believe in that Jesus. And when I finished the prayer I didn't realize that I was still sitting on a stool. I opened my eyes and Harry was right there in my face leaning across the counter.

"Hey Campolo, you told me you were a sociologist. You're not a sociologist, you're a preacher. What kind of church do you preach at?"

It was just one of those moments when you come up with just the right words.

"I preach in a church that throws birthday parties for whores at 3:30 in the morning." I thought I was being so clever. Then he said something I will not forget.

"No you don't. You don't belong to a church that throws birthday parties for whores at 3:30 in the morning. I would go to a church like that."

I thought, *Wouldn't we all?* Wouldn't we all love to belong to a church that throws birthday parties for whores at 3:30 in the morning? Well, that is the kind of church Jesus came to create. I don't know where we got this other one that's half country club. We ought to be throwing birthday parties not just for whores but for little old ladies, for kids who don't have birthday parties... for so many people who never get celebrated. That is the task of the church. A church that brings celebration into the lives of those who have had nothing to celebrate.

JR: You make a good point, Tony. You're a powerful public speaker. I appreciate your sharing that story with our audience.

Rev. C: A career public speaker is not what I'm called to be. I'm called to be a critic.

JR: Thank you.

<h1 style="text-align:center">Bishop Spong
Re-evaluating Values</h1>

Bishop John Shelby Spong is a former Episcopal bishop from Newark, New Jersey.

Bishop Spong is a controversial figure who once scandalized Christendom by espousing positions at variance with traditional Christian dogma. Though many of his views are not in the mainstream of Christian thought and practice, some are debated a bit less often now. He retired in the year 2000 to his home in Morris Plains, New Jersey.

The Christian message, when ritualized and dogmatized by the church, as Spong explains his position, becomes a quickly outdated, man-made message obscuring the original core meaning of love. The Bishop is an iconoclastic messenger.

Jim Remembers... A Few Hail Marys

I remember going to confession every week because you couldn't have communion on Sunday unless you went to confession on Saturday. Our gang would get together on Saturday, and we'd all walk over to the church together. On the way we would chat with each other about what we were going to say.

"What are you going to tell the priest?" One of my friends would ask.

"I could say I disobeyed my mother, maybe once, during the week."

"Then I better make it two," somebody else would say.

"I took the name of the Lord in vain [swearing] once or twice, but maybe," I would say, "I should make it three or four." I would have to make it believable, but not too much. We would worry about how much atonement we're going to have to do. Then on the way home we compared notes about that.

"I had to do five Our Fathers and three Hail Marys," one of the guys would say, and then somebody else might want to top it with 10 and four or maybe brag about their own virtuous self with an easier atonement.

Today, we hear so much about scandals with priests in the church doing things they shouldn't have done. We never heard anything about that kind of thing going on. There was never a moment where I feared anything and neither did my friends. We would have heard about it. I still think all the priests were exactly who they were supposed to be, good men trying to do good work. They were important in our community, and our community was better off for their presence with us. We never had any doubt about looking up to them.

When I was growing up, going to church was an important part of my life. My parents made sure that my brothers and sisters and I went to church. My mother always had an envelope with a dime in it ready for us on the way to mass. We had to take it to church, and we had to go to catechism.

I had to walk from Love School to catechism class at St. James. I accepted what they were preaching because my mother and father believed that way. I figured, okay, this is the way to get to heaven. We would go to confession and we used to have fun there.

Kidding aside, I think the church's greatest contribution is to tell you the difference between right and wrong. It keeps order in society, basically. If nobody was there to tell you that you were committing a sin because you were doing this or doing that, the society would be chaotic. The church puts in a sense of guilt if you do something that they teach is wrong. If you disobey your mother and father, it's called a venal sin.

I pictured my soul and figured it had a few black marks on it. That impressed me enough to inspire me do right and to worry about other things, even swearing. It's necessary because people are searching for the answer to life, they really are. What are we doing here? Why are we here? What is our purpose?

I simply say to myself, "Well, I'm here." The best thing is to act righteously, respect your family and your friends. Respect the differences in people. I was so naïve when I went to college, for instance, and heard about the segregated South, that I was astounded. I asked the other fellows, "Why the hell are they doing that?"

I went to school with my neighborhood kids. I played with black kids and I went to their homes. They're nice people. Why did they drink from a different fountain down south? I just could not believe it. I got shook up watching the scenes during the civil rights era; the dogs, the billy clubs. I wondered why people caused all those frustrations. We only live here for a short time, the span of a fleeting moment. Why make it hard for anybody?

That's why I believe, in my time on the radio, if people learned something worthwhile that gave them a better feeling about living, if it improved their day somewhat, if it gave them a laugh or a sincere thought or some wisdom that was shared, then it was all worthwhile.

A Conversation with Bishop Spong

Jim Roselle: I grew up as a Catholic boy and went to catechism every week. I accepted what I learned. Now, I suddenly hear from you, Bishop Spong, that a lot of it is really something I should not believe in any longer, but look at it with a different mindset. That would be a difficult task for me. How do I except that?
Bishop Spong: I would never want to tell you not to believe it any longer. I think there is a difference between a God experience - which I think is eternal and real - and the way people explain the God experience.

JR: Do you think you disagree with how God was explained to me?
Bishop S: I think we ought to be free to let the explanations change over the years, as indeed they have.

If you look back in the early history of the Christian church, one of the great battles was whether Adam and Eve had navels. Now, I have never met anybody who wants to argue about whether or not Adam and Eve had a naval today, but that was a great big battle in the early life of the church. So the explanations of the God experience change through the ages.

The difficulty comes when religious people, and we are all prone to do it, fall in love with their explanations and they say this is the unchanging, infallible, eternal way that God is to be understood. Well, that is absolute foolishness. Something will happen the next day that will give you a whole new perspective on the way the world operates, and you have to process that into your explanation of God.

Remember, in the early years of Christianity, we assumed that if you got sick you were being punished for your sins. We didn't understand there were germs and viruses and tumors. Then we developed antibiotics to take care of some of the things that caused people to be sick. We discovered that antibiotics work just as well on sinners as on saints. It has almost nothing to do with your moral or spiritual behavior. You can operate on a sinner's malignancy just as well as you can operate on a saint's.

The whole area of seeing cause and effect as part of God's activity in human life has dissipated in an enormous number of ways in our society. The old explanations just don't work. That doesn't mean that God isn't real, or that God isn't present, or that God has ceased to be a reality. We've got to find a different language to talk about that experience.

JR: Did God make the earth in six days and then take a day of rest?

Bishop S: That's the primary Hebrew myth of creation. I would say no, but it's a beautiful story that can't be literal history. We know today, for example, that the earth is not complete. It is still evolving. Life is still evolving. Galaxies in this universe are still being formed.

The idea that there was a finished creation from which you can take a day off is a wonderful story and I think that people needed a Sabbath for rest every week. I think that brought that institution into being. Obviously that is not a literal story. And then there's Darwin… we know today from radioactivity measurements that this earth has been here 4 ½ to 5 billion years. Human life, at the very most, has been here only 2 million years. So if you condense all that history to a 24-hour clock, human life appears about 10 nanoseconds before midnight. We are very late developing creatures.

JR: But look at the impact it has had over the years, saying that it's a sin to work on Sunday. All that we have followed so - may I say it - religiously, if we did do it, was it out of a sense of guilt?

Bishop S: Well, yes, at least sometimes. The church does guilt better than we do anything else. We really are past masters at manipulating guilt. What happened is that the Jewish Sabbath - the seventh day of the week, the day of rest - became Saturday – the first day of the week - for Christians.

The Sabbath started Friday night at sundown, and we would stay resting until Saturday night at sundown. That organized Jewish life, and I think it's a wonderful idea. The Jews, remember, were slaves in Egypt. The Sabbath was terribly important because even the slaves got a day of rest. It was important for their well-being.

Now, Christians don't observe the Sabbath. We think we do, but we have gotten them confused. It's not the Jewish Sabbath. And it wasn't a day for refraining from work. It was the idea of Easter, the resurrection experience that marked the first day of the week, the Christian Sunday.

In the 16th century, John Calvin, who was sort of an uptight kind of man, put all of the Jewish Sabbath day restrictions onto the Christian Sunday.

When you and I grew up, I couldn't go to a baseball game on Sunday because that caused other people to work. I couldn't cut the grass, either, which really didn't bother me. My mother was really strict so I would sneak out to the baseball game on Sunday only if it was a doubleheader. Because whatever she did to me was worth it for a doubleheader, but for a single game it wasn't quite worth it.

JR: May I pause here Bishop Spong? Because we have messages… but not from God… these are commercials.

Bishop S: God speed, Jim.

Huston Smith
Many Wisdoms

Huston Smith is a religious studies scholar and the author of the book *"The World's Religions: Our Great Wisdom Traditions"* [HarperCollins, 1991. Originally titled *The Religions of Man* for the 1958 publication] which has sold more than 3 million copies.

Huston was born to Methodist missionaries in Suzhou, China, in 1919. He lived there with his family until he was 17, then moved to the United States to attend Central Methodist University and the University of Chicago. As a young man, Huston did not quite discard his traditional Christian understanding of the world, but broadened his world view to include various forms of mysticism. He later linked up with Timothy Leary and Richard Alpert (who later adopted the name, Ram Dass) at Harvard

University exploring psychological and spiritual experiences using LSD and other hallucinogenic substances.

Though his spiritual insights grew out of the religious traditions in which he was raised, his scientific research and scholarship both remained firmly focused in spirituality. He was also once the subject of a five-part series on *PBS* hosted by Bill Moyers called Wisdo*m of the Ages*.

Jim Remembers… The National Council of Christians and Jews

My religious experiences are not as varied as Huston Smith's, but I share his opinion that people from different faith backgrounds should be able to respect and learn from each other and then work together.

In 1983, I received the National Conference of Christians and Jews Brotherhood Citation at the 25th NCCJ Brotherhood Citation dinner of the Jamestown Chapter. I had worked closely with Temple Hesed Abraham in Jamestown on their many annual sports dinners to which they invited famous athletes, and with my boss, Si Goldman, a member of that congregation. I had also always worked very comfortably with people of every faith and denomination and we often accomplished good things for our community.

I was humbled by the 200 people there who applauded and even gave me a standing ovation. The NCCJ Award was presented by Senior Co-chairman Howard Brooke.

Max Robinson, the Buffalo sports broadcaster who had been a harness race announcer at Batavia Downs, hosted the dinner. He had also worked for WJTN from 1958 to 1965, so we had worked together and been friends for a number of years.

Dominic Loperiore, of the Jamestown Boys Club, thanked me for helping members of the Club reach their highest potential, a goal of membership for every boy there. He tried to single me out for always offering "…a smile and a lot of enthusiasm," but I certainly wasn't alone in that. Everybody there felt that way. At the time I was vice president of the board of directors at the Jamestown Club.

When I accepted the award, I said I couldn't help wondering about what I would do if I were Tevye the Dairyman, the main character in *Fiddler on the Roof*. "If I were a rich man," I told everybody, "I'd still want to be born to my wonderful parents, and I'd still want to have the same three sisters, three brothers, three children, wife and three stepchildren."

If the fiber of my life is brotherhood – which I think it is - it started in the neighborhood where I was born, on Franklin Street, in Jamestown, New York.

I also remember Dr. Robert Ney who spoke on behalf of his wife, cardiologist Lillian Vitanza Ney, thanking me for my role as chairman of the annual WJTN *Heart Radiothon*. In 1980, I was honored with the American Heart Association Award of the Year for fundraising. The honor was made even a little more interesting because Lillian's father, Peter Vitanza, was my family's doctor during the years I was growing up. His heritage happened to be Sicilian, too.

None of this is as much to my credit as this award might make you think. I did nothing on my own; I owed every success to the community I lived in. Our families were from everywhere. We were Italians and Swedes, blacks and whites, Christians and Jews. The brotherhood this award talks about is just how we lived.

I appreciated the goals of the NCCJ to help promote understanding and mutual respect between religions and to support working together on civic and social justice issues with education and dialogue.

A Conversation with Huston Smith

Jim Roselle: Huston Smith, it is interesting that you make no preparation for interviews. You just answer cold.

Huston Smith: Cold turkey! Here comes the first question… No information as to what corner of the universe that question is going to come from.

JR: Since you are at all times prepared to answer any question, when did you make the decision to bring together all the thoughts of all the world's religions?

HS: You put the emphasis on the wrong foot. It was not like I figured out a trajectory with a shopping list as if I had said, "First I will go into Hinduism and check that off, and so on."

It wasn't like that at all. It was rather that I followed the light where it led. It was at each step along the way something came at me sort of like a tidal wave of truth. It's kind of like a tidal wave in the Pacific Ocean when you are swimming and get caught in one of those. You go in a kind of food blender spin. It was like that.

First it was Christianity, of course. I was born into that, and it sort of matured along the way, gradually, step-by-step. I would have been perfectly content to just play out my life in the Christian tradition, exploring profundities which greater than any single light can get to the bottom of. I never stopped being a Christian. I came to believe that God is defined by Jesus, but not confined to Jesus.

I would have been perfectly content to stay right there if it wasn't that, all of a sudden, I bumped into a marvelous Vedantic Hindu swami who was both a great Sanskrit scholar and a very holy man. All of a sudden, when I opened the Upanishad [Hindu writings purporting to reveal truths of the nature of ultimate reality] I just sat back because this was so extraordinary. That took about 10 years to find out the mysteries of that particular tradition which I did not find at all in conflict with Christianity, but simply stated in a different idiom.

Then Buddhism came to the country. *The Dharma Bums* [The Viking Press, 1958] by Jack Kerouac came my way and then Gary Snyder the poet - my Dharma brother in Kyoto where we were studying in a Zen monastery together and meditating. That took about a decade.

The Sufis came along next. Here again it was the same transcendent message and the heavens opened over the Arabian skies, you might say, and another decade passed.

The last one was the Native American. I had ignored them because my teachers referred to the oral, tribal religions that didn't have a written text as "primitive religions." That word primitive was used like "The plumbing in England is rather primitive." I was young and gullible so I just believed what my teachers told me. Dangerous! Dangerous! I went through most of my early career just paying no attention. It was only when I moved to Syracuse University, and we bought a house, that I found our house was only five miles from the Iroquois Longhouse. Well, interesting!

In China, I had read about Hiawatha and all of that, so we went for an afternoon drive to the Onondaga Reservation. From that point on I realized that I had spent my life girdling the globe trying to understand the outlooks of different people, while there was a tradition right under my feet the entire time, that I hadn't given it the time of day.

Happily, that changed. In the course of my 10 years in Syracuse these "primal religions" – I often called them that because they preceded the historical religions that are only about 4000 years old – are about 30,000 years old. They escalated in my regard for them right up to the level of respect I hold for the historical religions.

JR: Is there a common denominator among all of those?

HS: Oh, sure! Namely, the ultimate, the divine, the infinite. Its presence pervades and saturates [everything]. Someone… came up to me and told me that she had an image for the transcendence and the immanence of God. Her image was a sponge in a basin of water. The water is God and the sponge is the material world, and we who are within it. The sponge is saturated with God. What a beautiful image. That's what's constant in all of these traditions.

JR: Thank you, Huston Smith, for sharing your insights.

HS: Namaste, Jim.

Chapter 17

The Music Makers

Jim Roselle has been spinning disks since the age of printed sheet music and continues to do so in the age of digital sound and computers. When it comes to music, he has heard it all by all the best and sent it all out over the airwaves to generations of listeners. Few singers have graced a musical note the way Judy Collins has. Jim interviews Judy, the songstress and the legend, whose songs he has aired countless times. Ray Evans, who grew up just down the road from Jamestown, may have contributed more, and tallied more millions of air-plays, than almost any other songwriter over the years. He inspired the whole world with his timeless tunes and lyrics.

Most of what we take as being important is not material, whether it's music or feelings or love…They're not material, but they're vitally important to us.

Judy Collins

Writing anything is terribly hard but, alas for me, because I am addicted, a heck of a lot of fun. I often am sorry I ever started writing prose, because it is so hard. But I can't stop.

Judy Collins

A rose must remain with the sun and the rain or its lovely promise won't come true.

Ray Evans

Judy Collins

Judy Collins

Judy Collins was born in Seattle but grew up in Denver where her musical life began by playing classical piano with a local orchestra. Surrounded by many musical influences, she soon turned to folk music and scored a big, early hit with *Both Sides Now*. Later, Stephen Sondheim's *Send in the Clowns* and a signature rendition of the beloved old gospel song, *Amazing Grace,* were among her most popular vocals.

The Golden Age of Radio returned to Jim's Chautauqua conversations when Judy Collins shared Golden Age memories of the varied musical influences she experienced on her father's radio show. He was Chuck Collins, a vivid radio personality in Denver, known for his unique, freewheeling and announcer-does-it-all style which was made all the more fascinating to his audience because he was totally blind. He had surrounded young Judy with an eclectic mix of musical styles. He had many musicians on his show, but he was also frequently his own featured vocalist and musician as well as the interviewer, the MC and the commercial announcer.

Jim's experiences as a broadcaster had begun by playing the popular music of his day, but eventually came to include interviewing, program hosting and more. He understood something about the versatility enjoyed by a broadcaster like Judy's father. Jim, like Judy, also came to know the musicians themselves.

A Conversation with Judy Collins

Jim Roselle: Welcome back to Chautauqua Institution, Judy Collins. We are delighted, pleased, privileged and excited to have as a guest a voice we have heard thousands of times, millions of times. Help me welcome Judy Collins.
Judy Collins: Thank you, I'm delighted to be here.

JR: We certainly are pleased you're giving us some time for our broadcast. Thank you for what you've done to inspire us and let us enjoy your wonderful talent. I've had the privilege of playing your songs many, many times.
I'm tempted to say here, and I'll paraphrase just a little bit, "Isn't it rich? Are we a pair? Me here on the grounds, you on the air. Send in the clowns!"
[Jim cuts to a recording of Judy's song, *Send in the Clowns*.]
JC: I recognize that voice.
JR: Is that your favorite song?
JC: Actually not. There are lots of favorites. How can you pick one? The favorite is always the one I am singing at the moment so I guess at the moment *Send in the Clowns* is my favorite song.
JR: Your first performances were classical, weren't they?
JC: Not really. That came later. My first performance was on my father's radio show [Chuck Collins was blind, a singer/songwriter, interview program host and radio DJ]. He taught me a lot about music.
I was probably about four or five years old. My dad had a great show. It was old-fashioned radio, it was in the Golden Age of Radio were you did everything. He played his own songs, he sang, he wrote songs and he interviewed all the stars who came to town, Jack Benny, George Shearing and Red Skelton and that strange couple - my favorites - who had the eight mina birds and the two parrots.
I also did study classical piano because my father said, "You have to have training in real music. I don't want you to make your living in pop radio." So I played quite seriously. I studied, and I had to practice a couple of hours every day. I was a pupil of the amazing Antonia Brico. I don't think Antonia ever was here at Chautauqua Institution, although I made a movie about her later on in 1974. She conducted the London Philharmonic and she conducted a lot of Mozart. She traveled a lot, too. Once she was conducting in Denver, and when I was only 13, I played a two-piano Mozart concerto for her with another young pianist.
So yes, I was a hotshot classical pianist. Before that, I was an up-and-coming singer of the Great American Songbook on my dad's radio show.
JR: You had a voice teacher who was so popular that, at first, you didn't even think he would take you as a pupil.
JC: He wasn't popular, he was just… difficult, very difficult. He did not want anybody around who wasn't going to be serious about it, so I had to be.
I had asked a couple of people about singing teachers in 1964 because I kept losing my voice. I was already on the road, and I had already made two or three records. I already had a big career.
I asked friends whom I admired. I asked Mordechai "Mordy" Bauman who ran Indian Hill Camp [a summer workshop in the arts in Stockbridge, Massachusetts]. He knew everybody. Then there was a pianist and guitarist I asked who played for Belafonte, Ray Bogoslav. I asked them because I knew that they would know, and they were not above learning. A lot of people in the folk world were. When they heard the words "music lesson" or "singing teacher", they would scream as they ran out of the room.
So I asked Mordy and Ray and they both gave me a name, Max Margulies. I wrote his phone number down. I was living in The Village [Greenwich Village, New York City] at that time, and then I moved uptown to W. 79th St.

I called Max, this famous, difficult man; famous, that is, within a small circle.

"No, no, no!" he said. "I don't want any more students. I've had enough of students. I'm not interested. I like these opera singers. They come all the way from Europe, and they stay a month and they come every day. I don't want any of these fly-by-night singers."

I begged and pleaded as best I could. Finally he said, "Oh well, maybe. Want to come by?" He gave me his address, and I walked out my door, turned right, walked by the elevator and knocked on his door.

You see? He had no excuse not to see me. Who could've guessed we lived in, not only the same building, but on the same floor. I stayed with him for 32 years. Before he died, he reminded me, "Now don't worry. You know what to do. Just remember, it's clarity and phrasing. That's all you have to know."

JR: Let's go back to when you select a song, or some arranger decides this is the song for you, or somebody discourages you about a song you like. How do you make that final decision?

JC: It is very much like falling in love. I can't really say it any more clearly than that. I don't sing songs I don't love and people don't make me do things I don't want to do. I have the luxury to be broad and eclectic in my choices. The only person who ever limited me was myself. Others might have tried, but I was always involved from top to bottom in the choice of songs, arrangements and the musicians who were playing. Choosing of the song is mine.

JR: Your latest book is called *The Seven T's: Finding Hope and Healing in the Wake of Tragedy* [The Penguin Group, 2007].

JC: I did a lot of writing before the incident that propelled us into "*Healing and the Power of Music*". Then in 1992 my son died. He took his life. I became an advocate for suicide survivors and their troubles and the need to break the taboo of suicide.

I've always been a rebel. I was a girl who grew up in the 40s and 50s and became an advocate for the antiwar movement and, by the 60s, for human rights. Activism for those ideas are typical of my family. My mother always told me, "You go do it, girl!"

My mother is 91 now, and she is still at it. She gets mad at all of us if we are not taking enough action for something we believe in and doing the right thing.

I am sort of the body-mind-spirit girl, a throwback to the 60s, to a holistic approach to mental health as well as physical health.

JR: We have a gentleman who got here very early to say hello to you. He worked on a stage where you were doing a protest performance back in the 60s. How active were you during the protest movements in the 1960s?

JC: I was working and I was marching and getting arrested. I was making my opinion known. *Amazing Grace,* which I recorded in 1970 and became a huge hit, said there was a spiritual aspect to the protest. It said that if you change yourself you changed the world.

JR: You mentioned earlier in our conversation something about George Shearing. May I say there is a personal side to that for me? I am a member of the Boys Club alumni, and we wanted to raise money for the club. We wanted to pay back what they did for us and our first concert performer was George Shearing.

JC: He is wonderful. He is still around and I go to a church in New York, St. Thomas, which he attends too. At Christmas I always go there. I saw him there this year.

JR: Once again, it's always interesting to see how people's paths can cross in the most unexpected of ways. And I'm delighted our paths crossed today, here on the beautiful grounds at Chautauqua. Thank you for this time together.

JC: Thank you, Jim.

Jim Remembers…Getting to Know Another Musician

We hired Stan Kenton for a Boys Club Thanksgiving Eve concert at the Jamestown Armory. A snowstorm hit us that night, and we were getting calls from people at the other end of the county and down in Pennsylvania who were canceling their tickets because of the blizzard. The weather didn't stop Stan from showing up for the show, though, and we still had a decent turnout. The event was a success, and when the concert was over, he asked me for a favor.

"Can you give me a ride back to the Hotel Jamestown?"
"Mr. Kenton, I would be delighted to give you a ride back."
"Well that would be real nice. Thank you." I drove him back to the hotel through the snowstorm that was still blanketing the town. In the lobby we passed the hotel café. It was open 24 hours a day, back then.
"Let's stop for a cup of coffee," Stan said.
We were there until 3 o'clock in the morning chatting about his career, his vocalists, what it's like to go on the road and a hundred other things. He gave me the pleasure of his company for those hours, but I didn't have a recorder or a camera with me. That's made me mad every time I've thought about it ever since that night.

Ray Evans
The Music and Lyrics of the 20th Century

Ray Evans, a native of Salamanca, New York, just east of Jamestown, along with his partner, composer/songwriter, Jay Livingston, won three Academy Awards for his songs: *Buttons and Bows*, *Mona Lisa* and *Que Sera Sera*, all written for Hollywood movies. They also wrote *Tammy*, *Silver Bells - the Christmas song*, *Dear Heart* and the theme music for the TV shows *Bonanza* and *Mr. Ed*.

Ray also collaborated separately with Henry Mancini, Max Steiner, and Victor Young for movie scores. The team of Evans and Livingston collaborated on many song projects over the years, 26 of which sold more than a million records each; total record sales of their songs is estimated to have topped 400 million. Ray Evans was inducted into the Songwriters Hall Of Fame in 1977 and the Evans-Livingston team was awarded their own star on the Hollywood Boulevard Walk of Fame in 1995.

Evans' career spans the musical eras from printed sheet music to Internet and MP3 downloads. Few, if any, songwriters have enjoyed such a long and productive career at the top of popular charts and success in the movies.

Jim's broadcast career also began in the age of printed sheet music. He played the vocalists and iconic Big Bands of Ray Evans' youth on his radio show. The kind of music Jim played included all the melodic models that influenced Ray's youthful musical dreams.

Jim Remembers… The Big Bands

I've been playing music on the radio for a lot of years. I played all the most popular vocalists from the time I started. I played Sinatra and Tony Bennett, Nat King Cole, Peggy Lee, Joe Stafford, Helen Forrest and all the rest, even the fellow some people confused me with – except that I can't sing – the popular Jimmy Roselli. I played the big bands, too, like Duke Ellington, Tommy and Jimmy Dorsey, Glenn Miller, Count Basie, even Shep Fields, Glenn Gray and Benny Goodman.

We hired the Duke Ellington Band for a Boys Club fundraiser on the club's 20th anniversary. I was going to introduce him to the audience, so I went backstage earlier in the evening to meet him and the band, but he was not there. Band members often show up for a gig individually because they live in different places, not always near each other. When they get an assignment, they just rush to the venue from all directions.

I was backstage, watching the guys chatting with each other and I saw one of the fellows who appeared to be very young.

"Are you with the band?" I asked.

"Yes."

"You look like you're in your 20s."

"I am."

"This is a Big Band. I didn't expect anybody so young to be playing with Duke."

"Well, I love the Duke, you know, and I do play with him."

I thought it was very interesting that his generation appreciated Duke's music, and Duke appreciated the talents of the younger generation.

Suddenly the backstage door flew open and Duke Ellington walked in. He was a very dapper dresser in his camel hair coat. Everybody rushed up to him and grabbed him. They hugged him and they kissed him.

"Wow! It looks like they haven't seen him in years," I said to the kid.

"That's because today is a special day. Today is the Duke's birthday. He's 60 years old." The date was April 29, 1959.

Duke Ellington spent his birthday night with us. All the band members were very loyal to him and they showed it in the respect and love they showed. He put on a great show. It was wonderful that the Boys Club could celebrate his birthday with him, right here in Jamestown.

A Conversation with Ray Evans

Jim Roselle: Good morning. It's 10:05 on Saturday morning and this is *The Times of Your Life*. Let's talk about Ray Evans.
Russ Diethrick: He'll put a little song in your heart.

> **JR:** Salamanca, New York, is mourning his loss.
> **RD:** The whole country is mourning the loss.
> **JR:** Ray passed away on February 15th in Los Angeles at the age of 92.

I had the pleasure last October - you were unable to be with me that day – of interviewing Ray in the dressing room at the Ray Evans Theater in Salamanca. He was there to present a program with Karen Benjamin and Alan Chapman, a husband and wife team that had been touring the country singing his song book.

Tomorrow Salamanca will pay tribute with a memorial for Ray Evans. Let me just play the beginning of that interview for our listeners.

[Pre-recorded segment begins]

Jim Roselle: It's a privilege and a joy that I have the opportunity to be with Ray Evans, a songwriter who has left, as far as I'm concerned - and I know the audience feels the same way - a legacy of songs that will be heard for generations to come. Ray Evans, you're never going to die.

Ray Evans: Well isn't that nice. I like to hear that because I'm almost 92 now. There is a calendar that says the years are going by, but I will take the compliment. Even if I'm not here, as you said, the songs will be here - and thank God, they will be here. Thanks for the nice words

JR: You have been part of my life, Ray Evans, because I have had the pleasure over these many years to do a show playing songs. I couldn't count the times that I have played Mona Lisa, or that I played Doris Day's *Que Sera Sera* or I have played Debbie Reynolds' *Tammy* or that I've played the Ink Spots and *To Each His Own*...

RE: [Enthusiastically takes over the conversation here] ...or by Eddy Howard, who did the original, and then Tony Martin, Freddie Martin, the Modernaires, and so many more. You've kept me happy and also you have kept my bottom line going. That's how I pay my bills and my income tax. Thank you, Jim. I don't know how much you made, but between you and ASCAP (*American Society of Composers, Authors and Publishers*), I'm a happy camper.

[Recorded segment ends]

Jim Roselle: Ray Evans was a happy camper. And right now, Russ Diethrick, we have Ray Evans' sister, Doris Feinberg, on the phone from Salamanca. Good morning Doris.
Doris Feinberg: Good morning.

JR: We thank you for this opportunity to talk about your brother, Ray Evans, who is going to be honored tomorrow in Salamanca. You just recently returned from California attending the memorial there. Please tell us what took place.
DF: It was a gorgeous affair, a sit down dinner with 300 people in Beverly Hills at the Hillcrest Country Club. They had pictures of Ray all over and entertainment by Karen and Alan Benjamin, Michael Feinstein and other great singers and friends of Ray.
RD: He was loved all over the country, wasn't he?
DF: All over the world. He traveled a lot and he heard his songs everywhere. It made him feel very proud. Jay Livingston, his partner, passed away two years ago.
RD: What kind of feeling do you get when you hear those songs on the radio or television?
DF: It's very emotional. I get sad at the loss of such a remarkable talent. My big brother was very humble about it, though.
JR: Growing up, did you suspect anything about his love for music?
DF: In high school he was passionate about music. He used to get up at 5 AM and practice long tunes on his clarinet for a couple of hours - which was not appreciated by the rest of us. He organized a band in high school that played at high school dances and games.

He was also very passionate about athletics. He played football, basketball, tennis and softball. He was still playing softball when he was in his 80s with a bunch of young guys.
JR: Did you think music would be the career he would finally wind up in?
DF: No! He went to the Wharton School of Business at the University of Pennsylvania. It was far from music.

He had been valedictorian of his class here in Salamanca, and they would not accept him at the University of Pennsylvania that year because he was too young. He was barely 16 when he graduated, so he had to go back and take a GED course to get in. Ray had good training at the Wharton School, and he was his own business manager. His mind was full of statistics, too, about every athlete in a country, and other things like the stock market.
JR: How did he keep in touch?

DF: He came home at least once a year, sometimes more than that. I went out there once or twice a year, too. We were very close, and he was a wonderful brother. He was kind and generous.

He has a gorgeous home in Beverly Hills on a 5 acre property. He built a private park on some of the land. It has been given to the *Ray Evans Foundation*. All of the royalties are going into his Foundation, too. He is also leaving something to the theater in Salamanca.

JR: Did he ever tell you what his favorite song was?

DF: He always maintained that he loved them all. He never really chose one. Of course the ones that won the Academy Awards, naturally, they would be very high on his list. He has extensive archives, too. He must have 100 scrapbooks.

JR: Thank you, Doris. I'm sure we can all agree that Ray Evans' music will never be forgotten.

A Small Gallery

Meet the Press Moderator Tim Russert

Author and historian Doris Kearns-Goodwin

David McCullough, Pulitzer Prizer winning author and historian

Jim admires a gift of art

Epilogue and Acknowledgements

I want to explain how this book came about. A lot of my friends and listeners over the years have asked me to "write that book". Some people want to know about the people I've interviewed, some are more interested in my career and family history and others are simply fascinated with the medium of radio.

On the other hand, this also has to be a story about our community, the people themselves; the curiosity, generosity and support that made possible what's been done at WJTN over the years. Many of them also contributed invaluable information, archival sound, images and personal recollections.

Media 1 Group and WJTN-AM's contributions have been indispensible. I wish to thank Jeff Storey, Vice President & General Manager; Andrew Hill, Operations and Program Directors; Larry Saracki, AM Sales Manager; Terry Frank, News Director, and Dennis Webster, *Saturday Morning Breakfast Club* host, for researching and releasing the WJTN audio archives and many of the images used here. Thanks also go to Russell E. Diethrick Jr., my co-host on *The Times of Your Life*. Additional audio and video material was generously provided by the Robert H. Jackson Center and co-founder, Greg Peterson, Esq., the Jamestown, NY, Rotary Club and Philip A. Cala, Esq.

Longtime Chautauqua County residents, patrons of local culture, history and the arts, Bill and Pat Locke – with unwavering encouragement and support – brought together a team, led by Walt Pickut, including Westfield resident, Leslie Rackowski, and Donna Charest, retired Falconer School District teacher and administrator, to work with me on this project.

Photo credits go to Matt Warren, WJTN's production assistant who worked with me every summer at Chautauqua Institution, along with friends and fans with cameras always at the ready, and to Wanita Bratton, wife of the Institution's late president, Dr. Daniel Bratton, for photos from the Soviet Union.

Ellie Harmon kindly granted use of her late husband, Ed Harmon's previously published cartoons recalling and sometimes even fondly lampooning my summer experiences at Chautauqua. Thanks also to Gary Peters, local artist and muralist, who allowed me to include my favorite *Jamestoons*, and Chris Anderson, webmaster for our www.jimroselle.com web site.

Thanks also to Stacey Hannon, owner and publisher of *The Jamestown Gazette*, for her patience and sense of humor while *Gazette* Editor, Walt, juggled his regular editing and assignments with seemingly endless archive delving, interviewing and writing for this project.

Kathy Roselle and Nancy Pickut, spouses extraordinaire, deserve credit for their patience, encouragement and partnership – over the long haul, throughout Jim's career, for Kathy, and over the shorter, but intense period of this writing project for Nancy.

Chautauqua Institution, an historic landmark and artistic and intellectual capital of the world, has generously allowed me and WJTN to introduce their guests to our Chautauqua County radio listeners, and to our nationwide Internet audience. Their contributions could be an entire book in itself.

Sixty years of broadcasting cannot be condensed into a handful of pages between the covers of a single book. As a result, most of my 1,800 Chautauqua and Jamestown interviews are simply not here. None, however, has been left out of my heart, my memory or my gratitude for the role they have played.

Many people who work with me on the air are volunteers who contribute out of friendship and loyalty. Often, I don't even have to go out and find guests. Friends just bring them to my Dew Drop Inn.

Bill Clinger, a Pennsylvania congressman for 18 years and a member of the board of directors at Chautauqua Institution, visits with me every Thursday and talks about the political scene locally, around the country and in Washington. Refreshingly frank and direct, he gives anyone an honest opinion no matter which party he is talking about. He doesn't hold back, and that makes good radio.

Maureen Revegno is the kind lady who escorts Chautauqua Institution's chaplain of the week to me every Tuesday. She introduces them to my audience and I know I have listeners who especially look forward to hearing Maureen's introductions.

Jane Gross brings me anyone at Chautauqua associated with the opera, whether a set-builder, costume designer or performer. Jane is from New York City. Across the highway from Chautauqua Institution's entrance stands the *Jane Gross Center* which is dedicated for the use of the opera performers for their rehearsals and practice. She also travels a lot. At the beginning of every summer she gives me a wonderful description of wherever in the world she went during the previous year.

Vivienne Benesch and Ethan McSweeny are two of the directors of the Chautauqua Theater Company. They bring me the lead actors or the supporting characters the actors in the week's play at the theater. They are often young people working their way up toward major, professional positions in acting. Sometimes they are college students in theater and drama.

Every Thursday morning, Jeffrey Miller brings me the author of the week, whose book has been selected as book of the week by the Chautauqua Literary and Scientific Circle, the oldest still-functioning book club in the United States.

Gerhard Popps is a retired professor from West Virginia University. He is now the host, and his wife is the hostess, at the Institution's Jewish Center. He recently brought me the Ambassador of the United States to Israel for a fascinating discussion. Professor Popps told me the next day at the ambassador was very pleased with the opportunity to speak to my audience.

Then there was the French ambassador who, on my program, presented the Medal of Freedom – the highest medal of honor France can award – to a local gentleman, George Lown.

Howard Sanders started what I call The Breakfast Club. Howard graduated from Temple University and then retired at an early age. I never inquired about how he was able to do that, but I suspect he must have done something right. He comes every morning. I made him Honorary President of the Breakfast Club. I also know he was one of the regular teenage dancers on stage with Dick Clark's *American Bandstand*.

George Loun and the Ambassador of France on the air with Jim at Chautauqua

Linda Perlis has a show called *Parents Perspective* about schooling and children and parents' responsibilities. The show aired in Washington DC. She gave me a recorded copy of her show one day and asked if I could run it. We put it on Sunday mornings and gave it some airplay. It turned out to be very popular. She comes to the Breakfast Club almost as faithfully as Howard Sanders does.

I call Howard and Linda my "Breakfast Clubbers" and I am grateful for their loyalty.

Then there are Mort and Iris November, affectionately known as Lord Mort and Lady Iris. I've enjoyed Mort's famous, incomparable pancakes at his home and admired Iris's collection, probably the most extensive and beautiful of its kind in the world, of Statue of Liberty replicas, now at home in the Strong Museum in Rochester, New York.

Jim and Kathy Roselle with Mort and Iris November

I don't only count on these personalities, but I lasso people visiting Chautauqua, and some of them lasso me, too. I'm surprised and gratified by how many Chautauquans stop by to tell me they have someone they'd like me to meet, someone who would be very interesting on the air. One day, for instance, somebody told me about a friend who wrote a book on baseball. "I'll bring him over," the gentleman said. He did, and it made a wonderful program.

Finally, and perhaps most importantly, I want to acknowledge Joseph and Josephine Roselle. I could write another whole book about my mother alone…but words would fail me in giving her all the credit she is due.

Farewell

Gerald Heglund, WJTN's *Swedish Hour* host, recorded this famous farewell many years ago. Every year, at the end of the Chautauqua season, Jim plays the recording at the conclusion of his last summer broadcast from Chautauqua Institution.

To Chautauqua: Moment of Farewell

Sometimes I wish that I could love you less,
For when the summer and this and I must go,
Almost it is a rending of my soul;
You are a part of me and I love you.
Some other moment I shall sit apart
To count the many reasons for my love-
The varying beauty under summer clouds
Of rippling water, of ravine and grove;
The quick light-hearted friendliness
We breathed in with the air, the joy
Of learning, peace of wisdom
Yes – another time I'll meditate on these.

But not today. Today
I only know I leave you,
And I am silent with too much to say.
I shall remember lovely, little things-
I shall hear echoes on far
City streets-
Sometimes I wish that I could
Love you less.

Rebecca Richmond (1883-1961)
From her notebook in the Chautauqua historical collection.

Thank you for your company, take good care of this day. Live, love and enjoy.

Jim Roselle's daily sign-off

Appendix I

The Boys of the Boys Club

The Boys Club played a major role in shaping the lives of the many young men who once lived among Jamestown's South Side ethnic communities.

Jamestown Boys Club opened its doors on Monday, April 24, 1939, at 207 Prendergast Ave. The event, two full years in the planning, centered around a luncheon meeting of the founding sponsor organization, the Jamestown Rotary Club, in collaboration with the City Court and the Jamestown Police Department. Rotary President, Daniel F. Lincoln, who was also the second vice president of the Boys Club's Board of Directors, ceremonially presented the keys to Donald McGeorge, Boys Club Board President.

The plan was simple: "... To help make the city a better place for future generations of citizens."

President Herbert Hoover, 31st President of the United States, only six years out of office and by then Chairman of the Board of the Boys Clubs of America, sent a personal letter of congratulations to welcome Jamestown into the fellowship of 180 other American cities that already proudly hosted Boys Clubs.

Jim Roselle was one of the original 126 original members on that opening day. Seventy-five years later Jim is still able to name most of them and regale any willing listener with tales of their exploits. They had all become brothers.

Mr. Robert Clemments

The first managing director of the Jamestown Boys Club on opening day in 1939 was Robert Clemments, a native downstate New Yorker from New Rochelle. His wife, Rose, came to Jamestown from Springfield, Massachusetts, where she met her husband, who was the supervisor of the city's recreation centers. His directorship in Jamestown began on March 20th, about a month before the Club's official opening.

Six years later, in 1945, Clemments resigned his position in Jamestown to accept a similar position in Brooklyn, New York. He was succeeded in Jamestown by Mr. Arthur Verry, another very capable and popular Boys Club leader. Mr. Clemments later moved to Harrisburg, Pennsylvania, where he supervised the Boys Club until his retirement in 1972. It was during Clemments' time in Harrisburg that he and Jim reconnected, and he was instrumental in Jim obtaining his first, full-time broadcasting job.

In September of 1973, Clements returned to the Jamestown area to attend a dinner at the Red Coach Inn in Lakewood, New York. He had come back, he thought, to honor Jim's success at WJTN. Upon his arrival, however, Jim turned the tables on his old friend and emceed the dinner for the real honoree, Mr. Robert Clemments.

At the Jamestown Boys Club's 50th anniversary reunion in 1989, members from the 1950s, a decade after Jim's charter membership years, made it plain that the Boys Club was still living up to its promise.

Dominic Loperiore, who had by then risen to assistant vice president of the First Trust Union Bank in Jamestown, said the Club "...was like a second home... those were great days." He once told a reporter for the Jamestown's *Post-Journal*, "My mother asked me, 'why don't you bring your bed down there?'"

The Loperiore family was like many of the families that made up Little Italy, including Jim Roselle's Franklin Street neighborhood. They had come to Jamestown from Italy in February, 1953, with brothers Dominic, Anthony and Michael. The Boys Club and the [now closed] Saint James Catholic School taught them all English in only five or six months. The Club had what he called, "a nice, structured environment with the freedom to be creative… You played all your games there, your life revolved around it. We couldn't wait for the school bell to ring and get down there… We had a good time. It's probably something that influenced all of our lives." Loperiore even credited his Club with helping him qualify for a Top-Secret clearance during his stint in the United States Army.

The old expression, "Idle hands are the devil's workshop," made a lot of sense to another 1950s Boys Club member, Jim Condella. He told one of the gang many years later that the Club was great for "… trying to keep out of trouble, most of all."

The Boys Club leadership always recognized and rewarded the boys' accomplishments. Anthony Prinzi, later a key member of the Jamestown Area Labor-Management Committee, recalled that he had won many awards for his achievements at the Club and was named Prep and Junior Member of the Year in successive years. He was proud of the skills he gained, earning a place as one of the top five ping-pong players in the state of New York in the 10 to 12-year-old bracket. He credited his time there as a time of character building.

Tom Mazzone joined the Jamestown Boys Club at the age of six in 1951. He became a systems analyst at the multinational Cummins Engine Company, still operating in the 21st Century in Jamestown with a million-square-foot manufacturing facility. Mazzone grew up on Hazard Street, an immigrant neighborhood not too different from Franklin Street. His was also a family of modest means. The local YMCA was simply too expensive for him and most of his friends. The Boys Club became a natural home for him, too.

Frank T. Costanzo, who eventually became Jamestown's Development Director, credited the Boys Club and the downtown Saint James Church as the two most important institutions in his life. Costanzo won many swimming trophies at the Boys Club. "Best of all," he recalled, "I lived only four doors away. I could jump out of the pool, run home in the wintertime and not even freeze." He also remembers watching Carl Caprino crank out 150 pull-ups while the rest of the boys struggled to do 10.

A successful Jamestown attorney, Douglas A. Spoto, also a Boys Club graduate, had joined in 1953. He was another one who appreciated the inexpensive membership. His friends were "mostly the poorer kids" from many ethnic groups around town. He recalled that prejudice was nonexistent, as far as he could tell, within the safety of the Club.

Spoto recalled, "They made men out of boys very quickly…and most of the fellas I knew there grew up to be responsible members of our community."

Tony Zerbo, an original 1939 member who joined the club with Jim, had moved to California where he enjoyed a long, successful career in teaching and school administration. He joined in the 50th anniversary celebration saying, "I'll never forget the excitement it brought to me to be a part of a group of boys and close friends who I grew up with and will cherish forever…the friends I made at the club were like brothers."

A signature feature of the Jamestown Boys Club was the giant U.S. flag that flew over the building. The Jamestown Boys Club – now joined by the Girls Club – had been, and still is, a cornerstone of character building and good citizenship in the community.

Appendix II

A Poem

Jim Roselle's listeners usually come to know him as more than a radio personality. He is a friend, a neighbor and an honored member of their community. Listener Kathleen Joy penned this poem of tribute, which hangs in a place of honor on the wall of Jim's WJTN office.

Jim Roselle

I know a man from Jamestown
He's been here all his years
And this is just the perfect time
To give him all your cheers.

Jim Roselle is the guy
He's of whom I speak
Knows just how to say the words
He's always at his peak.

He's the "Voice of Jamestown"
The radio is his way
Of keeping all folks up-to-date
As they start their day.

He has his "Cup of Happiness"
It's his own thing-with style
We sit at home and join him
As he brings us a smile.

You see, his heart is full of gold
It's seen in every story
Local folks and big names too
They all get equal glory.

In the summer, Bestor Plaza
Is where Jim can be found
To share Chautauqua with the world
No other can be found.

And now it's 55 years
That Jim's been on the air
And we want 55 more
We think that's only fair.

So each and every morning
We all wake up with Jim
And since he gives his heart to us
We now give hours to him.

And if so our biggest wish for you
We know that you'll employ
When you go through life each day
Just *live, love, and enjoy*!!!

Kathleen Joy
September 20, 2008

Appendix III
Timeline – A few of Jim Roselle's Life Highlights

1875	Birth of Joseph Roselle, Jim's father.
1888	Birth of Josephine Parsaliti, Jim's mother.
1926	April 15. Jim is born on the nation's 13th Income Tax Day.
1938	First Surgery: Spinal Restructuring.
	Love School Graduation (Elementary).
1941	Washington School Graduation (Junior High).
1942	Second Surgery: Triple Arthrodesis, right Foot.
1944	Jamestown Graduation (High School).
1945	Jim's father, Joseph Roselle, dies at age 70.
1949	Graduation from St. Lawrence University.
1950	Jim buys a tape recorder.
	Starts part-time at WJTN-AM, Jamestown, NY.
	First on-air sports play-by-play.
	Start of *Alley Dust* bowling show.
1951	Starts at WHGB-AM, Harrisburg, PA.
1953	WNAE-AM, Warren, PA, 3 months in summer.
	Starts full-time in September at WJTN-AM, Jamestown, NY.
1954	Jim creates *Roselle's Record Room* afternoon music program.
	First Election Night remote broadcast from Democratic headquarters, still continuing.
	First marriage: to Lillian Dos Santos of Harrisburg, PA.
1955	Daughter Julie born.
1956	Daughter Mary Jane born.
1958	St. James Friday night Sock Hop starts (continues for 3 years).
1959	Ss. Peter & Paul Saturday night sock hop starts (continues for 5 years).
1960	Midway Park Wednesday night sock hop starts (continues for 8 years).
1961	Warren, PA. Knights of Columbus sock hop starts (continues for 5 years).
	Son Jim Jr. born.
1971	Jim's mother, Josephine Roselle, dies at age 83.
1974	First broadcast from Chautauqua Institution.
1975	Second marriage: to Kathleen Billgren Nalbone of Jamestown, NY.
	Chautauqua Institution daily broadcasts begin.
1986	Jim broadcasts from Pasadena, CA, Rose Bowl Parade with Jamestown High School Marching Band. Trip arranged by Band Director, Lou Deppas.
1988 – 2010	Jim broadcasts from Moscow's Red Square with Chautauqua Institution.
	Two Macy's Thanksgiving Day Parades in New York City.
	Grand Marshall – Sherman Days Parade.
	Grand Marshall – Jamestown's Annual Holiday Parade.
	SeaWorld Ohio – Remote Broadcast.
	Johnny's Lunch first franchise opening, Toledo, Ohio – remote WJTN broadcast.
	Austria, Germany and France remote WJTN broadcasts, initiated and accompanied by conductor, Brian Bogey, and Jamestown High A Capella Choir.
2014	Jim celebrates: 40 years at Chautauqua Institution.
	60 years broadcasting for WJTN.
	Publication of *The Best Times of My Life* by Jim Roselle with Walt Pickut.